TRENDS IN DEPRESSION RESEARCH

TRENDS IN DEPRESSION RESEARCH

MAURICE J. HENRI
EDITOR

Nova Science Publishers, Inc.
New York

For permission to use material from this book please contact us:
Telephone 631-231-7269; Fax 631-231-8175
Web Site: http://www.novapublishers.com

LIBRARY OF CONGRESS CATALOGING-IN-PUBLICATION DATA

Trends in depression research / Maurice J. Henri (editor).
p. ; cm.
Includes bibliographical references and index.
ISBN 13 978-1-60021-394-6
ISBN 10 1-60021-394-4
1. Depression, Mental. I. Henri, Maurice J.
[DNLM: 1. Depressive Disorder--therapy. 2. Depressive Disorder --epidemiology. 3. Depressive Disorder--physiopathology. WM 171 T794 2006]
RC537.T75 2006
616.85'270072--dc22 2006024666

Published by Nova Science Publishers, Inc. ✢ New York

CONTENTS

Preface		**vii**
Chapter 1	**Group Psychodynamic Interpersonal Psychotherapy: Summary of a Treatment Model and Outcomes for Depressive Symptoms** *Giorgio A. Tasca, Samuel F. Mikail and Paul L. Hewitt*	**1**
Chapter 2	**Psychotherapy and Patient Preferences for the Treatment of Major Depression in Primary Care** *Patrick Raue and Herbert C. Schulberg*	**31**
Chapter 3	**Major Depression, Age and Antidepressant Utilization in the General Population** *Scott B. Patten*	**53**
Chapter 4	**Antidepressants in the Acute Treatment of Adolescent Major Depression** *Mauri Marttunen*	**61**
Chapter 5	**Managing Treatment-Resistant Depression: Focusing on Increasing Serotonergic Transmission** *Ali Saffet Gonul, Kerem Doksat, Çagdas Eker and Ozlem Donat Eker*	**87**
Chapter 6	**Support Reciprocity and Depression among Children** *Hirokazu Taniguchi and Mitsuhiro Ura*	**113**
Chapter 7	**Postpartum Depression: Latin-American Perspectives** *Johann Vega-Dienstmaier and Maria I. Zapata-Vega*	**125**
Chapter 8	**Stimulant and Depressant Behavioral Actions of Alcohol in Non-Selected Wistar Rats** *Fabiola Hernández-Vázquez and Milagros Méndez*	**145**
Index		**161**

PREFACE

The global community is negatively impacted on a large-scale with tens of millions of people worldwide suffering from major depression. Economic growth is being stunted and lifestyles and lives crippled. Unfortunately, it is not clear what the myriads of causative factors are. Is it stress alone or stress caused by medical or psychological disorders or unknown combinations of these and other factors? This new book tackles these issues head on by presenting the latest research findings in this pandemic.

Chapter 1 presents a summary of a new group therapy approach and a 16-session treatment manual for Group Psychodynamic Interpersonal Psychotherapy (GPIP). The group therapy manual on which this chapter is based (Tasca, Mikail, and Hewitt, 2002) was originally developed as part of a randomized controlled treatment study for Binge Eating Disorder (BED; Tasca, Ritchie, Conrad, Balfour, Gayton, Lybanon, and Bissada, in press). However, the intent of developing the treatment approach was that it be applicable to a wide array of problems including depressive symptoms. For this reason, a broad theory of interpersonal and psychodynamic assessment and diagnosis is presented here, which provides the basis of the GPIP treatment approach. In this chapter depression and depressive symptoms are used as examples of a symptom class that often has a specific cluster of interpersonal problems that underlie the disorder or that co-occur with the disorder. To demonstrate the efficacy of GPIP for the treatment of depressive symptoms, a brief review of outcome data from a randomized clinical trial for the treatment Binge Eating Disorder (BED) is presented.

The authors in chapter 2 describe the small body of research investigating the effectiveness of psychotherapy for treating major depression experienced by primary care patients, and the nature of patient treatment preferences and their impact on treatment adherence and outcome. They conclude that depression-specific, short-term psychotherapies such as CT, CBT, IPT, and PST effectively treat acute major depression in primary care practice and achieve one-year outcomes superior to those achieved by the primary care physician's usual care. No outcome differences emerge when psychotherapy alone is compared to antidepressant treatment alone, or to psychotherapy combined with antidepressant treatment. The majority of primary care patients prefer psychotherapy or counseling. While inconclusive, research to date has not documented a positive impact of meeting patient preferences on subsequent treatment adherence or clinical outcome.

Major depression has typically been regarded as an under-treated disorder. Most studies have found a high prevalences of major depression in younger age categories, but particularly low rates of antidepressant treatment in these groups. In chapter 3, the frequency of treatment was assessed using data collected from a longitudinal cohort representative of the household population in Canada. Whereas a very low frequency of antidepressant use was found in the under 35 age category in 1994, a rapid increase eliminated this difference by 2000. As of this date, there was no longer any evidence that the under 35 age category was treated less frequently than other age groups.

Major depressive disorder (MDD) is among the leading causes of morbidity and mortality among adolescents (Aalto-Setälä et al., 2001, Marttunen et al., 1991, Shaffer et al., 1996). Major depression is twice as common in adolescents as in children, with an estimated prevalence around 5 – 8 % (Kessler et al, 2001, Haarasilta et al., 2001). Approximately one third to one half of adolescents treated in psychiatric settings suffer depressive disorders (Aalto-Setälä et al., 1998; Pelkonen et al. 1997). During an episode of MDD, adolescents demonstrate poor interpersonal functioning in peer and family relationships, and impaired academic performance. An episode of MDD may endanger the development of interpersonal social skills, behavioral control, and the acquisition of academic skills, thus resulting in a delay of social and academic development. Recovery from major depression in clinical samples is often only partial (Emslie et al, 1997), and even after recovery youth may continue to show impairment e.g. in interpersonal relationships and global functioning (Birmaher et al, 1996; Lewinsohn et al, 1994). Adolescent depression tends to run a recurrent course and seems to predict subsequent depressive and other psychiatric disorders in young adulthood (Lewinsohn et al.1999; Aalto-Setälä et al. 2002a; Fergusson and Woodward, 2002). Despite the marked suffering and serious consequences of adolescent MDD, the disorder is underreconized and undertreated (Aalto-Setälä. et al., 2002b, Wittchen et al., 1998). Chapter 4 reviews the research on the efficacy of antidepressants in adolescent major depression. The focus is in published double-blind placebo-controlled randomized trials and meta-analyses. Supplementary data from unpublished ongoing studies and open trials will be presented Published articles were identified through a search in the PubMed database from 1960s through 2002. Reference lists from the main reviews and RCTs were further used as a source of previous studies. RCTs presented in recent congresses providing preliminary results were further searched. Only studies with samples of ten or more subjects using standardized diagnoses of MDD and standardized outcome measures were included.

Among the more challenging problems in the treatment of major depressive disorder is the lack of adequate response to adequate monotherapy. Only partial or no response to antidepressant treatment is observed in as many as 29% to 46% of depressed patients. For those patients, three treatment strategies are the main options for the clinicians; switching to another antidepressant, augmenting with other psychotropic agents, or combining antidepressants. In many of these strategies, the aim is to increase serotonergic transmission without increasing side effects. Augmentation and combination strategies may produce a more rapid response than switching, not only because of neuropharmacological potentiation, but also because the time lost discontinuing one drug and starting another is avoiding. Recent studies in chapter 5, showed that venlafaxine, which has a dual-inhibition effect on serotonin and noradrenalin reuptake might be a good alternative for depressed patients who did not show any improvement with other antidepressants, especially serotonin reuptake inhibitors (SSRIs). However, there are limited data about the augmentation or combination strategies for treatment resistant patients who showed partial or no response to venlafaxine. The authors' previous experiences give us an idea that adding an SSRI to venlafaxine might help patients who did not respond to previous venlafaxine treatment. In this study, 38 patients who were on

225 mg/day venlafaxine for 8 weeks and still not responding to venlafaxine were ordinarily assigned to into two groups, venlafaxine up to 375 mgday or 50-100 mg/day sertraline add on venlafaxine 225 mg/day. At the second week, a significant difference on HAM-D scores was emerged between the groups. However, at the end of the study (eight week) there was no significant difference between the groups. Eight (42.1 %) of 19 patients taking high-dose venlafaxine and ten (52.6 %) of patients taking sertraline-venlafaxine combination had responded to treatments. However, the difference was not significant. Remission was observed in 4 patients (21.1 %) in high-dose venlafaxine group and 7 patients (36.8 %) in sertraline add-on venlafaxine group. The difference between the groups was significant (p=0.02, Fisher's exact test). Drop-out rates were similar but one patient from the combination group showed mild symptoms of serotonergic syndrome which were ceased with the termination of treatment. Adding a SSRI to an ongoing venlafaxine treatment of treatment resistant unipolar patients might have benefits in faster onset of action and higher rates of remission rates compared to high-dose venlafaxine. On the other hand, the cost-benefit ratio of this combination should be kept in mind as there was no clear superiority of combination treatment observed at the end of eight week.

Chapter 6 examined the relationship between support reciprocity in relationships with both parents and friends and depression among elementary school, middle school, and high school students, taking specific account of the quality of parent-child relationships. The participants were 340 first-year high school students, 312 second- and third-year middle school students, and 317 sixth-year elementary school students. Consistent with predictions, it was shown that support reciprocity in friendships correlated significantly with lower depression only among high school students. Moreover, it was found that for high school students who perceived their parents as caring and affectionate, support reciprocity in friendships related significantly to lower depression but not for those who perceived their parents as distant and dismissive.

In the past two decades there has been increasing recognition that mood disorders, particularly depression, are a significant cause of pregnancy-related morbidity. Latin-American researchers have been actively contributing to the field of perinatal psychiatry. Chapter 7 presents a review of the scientific literature on postpartum depression, available in MEDLINE and LILACS/BIREME databases, developed in Latin-American countries including studies conducted mostly in Brazil, Peru, and Chile. Furthermore, due to the known vast migration of Latin-American individuals into developed countries, selected studies on postpartum depression in women of Latino heritage in the United States of America were also reviewed. Significant efforts involving the adaptation and validation of widely used instruments for the assessment of postpartum depression in Spanish and Portuguese language, such as the Edinburgh Postnatal Depression Scale, have been reported. Estimates of the prevalence of depression in puerperal women varied from 5.92% and 48% in different clinical settings. The time at which the maternal assessments were conducted ranged from as early as one day to after up to one year postpartum. Demographic characteristics, availability of social and financial resources, affective support from partners and family, history of depression and/or other psychiatric symptomatology, other pregnancy-related pathologies, premature births, and neonatal illness, among others, have been consistently identified as associated risk factors for the development of postpartum depression in different studies throughout Latin America. Similar findings, in addition to migration and acculturation factors, may play a role in the development of depression in Latino women in the USA. The impact of perinatal depression in the wellbeing of mothers and their children, and perinatal and pediatric care and beneficial interventions for risk groups such as premature children were addressed in other contributions. The need for appropriate assessment, diagnosis, and treatment of postpartum depression, and the development of preventive strategies and specific services are discussed.

Low doses of alcohol have been reported to induce psychomotor activation in rodents, whereas high doses produce sedation. However, locomotor responses to alcohol may be influenced by different factors, including the dose and route of administration, the duration of drug exposure, the distinct sensitivity of rodent strains, the light-dark cycle and stressful situations. The aim of chapter 8, was to investigate locomotor responses in Wistar rats in normal and reverse light-dark cycles, as well as the effect of different doses of alcohol. Behavioral responses were assessed in an activity meter and scores of slow and fast horizontal movements, as well as slow and fast stereotyped movements were recorded. Rats were habituated for 30 min, then received an intraperitoneal (i.p.) saline injection and saline or alcohol was administered (0.25, 1 or 2.5 g/kg i.p.) after 30 min. A control group of animals was registered but not injected. Animals in the reverse light-dark cycle exhibited a higher motor response than those in the normal cycle. Thus, behavioral responses to alcohol were studied in reverse cycle animals. Forty four and 49 % significant decreases in total horizontal movements were observed in response to alcohol at doses of 0.25 and 2.5 g/kg, respectively, versus the control group. In contrast, a 69 % increase was found with 1 g/kg versus the saline group. This dose also increased total stereotyped movements by 41 and 92 % versus the control and saline groups, respectively, whereas a dose of 2.5 g/kg induced a 38 % decrease versus the control group. Total activity (total horizontal movements plus total stereotyped movements) was significantly increased (40 %) and decreased (43 %) by alcohol doses of 1 and 2.5 g/kg, respectively, versus the control group. The stimulant effect of alcohol was even higher (a 78 % increase) when compared to the saline group. Opposite behavioral alcohol effects were observed, 1 g/kg stimulating motor activity and 2.5 g/kg exhibiting a sedative effect. The authors' results suggest that stimulant alcohol effects may be mainly due to fast horizontal and fast stereotyped movements. In contrast, the sedative alcohol effects may involve similar contributions of slow and fast horizontal, as well as fast stereotyped movements. Alcohol behavioral effects may be closely related to activation of brain dopaminergic circuits.

In: Trends in Depression Research
Editor: Maurice J. Henri, pp. 1-30

ISBN 1-60021-394-4

Chapter 1

GROUP PSYCHODYNAMIC INTERPERSONAL PSYCHOTHERAPY: SUMMARY OF A TREATMENT MODEL AND OUTCOMES FOR DEPRESSIVE SYMPTOMS

Giorgio A. Tasca[1], Samuel F. Mikail[2] and Paul L. Hewitt[3]

[1]University of Ottawa, Ottawa Hospital, Ottawa Health Research Institute, Carleton University, Canada

[2]The Southdown Institute, Canada

[3]University of British Columbia, Canada

ABSTRACT

This chapter presents a summary of a new group therapy approach and a 16-session treatment manual for Group Psychodynamic Interpersonal Psychotherapy (GPIP). The group therapy manual on which this chapter is based (Tasca, Mikail, and Hewitt, 2002) was originally developed as part of a randomized controlled treatment study for Binge Eating Disorder (BED; Tasca, Ritchie, Conrad, Balfour, Gayton, Lybanon, and Bissada, in press). However, the intent of developing the treatment approach was that it be applicable to a wide array of problems including depressive symptoms. For this reason, a broad theory of interpersonal and psychodynamic assessment and diagnosis is presented here, which provides the basis of the GPIP treatment approach. In this chapter depression and depressive symptoms are used as examples of a symptom class that often has a specific cluster of interpersonal problems that underlie the disorder or that co-occur with the disorder. To demonstrate the efficacy of GPIP for the treatment of depressive symptoms, a brief review of outcome data from a randomized clinical trial for the treatment Binge Eating Disorder (BED) is presented.

GPIP represents an integration of several theories of psychotherapeutic treatment including psychodynamic, interpersonal and group theories. In particular, the work of

[1] Correspondence: G.A. Tasca, Ph.D. The Ottawa Hospital 501 Smyth Road, Room 7300 Ottawa, ON Canada K1H 8L6 Email: gtasca@ottawahospital.on.ca

David Malan (1979) that focuses on the Triangle of Conflict and Triangle of Person is used as the basis for understanding the psychodynamic underpinning of symptoms. Malan's (1979) Triangle of Conflict is modified and renamed the Triangle of Object Relations to better conform to contemporary psychodynamic notions of object and selfobject relations (Gabbard, 1990) as the basis of human behaviour. This reformulated model is linked to the interpersonal treatment model of Strupp and Binder (1984), which defines Cyclical Relational Patterns (CRPs) by which problematic interpersonal transactions are perpetuated in people's lives and in therapy. Interpersonal circumplex models (Benjamin, 1996) are used for specific interpersonal assessment and diagnosis that informs the treatment approach for an individual. Circumplex models, through the principle of complementarity, also define the self-perpetuating nature of CRPs, and the manner in which personality is defined and developed through the introjection or internalization of one's history of interpersonal transactions (Benjamin, 1996).

This integrated psychodynamic and interpersonal approach to symptoms, interpersonal processes and therapy is considered within a group therapy context. Group treatment occurs, by definition, in an interpersonal context and Yalom (1994) uses the interpersonal group context to further therapeutic work. Group treatment is defined within a phase model of treatment that provides guidelines for specific therapeutic interventions and therapist stances at different points in the group's development.

A Psychodynamic Focus: Malan's Two Triangles

Malan's (1974) two triangles represent a useful heuristic model for understanding symptoms form a psychodynamic point of view. In this model, the Triangle of Conflict consists of Impulse, Anxiety and Defense elements (Figure 1). The Triangle of Person consists of parallel relationship themes among relationships with Past others such as parents, Current others, and the Therapist (Figure 1). Malan suggested that the triangles stand on their apex because the element at the apex is historically earlier and is more likely out of awareness. In the Triangle of Conflict, the Defense is typically a coping strategy, symptom and/or behavior that is an attempted solution to the problem of unwanted Anxiety or Affect. It is a means of avoiding the unwanted experience. Anxiety is often generated by an unconscious Impulse, which tends to be sexual or aggressive in nature.

Although an important heuristic device, Malan's (1974) model is representative of drive theory or dual instinct theory of psychoanalysis (Pine, 1988). Drive theory has been consistently criticized by contemporary psychoanalytic thinkers as outdated and increasingly less relevant because it is not representative of female development (Lang, 1990), and because more current trends in psychoanalysis focus on the need for relating and connecting to others as the basis for human development (Ornstein and Ornstein, 1990). The latter, in particular, is consistent with an attachment theory approach that underscores the inherently biological and primary nature of the need to attach in order to survive and develop (Bowlby, 1988). Another important aspect that is missing from Malan's (1974) model is the implication for one's sense of self or introject. McCullough-Vaillant (1997) points out this shortcoming in Malan's (1974) model, and she has integrates this into her scheme of Triangle of Conflict. McCullough-Vaillant (1997) suggests that the total experience of Impulse, Anxiety, and Defense defines one's self experience.

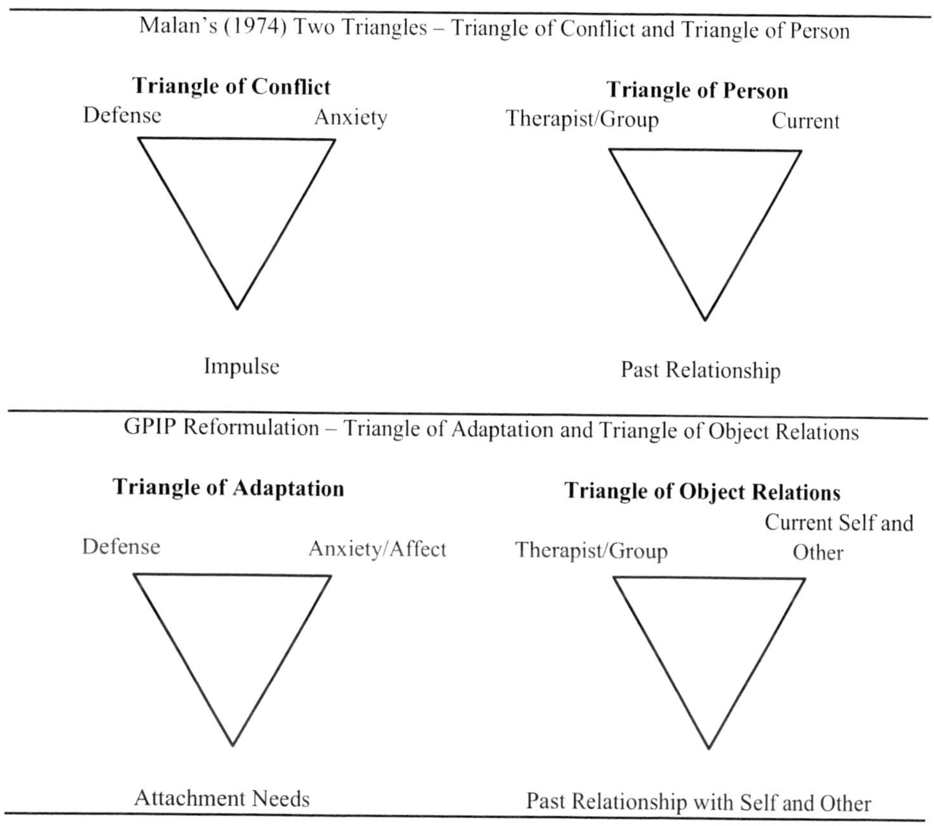

Figure 1.

In the GPIP redefinition of the Triangle of Conflict, attachment Needs take the place of sexual and aggressive impulses as the primary and often unconscious movers of human thoughts, emotions and behaviors. Generally, these are historically rooted needs that may or may not have been met adequately throughout one's life. Attachment needs are expressed in both current relationships as well as internalized relationships with significant figures from one's life. Unment attachment needs give rise to anxiety and problematic affect. In many instances fears of rejection and abandonment are the root of anxiety, anger, hostility or emotional numbing. This negative affect results in the development of defenses that protect and maintain the self-esteem and self-concept. Defenses are interpersonal in nature and define relational styles that tend to be consistent across interpersonal situations. Similar to McCullough-Vaillant (1997), the total experience of the self is defined by Needs, Anxiety/Affect and Defense. Because of the focus on relationships, both internalized and current, we call this model the Triangle of Adaptation (see Figure 1).

Although Malan's (1974) Triangle of Person adequately represents relationships with others, it does not represent internalized relationships or relationships with one's self. Benjamin (1996) argues that one engages in consistent relationship patterns with one's self that parallel relationship patterns with others. Benjamin calls these internalized patterns and relationships Introjects (Figure 1). Strupp and Binder (1984) integrated this notion in their interpersonal therapy when they stated that the experience of the self (Introject) is defined as the end product of ongoing typical interaction patterns. More is presented about introjected and complementary relationships with self and with others when Benjamin's (1996) and Strupp and Binder's (1984) models are discussed below.

The Cyclical Relational Pattern

The Cyclical Relational Pattern (CRP) for clients seeking psychotherapy is an hypothesized process whereby an individual experiences some affective state that is disquieting, distressing, overwhelming, or chaotic, and responds defensively to that affect in some interpersonal fashion. Defensive responses involve relating to others and self in a particular stylistic way. These interpersonal responses provide relief in the form of dispelling or dissolving the aversive affective state or by simply banishing the affect from awareness. This has a real cost in terms of creating psychological difficulties for the person as the "relief" is temporary and the source of the affective disregulation is never truly dealt with in an adaptive fashion. This notion is, essentially, the Triangle of Adaptation, which was outlined earlier.

We extend the Triangle of Object Relations by incorporating work from two sources: the brief psychodynamic literature, and the interpersonal models of psychotherapy and psychopathology. First, with respect to psychodynamic theorizing, the components of the CRP in this approach derive from Strupp and Binder's (1984) work, and they incorporate four facets of behaviour. These include: behaviors in which the client engages (Acts of Self), expectations of others' internal reactions to the client (Expectations of Others), others' overt behavior (Acts of Others), and finally, the incorporation of a model of the self that is based on the previous three facets (Introject). Second, the component from interpersonal theory involves an explication of the interpersonal style or stance the client takes in dealing with the aversive affective states. This is based on interpersonal models developed by Leary (1957) and Benjamin (1996).

Establishing the CRP is paramount in this therapeutic approach for numerous reasons. First, the CRP provides a framework or explanatory model that allows the therapist to make sense of clients' interpersonal behaviours. The CRP spells out the needs, resultant affective states, and defenses. The CRP also identifies overt behaviors in which the client engages, the client's expectations of others (including the therapist), and how the client relates these behaviours to his or her self-concept. Second, it provides information for the therapist to understand process issues in the therapeutic context. That is, information about the interpersonal intent, underlying motivation, affective communication and metacommunication becomes clearer by understanding the client's CRP. Third, the CRP provides the therapist with an important therapeutic tool for identifying effective interventions. Fourth, the CRP can be pointed out to the client (through didactic and experiential means), thereby deepening the client's understanding of his or her behaviour. Such cognitive and emotional awareness expands individuals' available resources in their efforts to make more adaptive choices that lead to more rewarding interpersonal patterns.

Components of the CRP

The CRP incorporates facets of clients' behaviour that fall in four categories outlined by Strupp and Binder (1984; Strupp and Binder refer to this as the Cyclical Maladaptive Pattern). It is important to view these components as working in a dynamic and interactive fashion, with each component having an influence on the other components rather than as static parts.

Acts of Self

This facet of the CRP includes all behaviours in which the individual actually engages covertly and overtly. It can involve needs, wishes, desires, affective states, cognitions, perceptions, and so forth. It includes all domains of behaviour including public and private (e.g., feeling angry and expressing anger), and the behaviours may be more or less available to conscious awareness.

Expectations of Others

This facet involves what the client expects or imagines other people will experience (i.e., think, feel, perceive, and so forth) in response to the client's behaviour. This can include the imagined reactions of others that are fully available to the client's awareness or may not be conscious. The verbalizations that characterize this facet often involve if-then statements whereby there is an expected inner experience of another person based on the client's acts. For example, "If I did this, then others might…".

Acts of Others

This component involves the actual observed reactions of others that the client reports or that the therapist sees. They are observed acts that can occur in relation to or as a response to the client's Acts of Self. The client appears to evoke these responses from others and the acts can include all domains of behaviour as described within the Acts of Self.

Acts of Self Toward Self (Introject)

This is an important facet of the CRP that involves the incorporation of the Acts of Self, and Expectations of Others' reactions and Acts of Others in relation to the self, into the client's self system. That is, it describes how clients treat themselves in relation to the other components of the model. It often takes the form of: "When _____ occurs, then I (am, feel, think, experience…)_________." These represent core self-concepts that are the ultimate target of this therapy.

The above categories of behaviour are synthesized into a transactional pattern whereby each component influences other components. The synthesis provides the initial focus of the

CRP and this is the framework for understanding the client's interpersonal and intrapersonal behaviours, reactions, and symptoms. The pattern does not meet the needs of the individual, and can actually take the person far from meeting his or her needs. It is important to understand that the pattern is currently maladaptive, *but* at some point in the client's development, when the pattern was first established, this style of behaviour may have been adaptive.

Interpersonal Theory

Interpersonal theory is based on a number of assumptions, all of which revolve around understanding and working with the client's relational pattern. At the heart of interpersonal theory is Sullivan's construct of the self-system. Sullivan (1953) conceptualized the self-system as an anti-anxiety system, having as its primary objective the maintenance of "felt interpersonal security" (p. 109). In more contemporary terms, the self-system refers to an individual's self-concept and the unconscious mechanisms that maintain the self-system (Talley, Strupp, and Morey, 1990). Interpersonal theory posits that each of us seek out relationships that confirm our self-concepts. Thus, an individual's pattern of communication and style of relating pull for responses from others that are congruent with his/her view of self (e.g., complementarity). The self-concept has its foundations in early interactions with parental figures. The responses of such figures to one's behaviors become the basis for one's view of self and ultimately, the Introject, or one's relationship with the self (Bretherton and Munholland, 1999). Over the course of one's life, the self-concept is maintained through a process of selective attention and engagement. Interpersonal encounters that fall outside of what is familiar evoke feelings of insecurity and intense anxiety. Thus, each of us strives to create an interpersonal world that is familiar and predictable, even when doing so creates problems in living and relating.

The Interpersonal Circumplex Model

Relational patterns or interpersonal styles can be represented on the interpersonal circumplex as diagrammed below. For the purposes of developing the CRP, the circumplex as defined by Leary (1957) and elaborated by Kiesler (1996) is presented in Figure 2.

First, in Figure 2, interpersonal behaviours, and in this case styles, can be ordered on two orthogonal continua that reflect *power* (or status) and *affiliation*. The poles of the power axis (i.e., the vertical axis) reflect Dominance on one end and Submission at the other. The affiliation axis (horizontal axis) reflects Hostility on one end and Friendliness on the other. Due to the orthogonality of the two continua, they can be depicted as two independent axes of a circle.

Interpersonal behaviours can be explained using these two dimensions of power and affiliation. Any particular interpersonal behaviour can be ordered around the circumplex. For example, interpersonal behaviour whereby the individual listens carefully and empathically to others' problems in an effort to help the person deal with that person's problems can be seen to be both Dominant (i.e., takes a helper role) and Friendly. Thus, the behavioural style is located in the upper right hand quadrant of the circumplex (i.e., in the Friendly-Dominant quadrant; Figure 2). On the other hand, an individual who listens carefully to what others say about their problems and expresses blame toward the person with the problem would fall in the Hostile-Dominant quadrant (Figure 2).

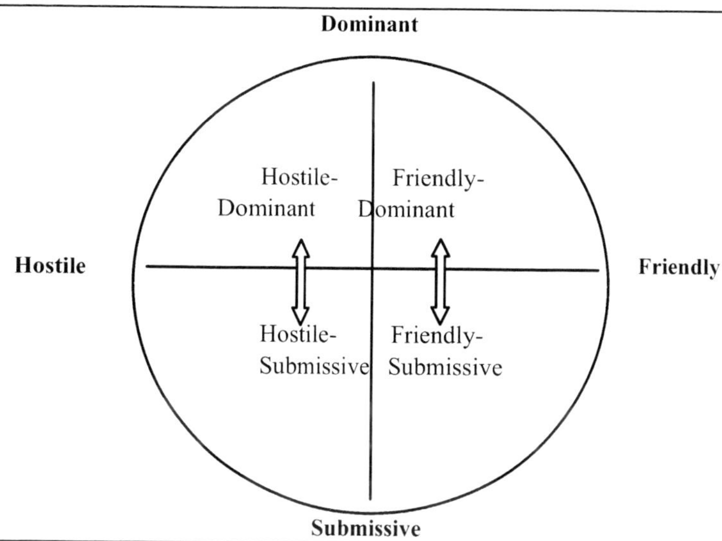

Note: Dominant-Submissive and Hostile-Friendly represent orthogonal dimensions. Quadrants represent elements of each dimension such as: Friendly-Submissive, Friendly-Dominant, Hostile-Submissive, Hostile-Dominant. *Complementarity* is represented by two headed arrows suggesting that Hostile-Dominant and Hostile-Submissive are complementary interactions, and Friendly-Dominant and Friendly-Submissive are complementary interactions

Figure 2. The Interpersonal Circumplex

Complementarity

A pivotal component of the interpersonal perspective is the principle of complementarity in interactions. The principle of complementarity suggests that an individual's interpersonal behaviours can evoke or pull a restricted set of interpersonal responses from another. For example, the individual who is ready for an important date after primping and preening for several hours, states to his roommate: "How do I look" is, of course pulling for a particular response, and the roommate is compelled to answer "Wonderful." This is an example of complementarity. According to Carson (1969), complementarity is defined on an interpersonal circumplex by an opposite response (i.e., reciprocity) on the control dimension and a corresponding response on the affiliation dimension. Reciprocity refers to a stance of Dominance in response to an individual who is Submissive or vice versa. Correspondence means that friendly behaviours tend to beget friendly behaviours, and hostile behaviours tend to beget hostile responses. Thus an individual will behave in a particular fashion with his or her preferred interpersonal style and this will produce a predictable response in other people, especially significant others. Represented within the circumplex, it can be seen that Hostile-

Dominant behaviours tend to evoke Hostile-Submissive behaviours or vice versa (i.e., reciprocal on the power dimension and corresponding on the affiliation dimension; Figure 2). This suggests that the person expressing their dominance and aggressive behaviours toward others, evokes others to take a Hostile-Submissive stance which might include angrily withdrawing, or engaging in passive-aggressive behaviour. Concurrently, Friendly-Dominant behaviour evokes Friendly-Submissive behaviour and vice versa.

Complementary interactions tend to continue unchanged and they are reinforcing to both interactants. When one person does not behave in a complementary manner, tension and anxiety is created in one or both participants because the Self Systems of one or both participants are being challenged. The interaction can then change to a complementary one in which one of the interactants changes their behaviours to complement the other person. Alternatively, the interaction could terminate if the level of anxiety caused by noncomplementarity is too high. (Complementary interactions are indicated by the two-headed arrows in Figure 2).

THE IMPORTANCE OF THE INTERPERSONAL STYLE TO PSYCHOTHERAPY

Understanding and explicating the interpersonal style of the client is extremely important in this model of treatment. First, due to the inflexibility of the defensive interpersonal style, it is assumed that the interpersonal style of the maladjusted individual will show itself in the therapy situation as it does in other interpersonal situations. Moreover, not only does the interpersonal style inform the therapist of the expected interpersonal behaviour of the clients, but it also provides a marker for a style of behaviour in which the therapist can choose to engage in order to either support the person's behaviour (complementary therapist response) or change the person's behaviour (noncomplementary therapist response).

For example, in the pre-group assessment and preparation, Jane had considerable difficulty providing details of what brought her to therapy. She admitted to symptoms of depression, but often spoke in generalities, which made it difficult for her therapist to clearly understand the social, family or interpersonal context of her problems. She complained that others were not interested in her problems, and they either became irritated with her or neglected her (Acts of Others). In fact, her relationship with her adult children had become increasingly distant. She, concurrently, reported significant low self esteem, feelings of worthlessness and poor self-evaluation when she compared herself to others (Introject). She was concerned that her problems weren't significant enough to warrant being in a group therapy, and she expected that others in the group would not be interested in her anyway (Expectations of Others). She also expressed concern that she was taking up the therapist's time (Acts of Self; Expectations of Others). Her hostile submissive manner resulted in the complementary response in the therapist of being much more directive than was typical, and he found himself feeling uncharacteristically irritated with her. The therapist then took a selectively complementary stance with her (e.g. he complemented her submissiveness with a measure of dominance in his overall approach, but he did not complement the hostility with counter-hostility). He suggested to her that if she agreed to join the group, it would be useful to her. However, he suggested that she might feel unworthy, may not likely take up much of the group time for herself at first, and this may lead to her feeling disappointed and angry (Acts of Self). She may also experience others in the group as neglectful of her or as irritated with her (Acts of Others). He took a dominant, though friendly stance when he suggested that one of her goals in the group will be to feel that she could take her rightful place in the group. This would be a sign that she saw herself as worthy of self care (Introject), and that she had something important to contribute.

Group Psychodynamic Interpersonal Psychotherapy

The following section summarizes the GPIP manual. GPIP is delivered in 16 sessions lasting 90 minutes each with 8 to 10 clients in each group. Prior to the start of therapy, clients participate in an individual pre-group preparation session. In this session, the interviewer collaborates with the client in developing a CRP formulation and this formulation is communicated to the client. Goals for the group treatment based on the CRP are articulated, and possible group therapy scenarios, based on the client's CRP, are discussed.

A Summary of the Manual

GPIP requires the therapist to enter into, and ultimately facilitate the alteration of the client's maladaptive interpersonal patterns, part of which involve shifting elements of the individual's self-concept (Strupp and Binder, 1984). For the client, this task is fraught with anxiety, as it requires changing significant components of the self-system. In particular, the client is asked to give up his or her "anti-anxiety" mechanisms and the felt sense of security that he or she has tried to attain over the course of development. It is the enormity of this task that makes psychotherapy so challenging. In order to facilitate the client's ability to tolerate such an arduous undertaking the therapist must create a secure environment characterized by mutual trust and respect. This is the essence of the therapeutic alliance and the process of engagement.

The Challenge of Complementarity in a Group Context

Establishing a therapeutic alliance within the context of group psychotherapy is a complex matter. On the one hand, the professionalism and training of the group therapist allows him or her to convey a stance of respect and trust with a minimum of distortion when approaching group members. Yet, the same cannot be assumed of the relationships that begin to develop between group members. In the initial stages of group formation most members of the group are likely to experience a high degree of uncertainty and anxiety. Group members have limited knowledge of the clinician as a person and no knowledge of one another. What is known is that the clinician has a certain amount of authority, power and influence. Members carry the hope that the therapist has a knowledge base and skill set that will be helpful to relieve their distress. Under conditions of uncertainty and perceived interpersonal threat interpersonal patterns and coping mechanisms become increasingly rigid. Security is sought through a retreat to what is most familiar. For example, an individual with histrionic traits is apt to present in a more dramatic and exhibitionistic manner. An individual with paranoid traits is likely to be more guarded, withholding and silent. Someone with obsessive-compulsive traits will hide behind the details of his or her story and a need for control. In the face of such disequilibrium each individual unknowingly pulls the therapist and other group members into responding in a manner that confirms the individual's view of self and the world.

Interpersonal theory posits that two dynamics are likely to emerge under these conditions. First, *the more rigid interpersonal styles will prevail.* In other words, these individuals are more likely to "succeed" in moving others into assuming a complementary stance. Second, *group members that have interpersonal styles that are naturally complementary will be more engaged and aligned with one another.* For example, an individual with a competitive interpersonal style (hostile-dominant quadrant of the interpersonal circumplex) will likely engage a group member with an unassured interpersonal style (hostile submissive quadrant). Group therapists that are able to attend closely to these early alliances will gain considerable insight into the interpersonal patterns and personality dynamics of group members. This will help in getting a clearer picture of the clients' Cyclical Relational Patterns (CRP).

Phases of Group Development

Models of group development serve to guide the therapist's conceptualization of group interactions. This includes identifying the optimal focus of group work, relevant therapist and member tasks, and expected interactions. Adhering to a model allows the therapist to steer the work of the group and to prioritize the type of intervention to be used.

We have found the concept of "phases" to have the greatest heuristic value. We suggest "phases" rather than "stages" in order to emphasize the fluidity of the process. Typically, it is a process characterized by a back and forth movement by members and the group-as-a-whole. The phases we have identified are: 1) Engagement and Pseudo-attachment, 2) Pattern Interruption and Reorganization, 3) Redefinition/Painful Authenticity, and 4) Termination.

Engagement and Pseudo Attachment: Phase One (Sessions 1 to 4)

The first hours of the group's life are dominated by an effort to define the task of the group. Although the focus of the group will have been discussed during pre-group preparation sessions, the anxiety inherent in the first few sessions contributes to an effort by group members to refine the primary objective of the group. For example, some members may state that their objective is to be free of depression, to improve their self-esteem, or to learn strategies aimed at extinguishing anxiety. Although each of these tasks is a legitimate focus for treatment, *the overriding assumption of the GPIP group is that clients' difficulties arise from problems in their important relationships.* Given this assumption the task becomes one of understanding, exploring and examining interpersonal patterns (CRPs) and the way in which these patterns interface with core aspects of the individual's self-concept (Introject).

During Phase One group members are also focused on identifying behaviours that are deemed to be acceptable within the group. Much of the communication that occurs in the group during this phase is therapist focused. In other words, members will typically direct their comments to the therapist and are most concerned with the therapist's judgment of them.

In their efforts to determine what is acceptable, members are most responsive to cues from the therapist and much slower to engage directly with peers. A related task revolves around members' search for a structure.

At an emotional level group members are faced with a number of challenges. Each must accommodate a shift in status from being an individual in relation to the therapist to being a group member, a process that may recapitulate early family dynamics. Members must explore the extent to which dependence on the group therapist is acceptable and/or tolerable. Members will seek out information regarding behavioral expectations such as expected level of self-disclosure, amount of historical material to be shared and how to handle tension that emerges. For most people clarity on these issues emerges through hesitant participation. While it is important for group therapists to respect the pace of each member, the therapist must also serve as catalyst and guide.

Therapist Tasks

In the first phase of group development the therapist has two primary objectives. At the *level of the individual*, the task is to help each group member to increase his/her capacity for self-observation. At the *level of the group-as-a-whole*, the primary objective is to foster the formation of a group identity that moves beyond pseudo attachment. The therapist begins by inviting group members to introduce themselves. The manner in which members approach the introduction reveals important aspects of their CRP. For example, some members might choose to focus on the nature of their work. Others may introduce themselves by emphasizing the target problem that has brought them to the group. Others yet, might speak to the various forms of treatment in which they have engaged.

Each introduction offers a glimpse into the inner world of the speaker, the ways in which he/she has come to define the self and the adaptive strategies that have been relied upon to preserve the self-concept. Similarly, each introduction will have a particular interpersonal impact. It may draw others near, push others away, or convey a stance of dominance or submission. The therapist can draw on this information in an effort to further his/her understanding of the manner in which each individual is likely to relate to others in the group. However, at this point in the life of the group, such information should be used to expand the therapist's conceptualization of individuals' CRPs and the group as a whole. The therapist's understanding of a given member's interpersonal and personality dynamics (CRP) are not yet shared in the form of interpretation or observation.

It is important to establish and model appropriate norms that will facilitate the group's efforts to establish authentic attachments. The therapist encourages group members to tolerate the discomfort of intense affect. One of the therapist's primary objectives is to create a sense of safety and cohesion. Thus, interpretations of either individual or group CRPs would be ill advised. Rather, the adaptive components of members' communication and defenses are emphasized. In doing so, the therapist can draw on Benjamin's (1996) view that defense mechanisms and rigid interpersonal patterns emerge out of an effort to protect the integrity of the self.

Typically, defense mechanisms are triggered by a perceived threat or a heightened sense of stress. The early phase of group formation, particularly the first session, is very stressful. Although individual group members may have met the therapist, other group members will be entirely unknown to them. Thus, as Beck, Dugo, Enge and Lewis (1986) suggest, members are focused on assessing each other, with each estimating his/her ability to cope with the experience of the group. The templates through which these assessments are made reflect core components of the CRP. As stated earlier, the CRP comprises an explication of the individual's Acts of Self, Expectations of Others, observed reactions of others (Acts of Others), and the Introject.

Creating a Sense of Safety

Using the Triangle of Adaptation, the level of safety can be fostered by emphasizing two components of the triangle: shared needs and shared anxieties or affect. In doing so, the therapist begins to connect group members to one another. Thus, common struggles, fears, hurts, wishes, and hopes can be underlined.

Binder and Strupp (1997) demonstrated that the emotional tone of the first three sessions is critical to treatment outcome. Sessions that are characterized by hostility and the use of pejorative language by the therapist are associated with negative outcome. Furthermore, reversing such a trend once established is extremely difficult. These findings speak to the importance of focusing on the adaptive aspects of each group member's interpersonal style. At times this may be a challenging task, particularly when the therapist is faced with a member or members that engage others through hostility and attack (Hostile-Dominance). The temptation is to shut down or silence these group members. However, doing so may be experienced as a form of reciprocal hostility. When faced with such an individual the therapist should endeavour to identify the fear that is buried beneath the hostility. Alternatively, one can focus on the intrapersonal intent of the hostile action (i.e. the need to create an internal state of safety). An example of an intervention depicting the latter process would be: "*Although a part of you would like to connect to others in here, it seems that most of your energy is going into simply trying to feel safe with us*". This intervention focuses on frustrated attachment needs of the Triangle of Object Relations (Figure 1).

In contrast to anxious hostility, some group members may assume a stance of rigid friendliness (Friendly-Dominant or Friendly-Submissive). This is a defensive posture aimed at the dilution of intense affect and the avoidance of interpersonal conflict and intimacy. In some ways this interpersonal style can be more difficult to manage therapeutically. For one thing, being friendly, particularly in the early stages of social engagement, is consistent with accepted social norms. The acceptability of this Act of Self, combined with the ease that it evokes in others, may obscure the defensive and maladaptive elements of this interpersonal posture. Therapists are likely to be drawn to complementary interactions with clients who assume this interpersonal style, particularly at times when therapists are feeling uncertain or anxious. Conversely, therapists that attempt to interpret this relational style in the early phase of group formation run the risk of alienating group members and evoking defensiveness. Members might begin to feel that every aspect of their behavior is open to interpretation, thereby leading to a lack of safety.

Rigid friendliness can be handled in a similar way as hostility. Emphasis should be placed on the adaptive component of the behavior (i.e., the need to diminish the Expectation of Others as attacking and/or rejecting). The fear of intimacy is driven by a belief that the self is deficient (Introject). The therapist can comment: "*It seems that you are taking care to get a feel for people in here in order to get a sense of where you stand.*" Comments such as this normalize the client's behavior and give members permission to assess the climate before jumping in blindly.

Establishing Adaptive Norms

During the early phase of group formation the group therapist is also focused on an intense effort to establish a set of norms that will facilitate the attainment of therapeutic objectives. The most central norms include: 1) a willingness to be self-disclosing and self-reflecting; 2) the verbal expression of affect, fantasy and needs; 3) the sharing of interpersonal feedback with other group members and the therapist; 4) the respect of interpersonal boundaries; and 5) a willingness to remain in the here-and-now. Although the importance of each of these norms were discussed in pre-group preparation, group therapists usually have to continue actively reinforcing these behaviors in the first half of the group's life.

Self-Disclosure and Self-Reflection

Self-disclosure in a group is difficult for many people. Clients with interpersonal difficulties harbor feelings of shame. Statements about the self are likely to be guarded and superficial, reflecting a fear of rejection and criticism (Acts of Self). Repeated and frequent interpersonal difficulties may contribute to a firm belief that the self is flawed, bad and undesirable (Introject). Conversely, affirmation and compliments by the others are likely to evoke discomfort and an internal state of dissonance. Such statements are experienced as being non-complementary and therefore discordant with the negative Introject. The resulting state of dissonance is often resolved through a variety of defensive operations including the dismissal of positive interpersonal feedback, interpersonal retreat, use of contradiction, or an escalation of behaviors that have the effect of pushing others away. These over-learned responses are likely to operate outside of the individual's awareness in a manner that is automatic and reflexive. Such behaviors are directed at the task of maintaining the integrity of the individual's self-system (Sullivan, 1953), thereby allowing a state of homeostasis that minimizes felt anxiety and inner tension.

It is critical for group therapists to note and respond to these defensive operations in the early stages of the group's life. Failure to do so allows for the emergence of norms that reinforce maladaptive patterns of relating to the self and others. It is important to address the criticisms that group members make toward the self or other group members. In doing so, the challenge of the therapist is to diffuse the client's hostility without reprimanding or sounding confrontational or hostile. Rather, therapists must fix their gaze rigidly on the tripod of: 1) solidifying the therapeutic alliance; 2) establishing adaptive norms; and 3) creating an atmosphere of safety.

An equally effective intervention involves identifying the interpersonal intent of a client's statement or behavior. This can be used when the therapist is attempting to keep two or more group members focused on either the affiliative or hostile elements of their engagements. In the early phase of group development voicing the intensions that give rise to affirming statements can create a positive state of tension. For example: "*You want to get close to her. If you like her can you tell her directly*?" Similarly, highlighting the self-protective components of hostile behavior can abort the process of attack and counter-attack that can create distance and a chronic state of threat within the group. The therapist can address a client's retreat by giving voice to both sides of the ambivalence: "*Part of you is hungry to hear more of the kind of thing that she is saying to you* (Attachment Needs), *but part of you is terrified and unsure* (Anxiety) *of the risk involved in seeing yourself through others' eyes.*"

The "public" nature of group therapy leads to a multitude of negative reactions in response to invitations to engage in self-reflection and self-disclosure. These include feelings of anxiety, fear, irritation, or numbness. Most group members are likely to experience a tension between their expressed desires for change and the feelings of safety and familiarity afforded by guarding prototypic ways of being (Acts of Self). The resulting tension is manifested in the appearance of interpersonal ambivalence and a near constant variability in degree of engagement. If allowed to continue without comment, such a climate dilutes individual members' commitment and identification with the group. Group therapists can move the process forward by looking for opportunities to give voice to the inner tension percolating within each member. In doing so, the group's ambivalence is normalized within a frame of adaptation. The therapist may make a comment that strikes at the heart of the ambivalence: "*People are sizing each other up. The group is anxious about connecting*".

Therapists' use of group-as-a-whole interventions in the early phase of group development invites individual members to view themselves as being part of a collective, thereby injecting a tone of "we-ness". Typically, these are interventions aimed at connecting members to one another and ultimately aimed at increasing identification with the entire group. The impact of group-as-a-whole interventions is somewhat paradoxical. They communicate empathic attunement with a subjectively felt experience while underlining the universality of an experience in a manner that builds on the collective identity of the group.

Building Cohesion

Building a sense of "we-ness" is critical in the first phase of group development. Research has demonstrated that cohesion is positively correlated with treatment outcome (Marziali, Munroe-Blum, and McCleary, 1997). A number of interventions can be used to foster a sense of cohesion. For example, research in social psychology has demonstrated that people who perceive themselves as having shared experiences or goals tend to feel a great degree of connection to one another (e.g. Widmeyer and Ducharme, 1997). The homogeneity of most time-limited groups is a decided advantage in this regard. The therapist can deliberately draw the attention of group members to various aspects of their shared experience: *"It's evident that a number of people have struggled with feeling of isolation and shame as a result of their appearance."* Cohesion can also be built by connecting smaller groups of individuals to one another: *"John it sounds like your experience growing up is very similar to what Pat described earlier."*

Pattern Interruption and Reorganization: Phase Two (Sessions 5 to 8)

This second phase in the group's life is marked by an increase in interpersonal tension. Members begin to compete with each other and the therapist for time, attention, and dominance. Individuals may become resistant to the roles and ideas of other members, leading some to be silent and passive (Hostile-Submissive) while others become increasingly vocal and hostile (Hostile-Dominant). From the vantage point of the individual the primary task is individuation. Individual objectives take on greater clarity and become framed as unique. Some group members may challenge the therapist's authority and assigned role. This dynamic is generally outside of the individual's awareness. It involves playing out one's usual CRP in a manner that confirms long-held views about the self (Introject) and the expected reactions of others (Expectations of Others).

Beck, Dugo, Eng, and Lewis (1986) termed this the stage of "personal influence and survival." This phase of group development is marked by an increase in both intrapersonal and interpersonal tension. The movement toward increased individuation generally emerges in response to the therapist's continued efforts to solidify the extent to which members identify with the group and its objectives. As individuals are exposed to the stories of others and the unifying statements of the therapist, they encounter an image of self (Introject) that is reflected in the painful disclosures of others. Such encounters are simultaneously comforting and disturbing. It is at this point that members are most vulnerable to premature termination. Each individual is faced with the difficult task of choosing between relinquishing the companionship and protection of well-learned defenses (Acts of Self) and self images (Introjects), or maintaining an unsatisfying equanimity that offers familiarity, predictability, and perhaps even a pseudo mastery. The high degree of anxiety emerging out of this state of conflict is apt to contribute to a marked increase in symptomatology and an amplification of maladaptive interpersonal patterns (e.g. CRPs).

Therapist Tasks

Group therapists cannot, nor should they avoid becoming mired in the complementary pulls group members' CRPs. Entry into the client's interpersonal world is an essential component of empathic attunement often involving the therapist responding to the client in ways that are all too familiar to the client (Acts of Others). There is no error in responding to the client's "pull" for brief periods of time. If error does occur, it typically results from the therapist's unconscious self-criticism and the accompanying punitiveness that stems from a perceived sense of failure.

Interpersonal theory postulates that there are two ways through which the resulting tension can be dissipated. The first involves a discontinuation of the interaction, with one or both participants leaving the interpersonal field. Alternatively, if the interaction continues one of the participants must yield to the other by assuming a complementary stance. In this scenario, accommodation typically occurs through a shift in the interpersonal behavior of the participant exhibiting greater flexibility and a broader interpersonal repertoire. It is for this reason that therapists are necessarily "pulled" into the relational world of group members.

In most groups there are likely to be two distinct patterns of interpersonal tension during this phase. Group members whose defenses are organized around a CRP characterized by hostile-dominance will react by challenging the therapist's authority and actively competing for his or her role. The hostile-dominant individual will feel threatened by the dominance of the therapist and will take every opportunity to either ignore or challenge the therapist and other group members who exhibit a capacity for dominance or assertiveness. Such challenges will take the form of "yes-butting", pointing out errors in logic, assuming the stance of expert, or simply ignoring the comments of the therapist. It is not unusual for therapists to feel as if their comments were not heard. At times the therapist may feel incompetent or insignificant, as if the group would do well without them. These countertransference reactions signify that the therapist, having touched the client's vulnerability, has been drawn into the client's maladaptive relational pattern (e.g. CRP). The primary task of the therapist is one of pattern interruption. The therapist works to avoid punishing or humiliating hostile-dominant responses, while protecting other members of the group. This can be accomplished by normalizing the individual's anxiety and felt sense of threat. For example, the therapist might offer the following comment: *"People are becoming increasingly anxious, particularly as each of you encounters parts of your own pain through the stories of others."*

Members exhibiting an interpersonal style clustered around the friendly half of the circumplex tend to be conflict avoidant. A friendly-submissive relational stance is aimed at dissipating the anger or hostility that inevitably finds its way in all intimate relationships. Thus, for these group members the increased tension characteristic of this phase of group development is generally more intrapersonal, or internally felt. Their coping style reflects a pattern of internalization, a process consistent with their tendency to be highly self-referent and with their self-critical Introject. Their Acts of Self can take one of two forms: a pattern of rescuing whereby they assume the role of peace-maker in response to criticisms levied toward the therapist and other group members; or sulking born out of a harsh internal critic and a propensity to personalize the comments of others. The first category of response is best dealt with through group-as-a-whole statements that point to the ongoing process of interaction: *"The group is showing a great deal of courage through your willingness to challenge the constant need to be polite and careful."*

Sulking and/or self-critical responses can be addressed through a variety of individual, subgroup and group-as-a-whole interventions, each of which targets the self-limiting elements of the individual's behavior. For example: *"I wonder if it is more tolerable to blame and even punish yourself than it is to express disagreement with John?"*

The primary themes of Phase Two are: "Do I count?", and "Am I safe from myself and/or others?" The conflict inherent in Phase Two is aimed at answering these two questions. In taking on the therapist, a group member unconsciously expects to encounter the thunderous backhand of criticism or the coldness of dismissal, styles of engagement that may have been all too familiar in childhood and adolescence. These are the foundation upon which Expectations of Others are formed within the context of the CRP. In some cases, such responses are internally generated, taking shape in images of self (Introject) and echoing throughout a member's internal dialogue. To the extent that the therapist is able to assume a friendly interpersonal stance that conveys acceptance and interest through inquisitiveness, he or she can begin to interrupt established patterns of behavior and expectation and challenge the CRP. In turn, group members will begin considering the possibility that the self is worthwhile.

Working with the Emotional Leader

Beck et al (1986) suggested that each group has an “Emotional Leader.” This is a member of the group who is most prepared and motivated to participate in the work of therapy. This person serves as the manager of the group's emotional processing, and is typically expressive, extraverted, and well liked by other group members. As conflict is resolved and the tone of hostility subsides, some group members become increasingly self-disclosing, revealing hidden parts of self and past experiences. During this phase in the group’s life the Emotional Leader becomes increasingly self-observing and more receptive to the therapist’s efforts to block maladaptive interpersonal patterns. This serves as a powerful source of modeling for other group members.

During Phase Two, one of the therapists’ primary tasks is to bring the group to conscious awareness of the harsh internal critic at the core of the self-concept (Introject) of the Emotional Leader and others like him/her, while moving group members toward greater self-tolerance.

Therapist Task

During this phase the therapist relies on two primary forms of intervention: emotional processing and process commentary. *Emotional processing* involves an invitation to all levels of the group, individuals, sub-groups and the group-as-a-whole, to enter into affective experience. This phase will be marked by the use of group-as-a-whole interventions. Therapists must be prepared for strong negative transference reactions in response to these interventions. The process of change is propelled by the therapist's ability to tolerate the expression of such emotion without retaliation or dismissal.

Group-as-a-whole interventions typically are aimed at the Emotional Leader of the group. As this individual enters more deeply into an examination and disclosure of hidden parts of self, the therapist's task will be both to support the individual and connect him/her to others in the group. The therapist must anticipate an increase in the use of both individual and group defenses. Typically these will include the use of intellectualization, rationalization, symptom escalation, problem solving and a general focus on cognition. At such junctures the therapist is encouraged to examine gently with the group the process concealed by the defense. Examples include: *"What did John's comment touch in you?"*

These types of interventions are intended to connect members of the group to their inner experience. Clearly, the emphasis is on affect, although at times it may be helpful to explore core beliefs and assumptions (Expectations of Others or Introjects): *"When Jack tells you that he wants to get closer to you, how does that impact the way you see yourself?"*

Process commentary involves meta-communication. These are statements that focus on what is happening at the level of the relationship. In process commentary, *content* is under-emphasized and the accent is placed on the interpersonal impact of the message (i.e. *process*). It may be helpful for the therapist to imagine placing him/herself on both sides of a member's comment. In other words, what would it be like to be on the receiving end of the comment and what would it be like to have made the comment?

An example of a process comment includes: *"You sound frustrated because she won't defend her position"*

Process commentary can also focus on elaborating the impact that the message has on the speaker. This can include either interpersonal or intrapersonal components. An interpersonal focus is very similar to the above example: *"It sounds like you want to stop her from getting any closer to you."*

The *intra*personal focus targets the effect that the speaker's communication has on his or her sense of self. When such interventions are well timed they move the individual, and the group, to a deeper awareness of the individual's introject. *"I wonder if you are afraid that if you let Julie be right in her understanding of you, you will be engulfed by her?"*

Redefinition/Painful Authenticity: Phase Three (Sessions 8 to 12)

This phase of the group's life is a time of deep inner work aimed primarily at the Introject. The emotional upheaval that occurred in the early part of Phase Two may re-emerge, but in a different form. As desired as change and growth are, they seldom occur in the absence of pain, anxiety, uncertainty, and a transient yet intense wish to put it all back as it once was. If conflict emerges it usually involves a conflict with internalized images of self and parental figures. Beck, et al. (1986) refer to this aspect of the process as "self-confrontation in the context of interdependence" (p. 619). Individual group members begin to move toward conscious awareness of unwanted parts of the self and others. If interpersonal conflict was managed skillfully during Phase Two, the individual comes to the realization that his/her emotions are not destructive, thereby contributing to a deepened tolerance of previously feared and denied parts of the self. Negative aspects of the Introject are redefined. Through this experience of expansion, the individual's assumptions about relationships are transformed, resulting in a decreased need to impose a particular view of the world onto others. Group members are more ready to withdraw their projections (Expectations of Others), while taking greater ownership of their contribution to interpersonal difficulties. Interpersonal learning and authenticity are at a maximum. By this point the group has achieved a solid sense of trust, characterized by mutuality and respect. Interpersonal feedback is more carefully considered rather than being deflected or contradicted. Members begin to explore themes of intimacy, connection, attraction and sexuality. A broader range of affective expression is exhibited, reflecting more tolerance of one's emotions and the emotions of others. During this phase of the group interpersonal confrontation is not viewed as a threat to the integrity of the individual or his or her relationships. When confrontation occurs, it is typically less hostile than Phase Two confrontations. These encounters are an important component of learning to tolerate differences and accept the limits inherent in all relationships.

Phase Three also includes a certain amount of grief work in which members begin to relinquish long held fantasies about wished for relationships with significant others. As group members soften their defenses and become increasingly receptive to the affirmation and acceptance of others, there emerges a complex mix of feelings. On the one hand, they may feel the elation and excitement that accompanies experiences of acceptance and belonging. At the same time they may feel anger, bitterness, and deep sadness that such experiences were absent throughout much of their lives. It is through this admixture of emotions that group members develop an acceptance of others' limits and imperfections.

As group members work through these complex themes they will hopefully emerge with a balance between autonomy and interdependence. Often this will take the form of a readiness to stand separate from old ways of relating to one's family of origin. Some people go through a period of time in which they distance themselves from family members, feeling that they need time to solidify the changed introject that has emerged through the therapeutic process.

During Phase Three members are able to enter more easily into a mode of problem identification and engage in constructive problem solving. The tendency to externalize blame lessens. The therapist may note a redefinition of individual objectives, with group members growing in their acceptance of the limits of what participating in the group can achieve for them. This is a parallel process to the realization that significant others are limited in what they are able to give. It represents an instance of reverse generalization. In other words, a group member may begin to generalize what he or she has come to accept in intimate relationships to relationships encountered in the group. The group and its therapist are no longer idealized, but viewed compassionately and realistically. Thus, Expectations of Others are altered. For many therapists this shift can be a source of narcissistic injury. The greatest challenge to the therapist is to allow him or herself to appear both human and professional.

Therapist Tasks

During Phase Three the therapist is much less active. By this point in the process most of the interactions involve member-to-member exchanges. Ideally, Phase Three is a time during which members integrate affect and cognition. The therapist's task is to facilitate the process of re-scripting. In GPIP terms this is the time when shifts in the CRP begin to be internalized to alter the Introject. If an individual is able to experience a shift in at least one of the components of the CRP, then the stage is set for realignment of the remaining components. The therapist can facilitate this process by highlighting the subtle changes that are occurring. For example, the therapist might comment: *"It seems that you are more confident that your anger won't destroy John or your relationship with him."*

Although the therapist may be less active during this stage, the nature of his/her interventions remains critical. As stated above one of the therapist's primary tasks is to model the integration of being both human and an authority figure. This is accomplished most effectively through a willingness to accept and acknowledge one's limits as a helper. Invariably, there will be times when the group or one of its members feels that the therapist has made an error in judgment. Typically this may be in response to administrative decisions, a failure to empathize, or a mistimed interpretation. Some group members become quite anxious when a given individual becomes critical of the therapist. They react by actively protecting the therapist, offering explanations and rationalizations or blaming the member with the complaint. Others react by distracting the group from focusing on the conflict or disappointment, perhaps by inciting a crisis. Such crises can take many forms including an escalation in symptoms, a conflict with another member, a focus on a circumscribed problem, and so on. In these situations it is critical that the therapist employ process statements as a means of bringing group members to a conscious understanding of the unfolding dynamic: *"I wonder how Sue's disappointment in me is affecting others"*.

In inviting the group to examine such questions the therapist initiates the process of re-scripting their CRP. For it is in trying to wrestle with such questions that members must examine their assumptions about the self and their expectations about other's responses toward them. The therapist's willingness to amplify a group member's disappointment or criticism offers the group-as-a-whole an unfamiliar, yet welcome experience of another in authority. Such encounters, when repeated over time, eventually allow members of the group to shift their "observed reactions of others", and ultimately their CRP.

Termination: Phase Four (Sessions 3 to 16)

The time span identified with the termination phase may seem odd. Yet, in time-limited treatment, once members move past introductions and the initial anxiety of being in a group, they are likely to struggle with termination related themes throughout the life of the group (c.f. Piper, McCallum, and Azim, 1992). A unique aspect of this experience is that the time limits are not in any member's control. The therapist established the meeting time, the length of each session, the frequency of sessions and the number of sessions. This degree of structure "pulls" for the emergence of certain themes. For example, for individuals whose relationships with parental figures were enmeshed or relationships in which they were parentified, such containment and boundary setting may offer a sense of relief and security. Conversely, individuals familiar with emotional abandonment in which parental figures were seldom accessible may respond to these limits with mistrust, resentment, anger, hurt and feelings of deep loneliness.

The work of termination includes making such reactions overt so that they can be processed without distortion. Their resolution requires that they be voiced, felt, and given legitimacy by a receptive and empathic audience. Often group members are tempted to dilute the impact of the feelings that begin to emerge at the end of treatment. They may look for ways to extend the life of the group by discussing the possibility of informal get-togethers after therapy has ended. Or they may suggest that they exchange numbers, hold "anniversary" meetings, and so on. Such suggestions speak to the extent to which members have valued the experience. At the same time, these suggestions represent an unconscious effort to avoid the pain of the current, as well as past separations. In fact, in the last few sessions some members recount previous losses - the death of parents or other significant figures, experiences of divorce or separation, experiences of relocation or moving, or the loss of a valued job. Compelling as these stories are, it is critical for the therapists to connect them to the experience of the group in the moment. In response to a painful story in which a member tearfully recounts details of a divorce that occurred seven years previously the therapist may comment: *"Perhaps the group is silently struggling with the anticipation of our imminent separation"*

Therapist Tasks

As members begin to say goodbye to each other there is a strong pull to idealize the group encounter. It is not unusual for groups to engage in a "go-around" in which each member says goodbye by sharing personal experience of other members, including the therapist. Frequently, these summaries are restricted to the positive elements of each member's experience. It is natural for group members to feel that they want to leave on a good note. It is also natural for therapists to want to resist stirring up previous conflicts with the knowledge that there may not be sufficient time to fully resolve them. Authentic relationships, however, are multi-layered and encompass many unresolved experiences. What makes them authentic is the readiness of the participants to encounter the multitude of layers and to acknowledge the differences that can lead to a lack of resolution. The challenge of the therapist is to encourage each member to express the disappointments, frustrations, sadness, joy, and pain each feels in relation to the experience of others in the group.

An important task for therapists in this phase is to reinforce and acknowledge changes made in clients' CRPs. For example, as result of therapy, a friendly-submissive client may be engaging for the first time in more assertive interactions with others (Acts of Self) that reflect a greater respect for the self and less criticism of perceived personal shortcomings (Introject). At these times, other members often recall past interactions in the group that represent pivotal moments of change for the friendly-submissive client. These past interactions may have involved such a client nervously standing up for their own opinion in the face of a more dominant client's assertion. Ideally, it is the more dominant member who raises this example as a celebration of an important change in the friendly-submissive client's behaviour and view of self. Concurrently, the more dominant client may have learned to allow others their opinion and to listen empathically (Act of Self) without feeling the need to control others. The friendly-submissive member may have become less weary of the dominant client's opinions, which are no longer experienced as being overbearing. Changes to the dominant client's introject may include a sense of self as being more caring and more empathic. Ideally, the accumulation of these important group interactions become internalized into a more forgiving and empathic introject for all individuals in the group.

The group therapist is also faced with the task of saying goodbye to the group. Typically, this is an opportunity to express gratitude to members of the group in response to the gift of having invited the therapist into the sanctity of their most intimate struggles. The therapist may wish to underline the courage that members have demonstrated in their efforts to face their pain and fears. It is also important for therapists to give voice to their own disappointments, concerns and cautions to the group. It is a matter of individual comfort and style whether a therapist chooses to make a brief comment to each member or to address the group as a whole. Some therapists prefer to preserve the sense of collective identity that the group has achieved as a means of aiding members in their efforts to internalize the experience and carry it with them beyond the life of the group. Others feel it is important to model how one brings closure to an encounter in an immediate and personal way.

GPIP and the Treatment of Depressive Symptoms

The focus on both the introject and on relationships with others suggest these two areas are key targets for interventions in GPIP. Indeed numerous theorists have suggested that both the relationship one has with others and the relationship one has with the self are not only determinants of psychological difficulties, but also can be important focuses for therapy (e.g. Sullivan, 1953). These therapeutic focuses may be particularly pertinent for individuals who experience a variety of disorders and symptom patterns that can be produced and/or maintained by self- or other-relational difficulties (e.g., borderline personality disorder, social anxiety). One symptom pattern or syndrome that has been conceptualized as involving self- and other-relational difficulties is clinical and subclinical depression. A brief discussion of this model of depression is contained below.

Psychodynamic and Interpersonal Models of Depression

Although there are numerous disorders and symptom patterns that are consistent with both self-related (i.e., introjective) and interpersonal components (e.g., Blatt and Schichman, 1983), theorists over the years have incorporated both of these components in the understanding of depressive symptomatology. For example, Arieti and Bemporad (1980) described personality/interpersonal styles that underlie patterns of depressive symptoms and that focus on external supports for self-esteem. They described a typology of three forms of depression. The first is based on interpersonal relationships and is known as "dominant other", whereby the depression-prone individual relies almost totally on another person or persons for nurturance, meaning, gratification, and self-esteem (c.f. Chodoff, 1973). The second, known as "dominant goal", occurs when the individual derives self-esteem and meaning predominantly from achievement domains by focusing on achievement goals to the exclusion of other aspects of their life (c.f. Bibring, 1953), most especially, relationships with others. Indeed, the individual is seen as creating a self-esteem through performance in this domain and almost fanatically pursues the attainment of the goal. The third form of depression involves a characterologically flawed personality that is characterized by chronic hopelessness and futility. These personality/interpersonal patterns, at least the first two, clearly have two different focuses that are consistent with the model outlined above, and each creates a vulnerability or predisposition that can cause and maintain depressive symptoms (also see Beck, 1983).

Perhaps the most extensive conceptualization of these two patterns in the depression literature derives from Sydney Blatt and colleagues. This model, and a review of relevant research, is contained in Blatt and Zuroff (1992) and Blatt (2004). Briefly, Blatt describes two trajectories to depressive symptoms. The first, known as anaclitic, has a focus on interpersonal or connectedness issues with strong themes of abandonment, loneliness, and excessive dependency on others. The second, known as introjective, involves a focus for the individual on self-definitional issues (Blatt and Zuroff, 1992). This focus also forms a core aspect of the individual's identity, and a great deal of energy is expended on meeting unrealistic self-expectations, harsh self-judgments, self-loathing, and blame.

There is ample evidence to suggest that the introjective trajectory is very strongly associated with depression symptom severity (e.g., Blatt, D'Afflitti, and Quinlan, 1979) in clinical and nonclinical samples, and may be associated with symptoms of depression characterized by anhedonia, dysphoria, guilt, and self-criticism (Blatt, D'Afflitti, et al., 1976). Moreover, there is some suggestion that this pattern may become especially vicious in the presence of specific self-related or achievement-related failures and events. With respect to the anaclitic trajectory, there is evidence that this pattern is associated with depression symptoms such as somatic complaints and other non-cognitive depressive features, (Blatt, D'Afflitti, et al., 1976). Finally, there is evidence that this pattern may result in depression symptoms in the presence of interpersonal failures or events.

That these different personality/interpersonal styles are both associated with depression symptom severity suggests that both may be important focuses in treatment (Blatt, Shahar, and Zuroff, 2001). In order to address this issue, in the next section we present some data to support the idea that the GPIP treatment approach we have outlined, with its emphases on the relationship with self and relationship with others, may be particularly germane to the treatment of interpersonal issues that create vulnerability to depression.

Treating Depressive Symptoms with Group Psychodynamic Interpersonal Psychotherapy: Evidence from a Randomized Clinical Trial

The study reported here is taken from a larger randomized controlled trial of group psychotherapy for Binge Eating Disorder (Tasca, et al., in press). The randomized trial compared GPIP to Group Cognitive Behavioral Therapy (GCBT; Wilfley, Stein, Freedman, Beren, and Wiseman, 1996) and a wait list control condition. In the randomized trial, Tasca and colleagues (in press) showed that GPIP and GCBT were equally effective, and each was more effective that a control condition in reducing binge eating among those with BED. For the purposes of this chapter, we will focus on data comparing the GPIP and the Control condition. The main goal of this presentation is to assess the treatment effects of GPIP on problem areas that are purported to be specifically targeted by this treatment, namely, aspects of depression and of interpersonal problems.

BED is identified in the Diagnostic and Statistical Manual of Mental Disorders (DSM-IV; APA, 1994) as a potentially distinct disorder requiring further study. BED is associated with obesity, and is characterized by persistent and recurrent episodes of overeating, experience of loss of control during an overeating episode (i.e. a binge), and significant distress regarding binge eating, but with no compensatory behaviors (e.g. vomiting). It is estimated that between 1% and 3% of the general population, 8% of obese individuals, and 20% to 30% of obese clients in weight loss programs meet criteria for BED (Striegel-Moore and Franko, 2003). Individuals with BED report significant problems with depression (Marcus, 1993).

Research consistently points to negative affect such as depression, anxiety, anger and boredom as antecedents to binge eating episodes among obese individuals (Ganley, 1989), and among those with eating disorders including BED (Stickney, Miltenberger, and Wolff, 1999). One can also understand binge eating as a means of coping with negative affect. A number of writers suggest that those with Bulimia Nervosa (BN) or BED binge eat in order to distract themselves or cope with unwanted intense states of negative affect (Heatherton and Baumeister, 1991). Binge eating is often portrayed as a means of regulating one's mood states (Hawkins and Clement, 1980) and a number of researchers have found support for this assertion (Ardovini et al., 1999).

Researchers have also found that those with BED and BN tend to have an increased desire to binge eat after exposure to interpersonal stressors (Cattanach, et al, 1988). Wonderlich, Mitchell, Peterson and Crow (2001) argued that interpersonal patterns among those with BN are strongly related to negative mood, and that relationship styles may be a means of managing negative affect. The interpersonal characteristics of those with BED have received little attention to date in the literature. Madison (1997) reported that clients with eating disorders tend to cluster on two points of an interpersonal circumplex: the Hostile–Submission quadrant and the Friendly pole of the affiliation axis. Madison (1997) suggested that the sociable nurturant subgroup, i.e. those closer to the friendly pole of an interpersonal circumplex, may not acknowledge or know how to deal with conflict. This is similar to the results showing clients with BED may have problems experiencing and expressing anger (Eldredge et al, 1998). These individuals may try to satisfy key attachment figures by being overly nurturant at their own expense, which may represent a form of anxious attachment (Bowlby, 1988). According to the GPIP model, their introjects would be characterized by a sense of inadequacy, and of not being good enough for the attention and love of others. These individuals are overly nurturant at the expense of their own needs. On the other hand the hostile submissive subgroup, that is those closer to the hostile pole of an interpersonal circumplex, may exhibit attachment avoidance in which they withdraw in a passive manner to avoid threats to their self esteem (Bowlby, 1988). These individuals' introjects are highly self critical as they tend to blame themselves for achievement-related shortcomings. Blatt and Schiffman (1983) identified the overly nurturant and highly self-critical patterns as independent precursors to depressive symptoms (Blatt and Schichman, 1983).

Hence the purpose of this study is to assess if aspects of depressive symptoms and accompanying interpersonal problems that are purported to be common among those with BED are specifically ameliorated by GPIP treatment.

Participants were 88 individuals diagnosed with BED and randomly assigned to GPIP (n=48) or to a wait list Control condition (n=40). Clients had to report a minimum of two days of binge eating per week for at least the previous six months in order to qualify for the study. Exclusion criteria included: current problems with substance use, bipolar disorder, psychotic disorder, current suicidality, current other treatment for BED, a history of an eating disorder other than BED, current purging behavior, and being under 18 years of age. Potential participants also had to agree not to engage in any new treatment, psychological or pharmacological, while they were waiting for or actively receiving treatment in this study.

Participants were screened by telephone by a research coordinator who: described the nature of the study, screened for exclusion criteria, and assessed for the presence of binge eating and for DSM-IV diagnostic criteria for BED with a semi-structured interview. If clients met DSM-IV diagnostic criteria for BED as assessed by the research coordinator by telephone, they received an in-person interview with a clinical psychologist who conducted a similar semi-structured interview. If there was agreement between the telephone interview and the in-person interview, then participants were randomized to one of the conditions. In the Control condition, clients were assessed, waited 16 weeks without treatment or any other contact from the center, and then they were re-assessed. Individuals randomly assigned to GPIP were assessed pre-treatment, given a pre-group preparation session, and then they were given 16 weeks of group therapy. In total, five GPIP groups were formed. Group therapy sessions were videotaped for supervision and for the assessment of therapist adherence to the GPIP manual. Clients provided informed consent, and the study was approved by the institution's research ethics board.

Depression was measured by using the Personality Assessment Inventory (PAI; Morey, 1991). The PAI has three depression subscales: Depression – Cognitive (DEP-C), which is associated with worthlessness, hopelessness, and a sense of personal failure; Depression – Affective (DEP-A), which is associated with sadness, loss of interest, and loss of pleasures; and Depression – Physical (DEP-C), which is associated with change in physical functioning, activity level, energy, and sleep. PAI data are expressed as T-scores, with a normative sample mean of 50 (*SD*=10) (Morey, 1991) (Table 1).

Interpersonal problems were measured using the Inventory of Interpersonal Problems (IIP; Horowitz, Alden, Wigging, and Pincus, 2000). The IIP has eight subscales with a circumplex ordering (similar to Figure 2) based on interpersonal theory (Leary, 1957): Domineering; Vindictive; Cold; Socially Inhibited; Nonassertive; Overly Accommodating; Self Sacrificing; and Intrusive. Unipsatised scores are expressed as total scales scores, with higher scores indicating more interpersonal problems. Table 1 indicates normative means and standard deviations.

Five therapists identified themselves as working primarily from within a psychodynamic or interpersonal therapy mode, and they each facilitated one GPIP group. Each therapist attended a two-day training workshop that focused on the relevant manualized treatment. Each therapy session was videotaped, and these were used for therapist supervision, which occurred weekly on an individual basis, and monthly in a group supervision format. Videotapes were used to assess therapist adherence to the treatment manual by two independent judges blind to the treatment modality. Tasca and colleagues (in press) reported very high adherence to GPIP treatment with no therapist showing less than adequate adherence.

Of the total sample of 88, 82 were women, 98% were Caucasian, 94.3% had at least a high school education, 48.2% were married, 45.6% were employed full time, and the median family income was between 50 and 59 thousand Canadian dollars per year. Mean age of participants was 41.58 (*SD*=11.01); mean body mass index (BMI), calculated as weight in kilograms divided by height in meters squared, was 39.22 (*SD*=9.06); mean years of binge eating was 18.62 (*SD*=8.42); and mean days binged per week at pre-treatment was 4.12 (*SD*=1.46). There were no differences between the GPIP and Control participants on any of these variables at pre-treatment.

All data were normally distributed and there were no univariate or multivariate outliers. Table 1 indicates the means and standard deviations for all BED clients in the study, as well as those of the normative samples for those variables (Horowitz, et al., 2000; Morey, 1991).

Independent samples *t*-tests for the means comparing the BED and the normative samples were conducted. As indicated, the BED sample had significantly higher T-scores on all depression subscales compared to the normative sample and the effects were large. Also, the BED sample had significantly higher scores on all interpersonal problems scales compared to the normative sample, and the effects were small for Vindictive; medium for Domineering, Cold, and Intrusive; and large for Socially Inhibited, Nonassertive, Overly Accommodating, and Self Sacrificing.

Table 1: Means (*M*) and Standard Deviations (*SD*) of the Binge Eating Disordered (BED) Sample and of Normative Samples on Variables in this Study

Variable	BED		Normative Samples			
	M	*SD*	*M*	*SD*	*t*	*d*
Depression						
Cognitive	65.67	13.80	50.00	10.00	13.60	1.51
Affective	68.62	14.31	50.00	10.00	16.08	1.79
Physiological	61.13	10.43	50.00	10.00	9.98	1.11
Interpersonal Problems						
Domineering	7.36	5.36	4.9	4.5	4.77	.53
Vindictive	7.35	5.60	5.3	5.1	3.54	.40
Cold	9.85	6.00	5.7	5.9	6.25	.70
Socially Inhibited	13.58	6.75	6.5	5.7	10.85	1.21
Nonassertive	16.25	7.11	7.4	6.1	12.70	1.43
Overly Accomodate	15.13	5.97	7.8	5.3	12.16	1.37
Self Sacrificing	14.51	5.82	8.2	5.5	10.16	1.14
Intrusive	9.50	5.26	5.7	4.8	6.98	.78

Notes: Depression scales expressed as T-scores from the Personality Assessment Inventory (PAI) Morey, 1991). Normative PAI data (N=1000) mean = 50, SD=10. Interpersonal Problems are unipsatized total scores from the Inventory of Interpersonal Problems (IIP; Horowitz, et al., 2000). IIP normative data N=800. BED N=88 at pre-treatment. *t*-values are based on independent samples *t*-tests. All *p*'s <.001. Cohen's *d* indicates medium >.50, and large >.80 effects.

Table 2 indicates the pre- and post-treatment means and standard deviations for the GPIP participants and for the Control condition participants. To assess change on the variables across the GPIP and Control conditions, univariate analyses of covariance (ANCOVAs) were conducted for the measures. Pre-treatment scores on a variable were entered as a covariate, and the post-treatment score was assessed as the dependent variable. Results in Table 2 indicated that the GPIP treatment yielded greater and significant change than the Control condition on the Depression – Cognitive and on the Depression – Affective scales from pre- to post-treatment. In addition, the GPIP condition resulted in greater and significant change compared to the Control condition on the following three interpersonal problem areas: Domineering, Cold, and Self Sacrificing (Table 2). Post treatment scores on Domineering, Cold, and Self Sacrificing (Table 2) were compared to the normative data (Table 1), to assess if post treatment scores were closer to the normative mean. Recall that all three scales were

Table 2: Means (*M*) and Standard Deviations (*SD*) at Pre- and Post-Treatment for Group Psychodynamic Interpersonal Psychotherapy (GPIP) and the Control Condition with *p*-values and effect sizes (η^2) from the Analyses of Covariance (ANCOVA)

	GPIP				Control					
	Pre		Post		Pre		Post			
Variable	*M*	*SD*	*M*	*SD*	*M*	*SD*	*M*	*SD*	*p*	η^2
Depression										
Cognitive	64.68	13.95	60.35	13.56	66.85	13.71	67.60	14.96	.007	.08
Affective	67.58	14.43	63.55	15.62	69.88	14.24	70.68	17.32	.035	.05
Physiological	58.83	9.17	58.31	10.59	63.90	11.27	63.20	12.46	.949	.00
Interpersonal Problems										
Domineering	6.78	4.94	5.49	5.05	8.05	5.82	7.45	5.13	.001	.09
Vindictive	6.87	5.31	6.97	5.25	7.92	5.94	7.72	4.91	.199	.02
Cold	9.22	5.71	8.23	5.89	10.61	6.33	10.62	7.26	.050	.05
Socially Inhibited	12.96	6.59	12.20	5.92	14.32	6.94	14.33	8.78	.252	.02
Nonassertive	15.84	7.23	15.53	6.49	16.74	7.04	16.82	8.67	.583	.00
Overly Accommodating	15.22	5.84	15.09	6.07	15.03	6.19	15.45	6.53	.514	.00
Self Sacrificing	14.95	5.71	13.06	5.56	13.98	5.97	14.64	5.57	.014	.08
Intrusive	9.36	5.09	8.00	5.01	9.67	5.52	9.07	5.31	.135	.03

Notes: Depression subscales expressed as T-scores are from the Personality Assessment Inventory (Morey, 1991). Interpersonal Problems subscales are the unipsatized scale total scores from the Inventory of Interpersonal Problems (Horowitz, et al., 2000). ANCOVAs for each variable compared the GPIP condition (n=48) with the Control condition (n=40) at post –treatment while using the pre-treatment value as the covariate. $\eta^2 > .06$ indicates a medium effect size. Post-treatment data represent intent to treat data with last observation carried forward for missing data significantly higher among the BED group at pre-treatment compared to the norm. At post-GPIP treatment: Domineering means were not significantly different from the normative sample (t=1.15, p>.05) and the effect was small (d=.13); for Cold means, the difference remained significant (t=3.82, p<.001) but the effect size of the difference was small (d=.43); and for Self Sacrificing means, the difference remained significant (t=7.86, p<.001) and the effect remained large (d=.88).

The results indicate that those with BED report very high levels of depressive symptoms and of interpersonal problems. Moreover, these problems appear to be evident across a wide domain of areas. These results are consistent with previous findings that individuals with BED report high levels of depression (Tasca, et al., 2002) and of interpersonal problems (Eldredge, et al., 1998), and that these problems occur over a wide domain of interpersonal functioning.

The main purpose of this study was to assess if specific symptoms of depression and interpersonal problems, purported to be specifically targeted by GPIP, would show therapeutic change compared to a no treatment control. With regard to depressive symptoms, it was evident that GPIP resulted in improvements in experiences of worthlessness, hopelessness and a sense of personal failure often associated with low self esteem. Concurrently, GPIP treatment was successful in reducing experiences of sadness and of low energy and interest. These symptoms are generally characteristic of depression, but they do not necessarily address whether the depressive symptoms are consistent with self-related or interpersonal components (Blatt and Schichman, 1983).

In order to address the interpersonal nature of GPIP treatment outcome, changes in specific domains of interpersonal problems were evaluated. Results indicated that compared to the Control condition, GPIP resulted in significant positive change in Domineering, Cold, and Self Sacrificing domains. Interpersonal theorists suggest that those with problems in the Domineering and Cold domains (dominant and hostile) tend to have more dismissing attachments (Horowitz, et al., 1993). These individuals likely are similar to those with self-related depressive symptoms (Blatt and Schichman, 1983). Hence, GPIP appeared to have a positive impact on these self-related aspects, so that these individuals likely were less distant and controlling in relationships. The results suggested that GPIP treatment resulted in positive shifts in individuals' depressive symptoms, and that these changes co-occur with reductions in self critical and avoidant types of introjects.

Self Sacrificing scores were among the highest obtained by those with BED on the IIP at pre-treatment, suggesting that attachment anxiety (Horowitz, et al., 1993) and interpersonal dependency (Blatt and Schichman, 1983) may be important elements that co-occur with their experiences of depression. GPIP resulted in significant and large positive gains in Self-Sacrificing, suggesting that at post-treatment these individuals tended to focus less on others' needs at their own expense, and likely they were more assertive in interpersonal interactions. These individuals' introjects may have become more positive with regard to their worth in relationships, and this may have attenuated their depressive symptoms. However, post-GPIP treatment Self Sacrificing scores were still very high compared to the norm, and so they likely continued to struggle with self assertion and a sense of self worth in relationships.

The results of this study suggest that GPIP resulted in positive changes in depressive symptoms and interpersonal problems among those with BED. The specific depression scales and interpersonal problems scales indicated change in aspects reflective of both self critical and interpersonal dependency patterns of depressive experiences (Blatt and Schichman,

1983). Although preliminary in nature, this study suggests that GPIP resulted in interpersonal changes for both avoidant and anxious attachment patterns, and that these changes co-occur with positive change in depressive symptoms.

CONCLUSION

This chapter presented an overview of a new Group Psychodynamic Interpersonal Psychotherapy (GPIP). The model is based on a re-formulation of Malan's (1977) Triangle of Conflict and Triangle of Person, and the reformulation incorporates interpersonal and attachment research and theory into a model of self and other. This model is situated within interpersonal circumplex theory. Cyclical Relational Patterns (CRPs; Strupp and Binder, 1984) provide the context within which patients' problems are conceptualized and treatment interventions are formulated. This treatment approach is presented within a group therapy context, and group treatment is seen as a natural arena for GPIP because of the notion that groups represent social microcosms (Yalom, 1994). GPIP is briefly extended to problems related to depressive symptoms, and outcome data on depressive symptoms and interpersonal problems are presented from a randomized clinical trial (Tasca, et al., in press). Preliminary data, suggested that the GPIP is effective in reducing both binge eating among those with BED, and in reducing symptoms of depression and accompanying self critical and dependency related interpersonal problems.

REFERENCES

American Psychiatric Association (1994). *Diagnostic and statistical manual for mental disorders* (4th ed.). Washington, DC: Author.

Ardovini, C., Caputo, G, Todisco, P, and Dalle Grave, R. (1999) Binge eating and restraint model: Psychometric analysis in binge eating disorder and normal weight bulimia. *European Eating Disorders Review, 7*, 293-299.

Arieti, S. and Bemporad, J.R. (1980). The psychological organization of depression. *American Journal of Psychiatry. 137*, 1360-1365.

Beck, A.P., Dugo, J.M., Eng, A.M., and Lewis, C.M. (1986). The search for phases in group development: Designing process analysis measures of group interaction. In L.S. Greenberg and W.M. Pinsof (Eds.). *The psychotherapeutic process: A research handbook.* New York: Guilford.

Benjamin, L.S. (1996). *Interpersonal diagnosis and treatment of personality disorders* (2nd ed.). New York: Guilford.

Bibring, E. (1953). The mechanism of depression. In P. Greenacre (Ed). *Affective disorders; Psychoanalytic contributions to their study.* (pp. 13-48). Oxford, England: International Universities Press.

Binder, J.L., and Strupp, H.H. (1997). "Negative process": A recurrently discovered and underestimated facet of therapeutic process and outcome in the individual psychotherapy of adults. *Clinical Psychology: Science and Practice, 4*, 121-139

Blatt, S.J. (2004). *Experiences of depression: Theoretical, clinical, and research perspectives.* Washington, DC: American Psychological Association.

Blatt, S.J., D'Affitti, J.P., and Quinlan, D.M. (1973). Experiences of depression in normal young adults. *Journal of Abnormal Psychology, 85*, 383-389.

Blatt, S.J. and Shichman, S. (1983). Two primary configurations of psychopathology. *Psychoanalysis and Contemporary Thought. 6*, 187-254.

Blatt, S.J., Shahar, G., and Zuroff, D.C. (2001). Anaclitic (sociotropic) and introjective (autonomous) dimensions. *Psychotherapy, 38*, 449-454.

Blatt, S.J. and Zuroff, D.C. (1992). Interpersonal relatedness and self-definition: Two prototypes for depression. *Clinical Psychology Review, 12*, 527-562.

Bretherton, I. and Munholland, K.A. (1999). Internal working models in attachment relationships: a construct revisited. In J. Cassidy and P.R. Shaver (Eds.). *Handbook of attachment: Theory, research and clinical applications* (pp. 89-114). New York: Guilford

Bowlby, J. (1988). *A secure base: Parent-child attachment and healthy human development.* New York: Basic.

Carson, R.C. (1969). *Interaction concepts of personality*. Chicago: Aldine.

Cattanach, L., and Rodin, J. (1988). Psychosocial components of the stress process in bulimia. *International Journal of Eating Disorders, 7,* 75-88.

Chodoff, P. (1973). The depressive personality: A critical review. *International Journal of Psychiatry,11*, 196-217.

Eldredge, K.L., Locke, K.D., and Horowitz, L.M. (1998). Patterns of interpersonal problems associated with binge eating disorder. *International Journal of Eating Disorders, 23,* 383-389.

Gabbard, G.O. (2000). *Psychodynamic psychiatry in clinical practice* (3rd ed.). Washington, DC: American Psychiatric Publishing, Inc.

Ganley, R.M. (1989). Emotion and eating in obesity: A review of the literature. *International Journal of Eating Disorders. 8*, 343-361.

Hawkins, R.C. and Clement, P.F. (1980). Development and construct validation of a self-report measure of binge eating tendencies. *Addictive Behaviors. 5,* 219-226.

Heatherton, T.F. and Baumeister, R.F. (1991). Binge eating as escape from self-awareness. *Psychological Bulletin. 110*, 86-108.

Horowitz, L.M., Alden, L.E., Wiggins, J.S., and Pincus, A.L. (2000). *Inventory of Interpersonal Problems manual.* The Psychological Corporation.

Kiesler, D.J. (1996). *Contemporary interpersonal theory and research: Personality, psychopathology, and psychotherapy.* New York: Wiley.

Lang, J.A. (1990). Self psychology and the understanding and treatment of women. *Review of Psychiatry, 9,* 384-402.

Leary, T. *Interpersonal diagnosis of personality*. New York: Ronald Press.

Madison, J.K. (1997). Interpersonal assessment and therapy of eating disorders: A clinical application of a circumplex model. In R. Plutnick and H.R. Conte (Eds.). *Circumplex models of personality and emotions.* Washington, DC: American Psychological Association.

Malan, D. (1977). *Individual psychotherapy and the science of psychodynamics.* London: Butterworths.

Marcus, M.D. (1993). Binge eating in obesity. In C.G. Fairburn, and T.G. Wilson (Eds.). *Binge eating: Nature, assessment, and treatment.* (pp. 77-96). New York: Guilford.

Marziali, E., Munroe-Blum, H., and McCleary, L. (1997). The contribution of group cohesion and group alliance to the outcome of group psychotherapy. *International Journal of Group Psychotherapy, 47*, 475-497.

McCullough-Vaillant, L. (1997). *Changing character: Short-term anxiety-regulating psychotherapy for restructuring defenses, affects, and attachment.* New York: Basic.

Morey, L.C. (1991). *The Personality Assessment Inventory professional manual.* Odessa, FL: Psychological Assessment Resources.

Ornstein, A. and Ornstein, P.A. (1990). The process of psychoanalytic psychotherapy: A self-psychological perspective. *Review of Psychiatry, 9*, Ch. 17.

Pine, F. (1988). The psychologies of psychoanalysis and their place in clinical work. *Journal of the American Psychoanalytic Association, 36*, 571-596.

Piper, W.E., McCallum, M, Azim, H.F.A. (1992). *Adaptation to loss through short-term group psychotherapy.* New York: Guilford Press.

Stickney, M. I., Miltenberger, R.G., and Wolff, G. (1999). A descriptive analysis of factors contributing to binge eating. *Journal of Behavior Therapy and Experimental Psychiatry, 30,* 177-189.

Striegel-Moore, R.H. and Franko, D.L. (2003). Epidemiology of binge eating disorder. *International Journal of Eating Disorders, 34* (Suppl.), 19-29.

Strupp, H.H. and Binder, J.L. (1984). *Psychotherapy in a new key: A guide to time-limited dynamic psychotherapy.* New York: Basic.

Sullivan, H.S. (1953). *The interpersonal theory of psychiatry.* New York: Norton.

Talley, P.F., Strupp, H.H., and Morey, L.C. (1990). Matchmaking in psychotherapy: Patient-therapist dimensions and their impact on outcome. *Journal of Consulting and Clinical Psychology, 58*, 182-188.

Tasca, G.A., Ritchie, K., Conrad, G.C., Balfour, L., Gayton, J., Lybanon, V., and Bissada (in press). Attachment scales predict treatment outcome in a randomized controlled trial of two group therapies for Binge Eating Disorder: An aptitude by treatment interaction. *Psychotherapy Research.*

Tasca, G.A., Mikail, S., and Hewitt, P. (2002). *Group psychodynamic interpersonal psychotherapy: A manual for time limited treatment of Binge Eating Disorder.* Unpublished manuscript.

Tasca, G., Wood, J., Demidenko, N., and Bissada, H. (2002). Using the PAI with an eating disordered population: Scale characteristics, factor structure and differences among diagnostic groups. *Journal of Personality Assessment, 79,* 337-356.

Widmeyer, W.N. and Ducharme, K. (1997) Team building through team goal setting. *Journal of Applied Sport Psychology. 9*, 97-113.

Wilfley, D.E., Stein, R.I., Friedman, M.A., Beren, S.A., and Wiseman, C.V. (1996). *Group cognitive-behavioral therapy for Binge Eating Disorder: Therapists manual.* Unpublished manuscript.

Wonderlich, S. A., Mitchell, J.E., Peterson, C.B., and Crow, S. (2001). Integrative cognitive therapy for bulimic behavior. In R.H. Striegel-Moore and L. Smolak (Eds.), *Eating disorders: Innovative directions in research and practice* (pp.173-195). Washington: American Psychological Association.

Yalom, I. (1994). *The theory and practice of group psychotherapy.* New York: Basic.

In: Trends in Depression Research
Editor: Maurice J. Henri, pp. 31-51

ISBN 1-60021-394-4

Chapter 2

PSYCHOTHERAPY AND PATIENT PREFERENCES FOR THE TREATMENT OF MAJOR DEPRESSION IN PRIMARY CARE

Patrick Raue*[*] *and Herbert C. Schulberg
Weill Medical College of Cornell University, NY USA

ABSTRACT

We describe the small body of research investigating the effectiveness of psychotherapy for treating major depression experienced by primary care patients, and the nature of patient treatment preferences and their impact on treatment adherence and outcome. We conclude that depression-specific, short-term psychotherapies such as CT, CBT, IPT, and PST effectively treat acute major depression in primary care practice and achieve one-year outcomes superior to those achieved by the primary care physician's usual care. No outcome differences emerge when psychotherapy alone is compared to antidepressant treatment alone, or to psychotherapy combined with antidepressant treatment. The majority of primary care patients prefer psychotherapy or counseling. While inconclusive, research to date has not documented a positive impact of meeting patient preferences on subsequent treatment adherence or clinical outcome.

Appropriate procedures for treating the major depression experienced by primary care patients have been the subject of randomized controlled trials conducted since the early 1980s by British and American investigators. Stimulated in part by the availability of valid and efficient procedures for diagnosing this mood disorder in the ambulatory medical sector, researchers have studied whether psychotherapeutic and pharmacologic interventions found efficacious with depressed psychiatric patients achieve similar outcomes with depressed primary care patients. The need to demonstrate cross-sector efficacy stemmed from ambiguities as to whether major depression diagnosed in the medical and psychiatric sectors has a similar etiology, symptom manifestation, severity level, and clinical course (Blacker and Clare, 1987; Schulberg, Block, and Coulehan, 1989). Randomized controlled trials (RCTs) exploring this issue with regard to pharmacotherapy have proceeded within the features of well-established methodologies, and have established that antidepressant medications are equally efficacious with primary care and psychiatric patients (Agency for Health Care Policy and Research Depression Guideline Panel, 1993). However, psychotherapy researchers investigating the impact of primary care-based psychosocial interventions within the methodology of an RCT have been confronted by unique challenges. Thus, they have had to deal with: (a) scientific complexities such as facilitating adherence to a psychologically-oriented treatment of the mood disorder even though patients expected to be treated for a physical illness; and (b) attracting the resources needed for costly randomized psychotherapy trials in the absence of generous fiscal support resembling that provided by the drug industry for pharmacotherapy research.

Given such scientific and practical challenges, an empiric base presently is available for determining when psychotherapy, medication, or a combination of the two is the treatment of choice for primary care patients experiencing major depression. This chapter first describes available depression-specific psychotherapies. We then highlight conclusions about psychotherapy's effectiveness that we judge valid even though derived from a limited knowledge base, and we emphasize clinical options still requiring further study. Finally, we discuss emerging directions in primary care including the consistent finding that the majority of depressed primary care patients state a preference for psychosocial rather than pharmacologic treatment of their mood disorder (Dwight-Johnson, Sherbourne, Liao, and Wells, 2000; Cooper-Patrick, Gonzales, Rost, Meredith, Rubenstein, and Ford, 1998; Churchill, Khaira, Gretton, Chilvers, Dewey, Duggan, and Lee, 2000). In light of these stated preferences, it is useful to examine whether granting a patient's choice of psychotherapy influences his or her adherence to this treatment, and the clinical advantages that it achieves.

Depression-Specific Psychotherapies

Earlier studies of whether a depression resolved when treated psychotherapeutically investigated such interventions regardless of whether they were generic in nature, e.g. counseling, or had incorporated principles and techniques specific to the mood disorder, e.g. cognitive therapy (Nathan and Gorman, 2002). As theoretical models of depression's etiology, onset, and clinical course have become increasingly refined, so have the psychotherapies based on them become increasingly detailed. This has led to the preparation of treatment manuals which guide the clinician through each of the therapy's sequential phases, and which seek to ensure that the clinician is adhering to the technical features deemed critical for the psychotherapy's efficacy. Treatment manuals have been developed by Beck, Rush, Shaw, and Emery (1979) for cognitive therapy, by Klerman, Weissman, Rounsaville, and Chevron (1984) for interpersonal psychotherapy, and by Hegel, Barrett, Oxman, Mynors-Wallis, and Gath (1999) who modified Nezu, Nezu, and Perri's (1989) problem solving therapy for primary care practice. These manuals provide detailed protocols that guide clinicians subscribing to each therapy's theoretic orientation on modes of

* Correspondence concerning this article should be addressed to Patrick J. Raue, Ph.D., Weill Medical College of Cornell University, 21 Bloomingdale Road, White Plains, NY 10605. E-mail: praue@med.cornell.edu.

interacting with their patients and techniques for focusing the treatment process. It is important to note that these manualized psychotherapies are all of short-term duration and thus remain relatively compatible with the restrictions imposed by managed care reviewers on psychotherapy's scope and duration.

Interpersonal psychotherapy (IPT) is strongly influenced by psychodynamic theory and emphasizes patients' current interpersonal relationships (Klerman et al., 1984). According to IPT, depression is related to one or more of these four problem areas: unresolved grief, role transitions, interpersonal disputes, and interpersonal deficits. The IPT therapist helps patients identify and clarify relevant problem areas, increase their awareness of how interpersonal relationships contribute to depression, and develop more successful strategies for dealing with current interpersonal problems. For example, a patient with a problem related to role transition would be encouraged to mourn and accept the loss of previously held roles, regard new roles as positive, and successfully cope with the demands of the new roles.

Cognitive and behavioral psychotherapies are more strongly rooted in learning theory (Beck et al., 1979). Cognitive psychotherapy considers depression an affective response to negative beliefs or interpretations of events. The cognitive therapist helps patients identify, challenge, and modify these unproductive beliefs. Behavioral therapy considers depression to result from a low rate of response-contingent positive reinforcements. The patient is encouraged to participate in pleasant activities or build the assertive social skills needed to elicit positive social responses.

Problem solving therapy (PST; Nezu et al., 1989), which is delivered within the principles of cognitive and behavioral therapy, was adapted to the needs of depressed primary care patients (PST-PC, Hegel et al., 1999). PST-PC teaches patients how to solve psychosocial problems within a seven-stage process during which a problem is defined, possible solutions identified, and preferred ones implemented. The goals of PST-PC are to increase patients' understanding of the link between life problems and depression, improve their ability to define and break down problems into discrete components, enhance their skill in applying problem solving procedures, and increase success experiences solving problems. Adaptations of this type of therapy to the primary care setting include shortening the treatment length to 4-6 sessions, shortening the session duration to 30 minutes, and broadening its implementation beyond mental health specialists to a range of health professionals (e.g., nurses, physicians) when given appropriate training.

The Primary Care Psychotherapy Evidence Base

Various criteria can be applied to the determination of whether a psychotherapy is sufficiently "evidence-based" or "empirically supported" to warrant inclusion in a compendium of treatments for depression (Westen and Morrison, 2001). Given the methodological flaws in earlier primary care psychotherapy research noted by Brown and Schulberg (1995), Schulberg, Raue, and Rollman (2002) proposed that, in addition to use of a depression-specific manualized psychotherapy, a randomized controlled trial must utilize standardized diagnostic instruments and an appropriate comparison arm for its findings to be judged meaningful. The Diagnostic Interview Schedule (Robins, Helzer, Croughan, and Ratcliff, 1981), the PRIME-MD (Spitzer, Williams, Kroenke, Linzer, deGruy, Hahn, et al.,

1994), and the PHQ-9 (Spitzer, Kroenke, and Williams, 1999) are all standardized instruments whose structured format facilitates their administration to primary care patients. With the growing interest in the effectiveness of depression-specific psychotherapy delivered in routine primary care practice, researchers now consider the "usual care" available from primary care physicians (which may or may not include counseling) a scientifically acceptable yardstick against which to compare psychotherapy's impact (Schulberg, Coulehan, Block, Lave, Rodriguez, Scott, et al., 1993).

With the diagnostic focus limited to major depression, eight clinical trials have incorporated the above methodological features. However, even within this restricted set of research reports, other key design elements differ markedly. Thus, (a) the time points at which investigators assessed outcome ranged from two to twelve months; (b) clinical outcome indices included absolute change in depressive severity, percentage of patients achieving a 50% or greater reduction in depressive severity, and/or the percentage of patients achieving recovery at a designated time point; (c) the intervention against which psychotherapy's outcome was compared could be either usual care provided by a primary care physician, an antidepressant medication, such a medication combined with psychotherapy, or a drug placebo; and (d) psychotherapy was provided either alone, or as one element of multi-modal care management. Given these differences, the database for assessing psychotherapy's effectiveness in primary care practice is quite variable on several key design features despite its conformance with minimal contemporary standards for a scientifically acceptable RCT.

Does Psychotherapy Alone Effectively Treat Major Depression Primary Care Practice?

The following analysis recognizes that psychotherapy's utility for treating major depression in primary care practice depends not only on its clinical outcomes but also upon its cost-effectiveness, availability of competent therapists, adequate insurance coverage, etc. (Schulberg et al., 2002). Nevertheless, for purposes of constructing consensus guidelines about whether and when to recommend psychotherapy alone or in combination with medication as the treatment for major depression in primary care practice, we focus our analysis and conclusions solely on the clinical findings drawn from available RCTs.

Six of the eight primary care RCTs conducted since the early 1980s were directed by British investigators (Blackburn, Bishop, Glen, Whalley, and Christie, 1981; Teasdale, Fennel, Hibbert, and Amies, 1984; Ross and Scott, 1985; Scott and Freeman, 1992; Mynors-Wallis, Gath, Lloyd-Thomas, and Tomlinson, 1995; Mynors-Wallis, Gath, Day, and Baker, 2000) and two by American researchers (Katon, Robinson, von Korff, Lin, Bush, Ludman, et al., 1996; Schulberg, Block, Madonia, Scott, Rodriguez, Imber, et al., 1996). Five of the RCTs investigated outcomes for patients treated with cognitive or cognitive-behavioral therapy (Blackburn et al., 1981; Teasdale et al., 1984; Ross and Scott, 1985; Scott and Freeman, 1992; Katon et al., 1996), two investigated outcomes for problem-solving therapy (Mynors-Wallis et al., 1995; Mynors-Wallis et al., 2000), and one for interpersonal psychotherapy (Schulberg et al., 1996). As was noted previously, primary care RCTs have utilized differing comparison arms for assessing psychotherapy's effectiveness. In the five

RCTs utilizing a primary care physician's usual care as the alternative to psychotherapy, two found cognitive therapy and usual care equally effective in markedly reducing depressive severity on the selected outcome index (Teasdale et al., 1984; Scott and Freeman, 1992). However, psychotherapy produced a significantly better outcome than usual care in the other RCT of cognitive behavioral therapy (Ross and Scott, 1985), in the study of cognitive behavioral therapy plus medication adherence (Katon et al., 1996), and in the study of interpersonal psychotherapy (Schulberg et al., 1996). When a medication placebo served as the comparison arm, problem solving therapy produced the clinically superior outcome (Mynors-Wallis et al., 1995).

The effectiveness of psychotherapy alone also has been compared with antidepressant medications, the first-line intervention typically utilized by primary care physicians when treating major depression (Pincus, Tanielian, Marcus, Olfson, Zarin, Thompson, et al., 1998). In the RCTs studying clinical outcomes for psychotherapy alone and such medications alone, investigators found similar improvement on the outcome index when the major depression was treated with either of these interventions (Scott and Freeman, 1992; Mynors-Wallis et al., 1995; Mynors-Wallis et al., 2000; Schulberg et al., 1996). The AHCPR Depression Guideline Panel (1993), the American Psychiatric Association (2000), and the Canadian Depression Work Group (Segal, Whitney, Lam, et al., 2001) judged psychotherapy alone effective but recommended that it be restricted as a monotherapy to mild-moderate episodes of major depression. However, Schulberg, Pilkonis, and Houck (1998) found interpersonal psychotherapy alone as effective as the antidepressant medication nortriptyline when treating the subgroup of primary care patients with more severe episodes of this mood disorder (mean baseline 17-item Hamilton Rating Scale for Depression score of 26; HRSD; Hamilton, 1960). This suggests the need for further research on the relationship between depressive severity and psychotherapeutic effectiveness in primary care populations experiencing both a mood disorder and physical illness.

In addition to comparing psychotherapy and pharmacotherapy as monotherapies for major depression, two primary care research teams have compared the clinical outcome achieved by psychotherapy alone and psychotherapy delivered concurrently with an antidepressant medication. Blackburn et al. (1981) found that 81.8% of patients provided cognitive therapy plus a medication recovered at five months compared to 72.7% of those provided CT alone, a nonsignificant trend. Mynors-Wallis, et al. (2000) found no differences in 12-month recovery rates among patients receiving problem-solving therapy alone or PST plus a medication (62% vs. 66%).

Given this small primary care data set concerning the relative utility of combined treatment, can findings from studies conducted with depressed psychiatric outpatients more definitively inform such practice in the ambulatory medical sector? Earlier reviews of pertinent research (Manning, Markowitz, and Frances, 1992; Robinson, Berman, and Niemeyer, 1990; Wexler and Cicchetti, 1992) almost uniformly concluded that combined therapy offers no clinical advantage over either intervention delivered as a monotherapy. More recently, Pettit, Voelz, and Joiner (2001) concluded that the advantage of psychotherapy combined with medication is modest and generally not great enough to influence choice of intervention during treatment's acute phase. However, some studies do indicate that combined therapy's effectiveness relative to monotherapy should influence treatment choice (Thase, Greenhouse, Frank, Reynolds, Pilkonis, Hurley, et al., 1997; De Jonghe, Kool, van Aalst, Dekker, and Peen, 2001; Pampallona, Bollini, Tibaldi, Kupelnick, and Munizza, 2004). Thase et al.'s (1997) "mega-analysis" of six RCTs conducted at the University of Pittsburgh found patients scoring >19 on the 17-item HRSD to benefit more from combined therapy than monotherapy, while there were no differences among less severely depressed patients. Since the major depression of primary care patients typically is of the less severe type (Coyne, Fechner-Bates, and Schwenk, 1994), combined therapy likely will be initiated with but a minority of the depressed primary care patients. Keller, McCullough, Klein, Arnow, Dunner, Gelenberg, et al. (2000) found an antidepressant medication combined with a cognitive-behavioral system of psychotherapy superior to monotherapy in treating chronic or recurrent depression. Again, however, this finding is minimally relevant to routine primary care practice since patients experiencing this mood disorder subtype will likely be referred to the specialty psychiatric sector.

Virtually all of the primary care and psychiatric studies of monotherapy versus combined therapy have focused on their efficacy during the acute phase of treatment. A recent review (Pampallona et al., 2004), however, concluded that patients receiving combined treatment benefit more than those receiving drug treatment alone, regardless of whether the treatment was acute or longer than 12 weeks. In addition, patients who received combined treatment lasting longer than 12 weeks were less likely to drop out of treatment, suggesting that one function of psychotherapy may be to keep patients in treatment. With regard to their relative advantages in preventing the recurrence of a depressive episode, two Pittsburgh RCTs achieved differing results. Frank, Kupfer, Perel, Cornes, Jarrett, Mallinger, et al. (1990) found three-year survival rates for midlife psychiatric patients treated with psychotherapy and medication during the maintenance phase to resemble those of patients provided pharmacotherapy alone. In a study of older psychiatric patients, however, Reynolds, Frank, Perel, Imber, Cornes, Miller, et al. (1999) determined that maintenance phase medication combined with psychotherapy is the optimal clinical strategy for preserving recovery.

Our analysis of the relative outcomes achieved by psychotherapy alone and combined therapy points to the complexity of designing and conducting such research (White and Walden, 2000) and the need for additional studies which control for key variables such as history of prior depression, severity of the episode at baseline, etc. While prior studies have investigated combined therapy delivered concurrently during treatment's acute phase, we also need to study combined therapy's efficacy when it is delivered sequentially. Thus, RCTs should investigate the impact of medication when used to augment psychotherapy that has produced only a partial response, or when serving as an alternative to psychotherapy that has produced no response. The currently available evidence about combined treatment's effectiveness as an augmentation or crossover strategy has been judged as equivocal by the Canadian Depression Work Group (Segal, Kennedy, Cohen, et al., 2001).

What implications do these reports have for the choice of psychotherapist? Outcome does not appear related to the psychotherapist's discipline since the clinicians achieving successful outcomes in the previously cited RCTs of psychotherapy alone, or as part of combined therapy, included psychiatrists, clinical psychologists, nurses, and general practitioners. Thus, individual competency with a particular psychotherapy rather than professional discipline should guide the selection of clinicians to deliver interventions of known efficacy, a principle that necessarily can be most readily implemented in urban areas and/or in geographic settings with access to extensive academic resources. We would note, however, that even in such locales primary care physicians are unlikely to obtain the training and schedule the practice time needed to deliver a depression-specific psychotherapy conforming to treatment manual standards despite evidence that physicians indeed can function at this quality level when so motivated and facilitated (Mynors-Wallis et al., 2000).

When patients are being treated concurrently with psychotherapy and an antidepressant medication, a decision is necessary as to whether both treatments should be delivered by a single clinician, or be split between the psychotherapist and a medication-prescribing physician. Past analyses of this issue focused on clinical and ideological parameters (Beitman and Klerman, 1991) but in recent years attention has shifted to the decision's economic implications. Thus, Goldman, McCulloch, Cuffel, Zarin, Suarez, and Burns (1998) argue that integrated treatment in a managed care network delivered by a single physician is no more costly than split treatment including a lower paid non-physician. It is highly unlikely, however, that a depressed patient can receive combined treatment from a single clinician in primary care practice unless management of the mood disorder is "carved out" to a behavioral health organization. When it is not, psychotherapy will likely be delivered by a non-physician, and pharmacotherapy by the primary care physician.

We conclude from the above analyses that a depression-specific psychotherapy (CT, CBT, IPT, or PST) provided alone by a competent clinician effectively treats major depression in primary care practice. It achieves outcomes in the 12 months following baseline that are statistically superior to those produced by the primary care physician's usual care, and are comparable to those achieved by an antidepressant alone. The clinical as well as statistical robustness of this conclusion is supported by the effect sizes achieved by the above treatments. They range from 1.66-2.32 when calculated in relation to the pre-post changes in the depression severity score, and from 1.39-2.05 in relation to a remission index. These magnitudes are indicative of true clinical change in pre-post depressive status. We acknowledge that the primary care database for deriving this conclusion about the effectiveness of psychotherapy alone is relatively small and restricted. Nevertheless, the findings are drawn from RCTs in which the outcomes were virtually uniform in their direction, subject groups met diagnostic criteria for major depression, and they experienced at least moderate levels of depressive severity. Psychotherapy alone also appears as effective as combined treatment for mild/moderate episodes of major depression, the predominant clinical pattern presenting in primary care practice.

What is the Framework for Determining Whether and When Psychotherapy Alone is Effective?

The determination of whether psychotherapy effectively treats the primary care patient's major depression and when maximal therapeutic benefit has been reached generally is based on the degree of symptomatic improvement occurring since baseline. As was noted previously, primary care RCTs have assessed a patient's clinical course in several ways. We suggest that absolute symptomatic change since treatment's onset, or a 50% reduction in depressive severity, is the pertinent criterion for judging whether clinical improvement is evident and continued psychotherapy alone is warranted. We consider the criterion of "recovery" (e.g. 17-item HRSD score <8) pertinent to the judgment of whether maximal therapeutic benefits have been achieved.

Our review of the eight primary care RCTs indicates that none directly addressed the above questions. Nevertheless, reasonably meaningful answers can be deduced from the published data since treatment intensity in these RCTs was adequate for this analysis. Thus, psychotherapy alone ranged from six sessions for problem-solving therapy (Mynors-Wallis et al., 1995; Mynors-Wallis et al., 2000) and cognitive therapy as part of a multi-modal intervention (Katon et al., 1996) to 10-15 sessions of cognitive therapy (Schulberg et al., 1993; Blackburn et al., 1981; Teasdale et al., 1984; Ross and Scott, 1985) and 12 sessions of interpersonal psychotherapy (Schulberg et al., 1996). While the cognitive therapy provided depressed patients in Katon et al.'s (1996) RCT was compacted into a six-week treatment episode, the psychotherapies delivered in the remaining RCTs extended over a 12-16 week duration. Thus, subjects in these studies met the six-eight session criterion for adequate exposure to treatment utilized by Howard, Kopta, Krause, and Orlinsky (1986) in their analysis of the dose-effect relationship in psychotherapy.

We found extent of clinical improvement after the initial 4-6 weeks of psychotherapy to range from a 20% reduction in baseline HRSD scores for patients provided interpersonal psychotherapy (Schulberg et al., 1996) to a 56% reduction in such scores for patients treated with problem solving therapy (Mynors-Wallis et al., 1995). While problem solving therapy produced the most immediate improvement, all psychotherapies produced steady improvement in clinical status over time. After four months, baseline depressive severity had been reduced by 50%-63% in all psychotherapy RCTs. Given this pattern of continuous clinical improvement during the initial 12-16 weeks of psychotherapy, we consider 6-8 weeks post-baseline an appropriate time point for gauging whether this intervention is proving beneficial and its continuation as a monotherapy justified. This recommendation is consistent with the finding by Shapiro, Barkham, Rees, Hardy, Reynolds, and Startup (1994) that 16-session psychotherapy has an advantage over 8-session treatment only for severely depressed patients (i.e. mean baseline Beck Depression Inventory score of 30; Beck, Ward, Mendelson, Mock, and Erlbaugh, 1961).

With regard to ascertaining when maximal therapeutic benefit has been derived from psychotherapy, fewer data are available for this judgment. Howard et al. (1986) determined that 46% of patients treated with long-term psychotherapy in mental health facilities improved after eight sessions and 73% after 26 sessions. However, primary care RCTs assessing clinical course for periods up to one year suggest that clinical status remains stable after four months of short-term psychotherapy (Lave, Frank, Schulberg, and Kamlet, 1998). This likely indicates that maximal therapeutic benefit has been achieved at this point with a time-limited treatment. We would caution, nevertheless, that psychotherapy not necessarily be terminated after four months since few data are available to clarify whether continuation or maintenance phase psychotherapy alone, even at a reduced level of intensity, protects against relapse. The need for research about psychotherapy's sustained effectiveness is underlined by Westen and Morrison's (2001) finding that only 36%-38% of depressed patients who improved remained improved up to 24 months post-baseline.

WHAT FACTORS PREDICT CLINICAL OUTCOME FOR PSYCHOTHERAPY ALONE IN PRIMARY CARE PRACTICE?

While 50%-60% of depressed primary care patients treated psychotherapeutically recover, the remaining 40%-50% provided this monotherapy do not. Distinguishing patient factors associated with the former and latter outcomes would possibly direct psychotherapists to customized interventions and, thereby, potentially improve recovery rates. Numerous investigators have sought to identify such distinguishing factors in studies of depressed psychiatric samples. For example, Sotsky, Glass, Shea, Pilkonis, Collins, Elkin, et al. (1991) identified six patient characteristics in addition to depressive severity predicting outcomes across both cognitive behavioral therapy and interpersonal psychotherapy. However, relatively few investigators have analyzed factors influencing outcome of depressed primary care patients whose symptom presentation is predominantly physical rather than affective, and who are experiencing physical illnesses of varying severity which could adversely influence the treatment process.

With regard to the small number of outcome-related studies conducted with depressed primary care samples, few are specific to psychotherapy. Thus, Schulberg, McClelland, and Gooding (1987) conducted an observational study of patients provided no standardized treatment of their depression. They found lifetime psychiatric symptoms positively related to persisting major depression six months post-baseline. Extensive psychopathology was similarly identified by Brown, Schulberg, Madonia, Shear, and Houck (1996) as adversely influencing outcome. Depressed patients with lifetime panic disorder had significantly poorer recovery rates regardless of whether they were treated with psychotherapy or an antidepressant medication. Patients treated with interpersonal psychotherapy were significantly more likely to have recovered from their episode of major depression at eight months when lacking a lifetime history of generalized anxiety disorder or panic disorder, and exhibiting no current Axis II personality disorder (Brown, Schulberg, and Prigerson, 2000). The adverse impact of personality factors on outcome was also detected by other investigators. Patience, McGuire, Scott, and Freeman (1995) found the presence of personality pathology to delay recovery from major depression across all treatment modes, and Katon, Lin, von Korff, Bush, Walker, Simon, et al. (1994) found higher initial neuroticism to significantly predict the severity of affective symptoms at four months in patients treated with antidepressant medications. In contrast to the previous reports that identified various patient-related factors associated with outcome, Mynors-Wallis et al. (1995) found no clinical, demographic, or psychosocial variables related to change in depressive severity among patients treated with problem-solving therapy. More recently, Alexopoulos, Katz, Bruce, Heo, Ten Have, Raue et al. (in press) found that comorbid anxiety disorders, hopelessness, and limitations in both physical and emotional functioning were associated with low remission rates among elderly patients treated with either antidepressant medication, interpersonal psychotherapy, or a physician's usual care. What judgments may be drawn from this limited database? It appears that the more extensive the co-occurring Axis I and Axis II psychopathology, the more difficult and delayed is the primary care patient's recovery from major depression.

Medical comorbidity is another factor hypothesized as adversely affecting the primary care patient's recovery from an episode of major depression. Earlier studies such as those by

Popkin, Callies, and Mackenzie (1985), Kukull, Koepsell, Inui, Borson, Okimoto, Raskind, et al. (1986), and Schulberg, McClelland, and Gooding (1987) found depressive outcomes significantly poorer for patients with comorbid medical illnesses. More recent studies such as those completed by Koike, Unutzer, and Wells (2002) and Iosifescu, Nierenberg, Alpert, Smith, Bitran, Dording, et al. (2003) continue to report such a relationship. Theoretical models to explain the manner wherein depression and physical illnesses interact to impede the patient's recovery from the mood disorder have been proposed by Katon (2003), and empiric tests of these formulations are now indicated.

Patient Treatment Preferences

A body of literature has developed in recent years regarding patient treatment preferences, and their impact on treatment adherence and effectiveness (van Schaik, Klijn, van Hout, van Marwijk, Beekman, de Hann, et al, 2004). Treatment preferences may be important in accounting for the significant number of patients who fail to become engaged in or adhere to interventions offered in primary care, whether they be antidepressant medication or psychotherapy. Nonadherence can be defined in numerous ways, including failing to initiate a recommended or prescribed treatment, limited use or misuse of treatment, failure to become engaged in treatment, and early termination treatment. Nonadherence or poor adherence can lead to compromised treatment efficacy and poor outcomes. Randomized clinical trials have reported remission rates that differ substantially when outcomes are compared for "intent to treat" and "treatment completer" cohorts, e.g., 49% vs. 69%, respectively, in Schulberg, et al.'s (1996) study of depressed mid-life primary care patient participants. In this study, only one-third of participants completed a full-course of psychotherapy.

A patient's decision not to initiate the treatment process, or to terminate it prematurely, often stems from his or her disappointment or dissatisfaction with not having a priori treatment preferences met. What is known about the preferences that depressed primary care patients bring to the clinical encounter? The most commonly stated choice of treatment by depressed patients is counseling or psychotherapy. In studies conducted by Cooper-Patrick et al. (1998), Churchill et al. (2000), and Dwight-Johnson et al. (2000), 50%-86% of depressed mid-life patients preferred a psychosocial intervention, while only a minority preferred medications as the initial intervention. In a randomized controlled trial conducted with older depressed primary care patients, Unutzer, Katon, Callahan, Williams, Hunkeler, Harpole, et al. (2002) found 51% to prefer counseling and 39% medications. Furthermore, 73% of the general practice patients interviewed by Zeitlin, Katona, D'Ath, and Katona (1997) judged antidepressant medications "very" addictive, and only 26% considered them "very" effective. Factors associated with choice of a psychosocial intervention in these studies were female gender, African American racial status, no prior medication treatment, concern that medications are addictive, and prior success with this intervention. Factors associated with preference for medication were greater depressive severity and prior success with medication.

Despite these findings, most depressed patients display limited understanding of the availability and efficacy of standard treatments for their mood disorder (Goldney, Fisher, Wilson, and Cheok, 2002). Based on this, an important issue regards the nature of information considered by patients in formulating their treatment preference, and whether interventions that involve education and that actively engage patients in a negotiation process lead to more informed preferences and subsequent adherence to the selected treatment.

Treatment Negotiation

The seminal body of research on treatment choice was conducted by Lazare, Eisenthal, and Wasserman (1975), who refined procedures for the patient and clinician to "negotiate" a "customer-based" treatment plan in the ambulatory psychiatric setting. Lazare et al. found that patients seeking help have one or more requests or preferences for treatment, including advice, support, insight, and medical treatment. Lazare et al. argue that one result of a clinician eliciting a patient's requests or preferences for treatment is that the patient will be more willing to listen to the clinician when he/she knows the request has been heard. This verbalization by the patient of a request for treatment is the first step in the treatment negotiation process. Lazare et al. describe this negotiation process as a mutual attempt by the participants to influence each other, with the patient educating the clinician about his/her needs, beliefs, and attitudes, and the clinician educating the patient about his/her formulation of the patient's condition and appropriate treatment options. The negotiation, while not necessarily providing patients what they initially want, actively solicits their participation in treatment planning. Adherence in this context refers to a mutually agreed-upon plan as opposed to a straightforward clinician recommendation.

Research has shown that the negotiated approach to treatment is associated with greater patient satisfaction, feeling helped, and feeling better following the initial interview (Eisenthal, Emery, Lazare, and Udin, 1979). In addition, negotiated, in contrast to non-negotiated treatment plans, were significantly related to patient adherence with the plan. Another significant predictor of adherence was the patient getting the treatment plan he/she wanted.

Related studies in the primary care sector (Brody, Miller, Lerman, Smith, and Caputo, 1989; Cooper-Patrick, Powe, Jenckes, Gonzales, Levine, and Ford, 1997; Dwight-Johnson, Unutzer, Sherbourne, Tang, and Wells, 2001) have supported the value of a negotiated treatment plan and the importance of the patient playing an active rather than passive role in formulating it. For example, Brody et al. (1989) found that primary care patients who perceived themselves as actively involved in their general medical care reported greater satisfaction with their physician, greater sense of control over their illness, and greater symptomatic improvement than did "passive" patients. Cooper-Patrick et al. (1997) conducted in-depth focus groups with depressed primary care patients and health care professionals about their attitudes about depression treatment, so as to understand patient help-seeking behavior and preferences for depression care. Patients expressed more concern than did health care professionals regarding the impact of spirituality, social support systems, coping strategies, life experiences, patient-provider relationships, and attributes of specific treatments (e.g., side effects, effectiveness, treatment length, etc.). In comparison to white patients, African-American patients raised more concerns regarding spirituality and stigma. Dwight-Johnson et al. (2001) found that a primary care quality improvement program designed to accommodate patient depression treatment choice increased the likelihood that these patients initiated treatment, compared to those receiving usual care. In addition, patients in intervention clinics were more likely to receive their preferred treatment approach.

Counteracting Biases about Treatment Risks

Another component of successful treatment negotiation involves consideration of how patients evaluate risks associated with a particular treatment. Tversky and Kahneman's (1974, 1981) groundbreaking work on decision making has demonstrated that people often make decisions without fully analyzing all relevant factors, and tend to rely on rules of thumb such as the availability bias (e.g., reliance on recent experiences). People also tend to avoid risk taking if the risk is framed as a potential loss as opposed to a potential gain. More recently, Ness (2002) has described how these biases operate in medical patients, particularly those with psychiatric problems like depression, and how physicians can counteract them when discussing treatment options. From this perspective, perception of the risks involved from a particular treatment option is heightened by irrational fears of unfamiliar approaches, lack of control, and possible harm to self. Depression and its associated cognitive and problem solving deficits may also result in negative, passive attitudes and a tendency to overestimate the risks of treatment while underestimating its benefits. Ness presents a model of treatment negotiation that extends beyond simple information giving to a mutual process involving the exploration of patient views and attitudes, educating the patient, counteracting his/her potentially biased judgments, and questioning how well the patient understands and evaluates the options. The ultimate goal of this process is to allow patients to make more informed decisions based on their own preferences, beliefs, and personality.

Negotiated Treatment and Outcomes

The previous literature, from many different but complementary perspectives, highlights the conceptual significance of the manner in which the treatment engagement process is negotiated, and the centrality of patient preferences to it. What is known, then, about the manner in which the treatment negotiation process relates to clinical outcomes? Only one such study has been conducted with a cohort of mid-life depressed primary care patients. The reports of Bedi, Chilvers, Churchill, Dewey, Duggan, Fileding, et al. (2000) of four-month outcomes and Chilvers, Dewey, Fielding, Gretton, Miller, Palmer, et al. (2001) of twelve-month outcomes with this population found generic counseling and antidepressant medication to produce similar improvement rates regardless of whether the patient had selected the treatment or been randomized to it. The investigators, therefore, concluded that accommodating patient preference in the treatment assignment confers no additional benefit. However, the study's methodology required that patients initially be randomized to either counseling or medication. Only patients refusing the randomized assignment were then offered their personal preference. Thus, the randomized subgroups likely included at least some patients whose a priori treatment preference was not met, but who nevertheless continued participating in the randomized treatment assignment despite their dislike of it. Outcome differences associated with a priori treatment preferences, therefore, could not be tested since the randomized subgroups were heterogeneous rather than homogeneous on the critical variable of a priori treatment preference. Innovative approaches such as the "partially randomized patient-preference design," which is rarely used in psychiatric research (Ten Have, Coyne, Salzer, and Katz, 2003), permit a more valid test of whether accommodating treatment preferences, or use of a more negotiated treatment approach improves adherence and clinical outcome.

DISCUSSION

Our review of primary care RCTs investigating psychotherapy's effectiveness leads us to recommend that physicians consider this intervention a meaningful option for patients experiencing major depression. The clinical outcomes produced by psychotherapy alone during the acute phase of treatment rival those of antidepressant medications alone when treating mild/moderate episodes of this mood disorder. Thus, findings from the primary care RCTs resemble those obtained with RCTs conducted in psychiatric settings (Gabbard, 2001). The AHCPR Depression Treatment Guideline Panel (1993), the American Psychiatric Association (2000), and the Canadian Depression Work Group (Segal, Whitney, Lam, et al., 2001) favor pharmacotherapy as the treatment of choice for more severe depressive episodes. However, the empiric basis for extending this preference to primary care practice is questionable. It may even be inappropriate given the finding by Schulberg et al. (1998) that psychotherapy and pharmacotherapy as monotherapies achieved comparable outcomes even with a subgroup of severely depressed primary care patients.

With regard to choosing between psychotherapy alone and this treatment combined with antidepressant medication, the primary care database is limited. We, therefore, should consider pertinent psychiatric RCTs for possible guidance. This latter body of research suggests that combined treatment as the initial intervention is most applicable to more severe depressive episodes (Thase et al., 1997) and to episodes with more chronic and recurrent features (Keller et al., 2000). Since such episodes are best managed in the specialty mental health sector, only occasionally is combined treatment likely to be the treatment of choice in routine primary care practice.

Given these findings about psychotherapy's effectiveness in reducing depressive symptomatology, we also must note that the proportion of individuals treated with psychotherapy for mood disorders in all settings declined from 71.1% to 60.2% between

1987-1997 (Olfson, Marcus, Druss, Ellinson, Tanielian, and Pincus, 2002). During this same time period, the proportion prescribed antidepressant medications increased from 37.2% to 74.5%. This national trend undoubtedly is associated with managed care's fiscal and practical constraints on the delivery of psychotherapy, and the advent of better-tolerated antidepressants readily prescribed by primary care physicians. The clinical and cost-effectiveness of this shifting treatment pattern remains to be determined, however. Lave et al. (1998) concluded from data gathered in the Schulberg et al. (1996) RCT that psychotherapy delivered by mental health specialists is more costly but also more effective than the "usual care" pharmacotherapy delivered by primary care physicians. Policy makers, therefore, must judge the propriety of further curtailing psychotherapy because of its higher costs and accepting the risk of poorer clinical outcomes associated with routine primary care pharmacotherapy (Sturm and Wells, 1995).

Our analysis of psychotherapy's effectiveness in the treatment of patients experiencing major depression undoubtedly would benefit from research on additional factors affecting its utility in primary care practice. Thus, we strongly suggest studying the impact of physical illness co-occurring with the mood disorder. Since the probability of persisting depression is related to the presence of co-occurring physical illnesses, is there a severity of such illness beyond which psychotherapy alone must be augmented with or replaced by antidepressant medication?

In a related vein, what is the impact of a patient's preference for psychotherapy or counseling on the treatment's effectiveness? Several studies (Dwight-Johnson et al., 2000; Cooper-Patrick et al., 1998; Churchill et al., 2000) found that 50-86% of depressed primary care patients prefer to be treated with a psychosocial intervention. However, Bedi et al. (2000) and Chilvers et al. (2001) found such patient preference to confer no additional benefit on outcome. Nevertheless, patient preference is a complex concept incorporating both psychological and methodological dimensions. For example, the manner in which a patient's preferences are elicited and the point in the recruitment and informed consent process when this occurs can profoundly influence the patient's stated preference. Ten Have et al. (2003), therefore, suggest experimenting with "reengineered" randomization designs that provide potential research subjects with differing degrees of autonomy in choosing the treatment to which they will be assigned.

We restricted the above review of primary care psychotherapy RCTs to those in which the psychosocial intervention was depression-specific given the increasingly refined theoretic models of the mood disorder's etiology, onset, and clinical course. However, psychotherapy or counseling provided in real world practice is most commonly of a generic, non-manualized format. Two recent British RCTs have successfully employed non-depression specific counseling when treating this disorder in primary care practice. That by Bedi et al. (2000) found generic counseling to achieve clinical outcomes comparable to that of anti-depressant medications; that by Ward, King, Lloyd, Bower, Sibbald, Farrelly, et al. (2000) found non-directive counseling and cognitive behavior therapy to achieve similar outcomes. A recent review (Bower, Rowland, and Hardy, 2003) of seven trials of counseling in primary care (including the above two studies) reported that counseling resulted in significantly more reductions in depression and anxiety than usual physician care in the short-term, but not the long-term (i.e., more than 6 months). These findings are intriguing given the complexities of recruiting and paying clinicians to provide depression-specific psychotherapy of treatment manual quality in primary care settings. At the least, these British studies force us to reopen the question of whether generic counseling as commonly provided in primary care practices is an effective component of the treatment armamentarium applicable to major depression in the ambulatory medical sector.

Another current direction in primary care is use of care managers to assist physicians in treating patients with major depression. Care managers function by making treatment recommendations, monitoring patient clinical status, and encouraging patient adherence to treatment. In some studies, care managers have provided manualized psychotherapy. An important question in this context is what training is necessary so that allied health professionals such as nurses and social workers lacking extensive psychotherapy experience can deliver the treatment effectively. In the PROSPECT study (Bruce, Ten Have, Reynolds, Katz, Schulberg, Mulsant, et al., 2004) where Interpersonal Psychotherapy was offered as an alternative to pharmacotherapy, care managers had varying levels of experience with depression in primary care and with psychotherapeutic approaches. An extensive 2-month training period was used to train all care managers in Interpersonal Psychotherapy, and ongoing supervision was provided (Schulberg, Bryce, Chism, Mulsant, Rollman, Bruce, et al., 2001). Similarly, efforts to train non-mental health professionals such as community nurses to administer Problem Solving Treatment in primary care (PST-PC) have been found to be feasible and effective (Mynors-Wallis, Gath, et al., 1995; Mynors-Wallis, Davies, Gray, Barbour, and Gath, 1997). These examples of care management approaches are particularly promising methods of treating depressed primary care patients, given the competing demands on physicians' time and the reluctance of many patients, particularly older ones, to follow up on referrals to mental health specialists (Waxman, Carner, and Klein, 1984; Ganguli, Mulsant, Richards, Stoehr, and Mendelsohn, 1997).

Author Note

Patrick Raue, Ph.D., Weill Medical College of Cornell University, 21 Bloomingdale Road, White Plains, NY 10605. Phone: 914-997-8684; Fax: 914-997-8650; E-mail: praue@med.cornell.edu

Herbert C. Schulberg, Ph.D., Weill Medical College of Cornell University, 21 Bloomingdale Road, White Plains, NY 10605. Phone: 914-997-5798; Fax: 914-997-8650; E-mail: HCS2001@med.cornell.edu.

References

Agency For Health Care Policy and Research Depression Guideline Panel, U.S. Dept. of Health and Human Services. (1993). *Clinical Practice Guideline, Depression In Primary Care: Vol. 2. Treatment of Major Depression. AHCPR Publication No. 93-0551.* Washington, DC: U.S. Government Printing Office.

Alexopoulos, G., Katz, I., Bruce, M., Heo, M., Ten Have, T., Raue, P., Bogner, H., Schulberg, H., Mulsant, B., Reynolds, C., and the PROSPECT Group (in press). Remission in depressed geriatric primary care patients: A report from the PROSPECT study. *American Journal of Psychiatry.*

American Psychiatric Association. (2000). Practice guideline for the treatment of patients with major depressive disorders (revision). *American Journal of Psychiatry, 157* (April Suppl.), 1-45.

Beck, A., Rush, A., Shaw, B., and Emery, G. (1979). *Cognitive Therapy of Depression.* New York: Guilford Press.

Beck, A., Ward, C., Mendelson, M., Mock, J., Erlbaugh, J. (1961). An inventory for measuring depression. *Archives of General Psychiatry, 4,* 561-571.

Bedi, N., Chilvers, C., Churchill, R., Dewey, M., Duggan, C., Fielding, K., Gretton, V., Miller, P., Harrison, G., Lee, A., and Williams, I. (2000). Assessing effectiveness of treatment of depression in primary care. *British Journal of Psychiatry, 177,* 312-318.

Beitman, B., and Klerman, G. (Eds.) (1991). *Integrating Pharmacotherapy and Psychotherapy.* Washington, D.C.: American Psychiatric Press.

Blackburn, I., Bishop, S., Glen, A., Whalley, L., and Christie, J. (1981). The efficacy of cognitive therapy in depression: A treatment trial using cognitive therapy and pharmacotherapy, each alone and in combination. *British Journal of Psychiatry, 139,* 181-189.

Blacker, C., and Clare A. (1987). Depressive disorder in primary care. *British Journal of Psychiatry, 150,* 737-751.

Bower, P., Rowland, N., and Hardy, R. (2003). The clinical effectiveness of counseling in primary care: A systematic review and meta-analysis. *Psychological Medicine, 33,* 203-215.

Brody, D., Miller, S., Lerman, C., Smith, D., and Caputo, G. (1989). Patient perception of involvement in medical care. *Journal of General Internal Medicine, 4,* 506-511.

Brown, C., and Schulberg, H. (1995). The efficacy of psychosocial treatments in primary care: A review of randomized clinical trials. *General Hospital Psychiatry, 17,* 414-424.

Brown, C., Schulberg, H., Madonia, M., Shear, M., and Houck, P. (1996). Treatment outcomes for patients with major depression and lifetime anxiety disorders. *American Journal of Psychiatry, 153,* 1293-1300.

Brown, C., Schulberg, H., and Prigerson, H. (2000). Factors associated with symptomatic improvement and recovery from major depression in primary care patients. *General Hospital Psychiatry, 22,* 242-250.

Bruce, M., Ten Have, T., Reynolds, C., Katz, I., Schulberg, H., Mulsant, B., Brown, G., McAvay, G., Pearson, J., and Alexopoulos, G. (2004). Reducing suicidal ideation and depressive symptoms in depressed older primary care patients. *Journal of the American Medical Association, 291,* 1081-1091.

Chilvers, C., Dewey, M., Fielding, K., Gretton, V., Miller, P., Palmer, B., Weller, D., Churchill, R., Williams, I., Bedi, N., Lee, L., and Harrison, G. (2001). Antidepressant drugs and generic counselling for treatment of major depression in primary care: randomized trial with patient preference arms. *British Medical Journal, 322,* 1-5.

Churchill, R., Khaira, M., Gretton, V., Chilvers, C., Dewey, M., Duggan, C., and Lee, A. (2000). Treating depression in general practice: factors affecting patients' treatment preferences. *British Journal of General Practice, 50,* 905-906.

Col, N., Fanale, J., and Kronholm, P. (1990). The role of medication noncompliance and adverse drug reactions in hospitalizations of the elderly. *Archives of Internal Medicine, 150,* 841-845.

Cooper-Patrick, L., Gonzales, J., Rost, K., Meredith, L., Rubenstein, L. and Ford, D. (1998). Patient preferences for treatment of depression. *International Journal of Psychiatry in Medicine, 28,* 382-383.

Cooper-Patrick, L., Powe, N., Jenckes, M., Gonzales, J., Levine, D., Ford, D. (1997). Identification of patient attitudes and preferences regarding treatment of depression. *Journal of General Internal Medicine, 12,* 431-438.

Coyne, J., Fechner-Bates, S., and Schwenk, T. (1994). The prevalence, nature, and co-morbidity of depressive disorders in primary care. *General Hospital Psychiatry, 16,* 267-276.

De Jonghe, F., Kool, S., van Aalst, G., Dekker, J., and Peen, J. (2001). Combining psychotherapy and antidepressants in the treatment of depression. *Journal of Affective Disorders, 64,* 217-229.

Dwight-Johnson, M., Sherbourne, C., Liao, D., and Wells, K. (2000). Treatment references among depressed primary care patients. *Journal of General Internal Medicine, 15,* 527-534.

Dwight-Johnson, M., Unutzer, J., Sherbourne, C., Tang, L., Wells, K. (2001). Can quality improvement programs for depression in primary care address patient preferences for treatment? *Medical Care, 39,* 934-944.

Eisenthal, S., Emery, R., Lazare, A., and Udin, H. (1979). 'Adherence' and the negotiated approach to patienthood. *Archives of General Psychiatry, 36,* 393-398.

Frank, E., Kupfer, D., Perel, J., Cornes, C., Jarrett, D., Mallinger, A., Thase, M., McEachran, A., and Grochocinski, V. (1990). Three-year outcomes for maintenance therapies in recurrent depression. *Archives of General Psychiatry, 47,* 1093-1099.

Gabbard, G. (2001). Empirical evidence and psychotherapy: A growing scientific base. *American Journal of Psychiatry, 158,* 1.

Ganguli, M., Mulsant, B., Richards, S., Stoehr, G., and Mendelsohn, A. (1997). Antidepressant use over time in a rural older adult population: The MoVIE Project. *Journal of the American Geriatrics Society, 45,* 1501-1503.

Goldman, W., McCulloch, J., Cuffel, B., Zarin, D., Suarez, A., and Burns, B. (1998). Outpatient utilization patterns of integrated and split psychotherapy and pharmacotherapy for depression. *Psychiatric Services, 49,* 477-482.

Goldney, R., Fisher, L., Wilson, D., Cheok, F. (2002). Mental health literacy of those with major depression and suicidal ideation: An impediment to help seeking. *Suicide and Life-Threatening Behavior, 32,* 394-403.

Hamilton, M. (1960). A rating scale for depression. *Journal of Neurology, Neurosurgery and Psychiatry, 23,* 56-62.

Hegel, M., Barrett, J., Oxman, T., Mynors-Wallis, L., and Gath, D. (1999). *Problem-Solving Treatment For Primary Care (PST-PC): A Treatment Manual For Depression.* Unpublished manuscript, Dartmouth Medical College.

Howard, K., Kopta, S., Krause, M., and Orlinsky, D. (1986). The dose-effect relationship in psychotherapy. *American Psychologist, 41,* 159-164.

Iosifescu, D., Nierenberg, A., Alpert, J., Smith, M., Bitran, S., Dording, C., and Fava, M. (2003). The impact of medical comorbidity on acute treatment in major depressive disorder. *American Journal of Psychiatry, 160,* 2122-2127.

Katon, W. (2003). Clinical and health services relationships between major depression, depressive symptoms, and general medical illness. *Biological Psychiatry, 54,* 216-226.

Katon, W., Lin, E., von Korff, M., Bush, T., Walker, E., Simon, G., and Robinson, P. (1994). The predictors of depression in primary care. *Journal of Affective Disorders, 31,* 81-90.

Katon, W., Robinson, P., von Korff, M., Lin, E., Bush, T., Ludman, E., Simon, G., and Walker, E. (1996). A multifaceted intervention to improve treatment of depression in primary care. *Archives of General Psychiatry, 53,* 924-932.

Keller, M., McCullough, P., Klein, D., Arnow, B., Dunner, D., Gelenberg, A., Markowitz, J., Nemeroff, C., Russell, J., Thase, M., Trivedi, M., Zajecka, J., Blalock, J., Borian, F., DeBattista, C., Fawcett, J., Hirschfeld, R., Jody, D., Keitner, G., Kockis, J., Koran, L., Kornstein, S., Manber, I., Ninan, P., Rothbaum, B., Rush, A., Schatzberg, A., and Vivian, D. (2000). A comparison of nefazadone, the cognitive behavioral- analysis system of psychotherapy, and their combination for the treatment of chronic depression. *New England Journal of Medicine, 342,* 1462-1470.

Klerman, G., Weissman, M., Rounsaville, B., and Chevron, E. (1984). *Interpersonal Psychotherapy of Depression.* New York: Basic Books.

Koike, A., Unutzer, J., and Wells, K. (2002). Improving the care for depression in patients with comorbid medical illness. *American Journal of Psychiatry, 159,* 1738-1745.

Kukull, W., Koepsell, T., Inui, T., Borson, S., Okimoto, J., Raskind, M., and Gale, J. (1986). Depression and physical illness among elderly general medical clinic patients. *Journal of Affective Disorders, 10,* 153-162.

Lave, J., Frank, R., Schulberg, H., and Kamlet, M. (1998). Cost-effectiveness of treatments for major depression in primary care practice. *Archives of General Psychiatry, 55,* 645-651.

Lazare, A., Eisenthal, S., and Wasserman, L. (1975). The customer approach to patienthood: Attending to patient requests in a walk-in clinic. *Archives of General Psychiatry, 32,* 552-558.

Manning, D., Markowitz, J., and Frances, A. (1992). A review of combined psychotherapy in the treatment of depression. *Journal of Psychiatric Research, 1,* 48-64.

Mynors-Wallis, L., Davies, I., Gray, A., Barbour, F., and Gath, D. (1997). A randomised controlled trial and cost analysis of problem-solving treatment for emotional disorders given by community nurses in primary care. *British Journal of Psychiatry, 170,* 113-119.

Mynors-Wallis, L., Gath, D., Day, A., and Baker, F. (2000). Randomised controlled trial of problem solving treatment, antidepressant medication, and combined treatment for major depression in primary care. *British Medical Journal, 320,* 26-30.

Mynors-Wallis, L., Gath, D., Lloyd-Thomas, A., and Tomlinson, D. (1995). Randomised controlled trial comparing problem solving treatment with amitriptyline and placebo for major depression in primary care. *British Medical Journal, 310,* 441-445.

Nathan, P., and Gorman, J. (Eds.) (2002). *A Guide To Treatments That Work* (2nd edition). New York: Oxford Press.

Ness, D. (2002). Discussing treatment options and risks with medical patients who have psychiatric problems. *Archives of Internal Medicine, 162,* 2037-2044.

Nezu, A., Nezu, C., and Perri, M. (1989). *Problem-Solving Therapy For Depression: Theory, Research, and Clinical Guidelines.* New York: John Wiley.

Olfson, M., Marcus, S., Druss, B., Ellinson, L., Tanielian, T., and Pincus, H. (2002). National trends in the outpatient treatment of depression. *Journal of the American Medical Association, 287,* 203-209.

Pampallona, S., Bollini, P., Tibaldi, G., Kupelnick, B., and Munizza, C. (2004). Combined pharmacotherapy and psychological treatment for depression. *Archives of General Psychiatry, 61,* 714-719.

Patience, D., McGuire, R., Scott, A., and Freeman, C. (1995). The Edinburgh Primary Care Depression Study: personality disorder and outcome. *British Journal of Psychiatry, 167,* 324-330.

Pettit, J., Voelz, Z., and Joiner, T. (2001). Combined pharmacotherapy and psychotherapy for depression. In M. Sammons and N. Schmidt (Eds.), *Combined Treatments For Mental Disorders* (pp. 131-160). Washington, D.C.: American Psychological Association.

Pincus, H., Tanielian, T., Marcus, S., Olfson, M., Zarin, D., Thompson, J., and Zito, J. (1998). Prescribing trends in psychotropic medications. Primary care, psychiatry, and other medical specialties. *Journal of the American Medical Association, 279,* 526-531.

Popkin, M., Callies, A., and Mackenzie, T. (1985). The outcome of antidepressant use in the medically ill. *Archives of General Psychiatry, 42,* 1160-1163.

Reynolds, C., Frank, E., Perel, J., Imber, S., Cornes, C., Miller, M., Mazumdar, S., Houck, P., Dew, M., Stack, J., Pollock, B., and Kupfer, D. (1999). Nortiptyline and interpersonal psychotherapy as maintenance therapies for recurrent major depression. *Journal of the American Medical Association, 281,* 39-45.

Robins, L., Helzer, J., Croughan, J., and Ratcliff, K. (1981). The National Institute of Mental Health Diagnostic Interview Schedule: Its history, characteristics, and validity. *Archives of General Psychiatry, 38,* 381-389.

Robinson, L., Berman, J., and Niemeyer, R. (1990). Psychotherapy for the treatment of depression: A comprehensive review of controlled outcome research. *Psychological Bulletin, 108,* 30-49.

Ross, M., and Scott, M. (1985). An evaluation of the effectiveness of individual and group cognitive therapy in the treatment of depressed patients in an city health center. *Journal of the Royal College of General Practitioners, 35,* 239-242.

Schulberg, H., Block, M., and Coulehan, J (1989). Treating depression in primary care practice. An application of decision analysis. *General Hospital Psychiatry, 11,* 208- 215.

Schulberg, H., Block, M., Madonia, M., Scott, C., Rodriguez, E., Imber, S., Perel, J., Lave, J., Houck, P., and Coulehan, J. (1996). Treating major depression in primary care practice: eight-month clinical outcomes. *Archives of General Psychiatry, 53,* 913-919.

Schulberg, H., Bryce, C., Chism, K., Mulsant, B., Rollman, B., Bruce, M., Coyne, J., Reynolds, C., and the PROSPECT Group. (2001). Managing late-life depression in primary care practice: a case study of the health specialist's role. *International Journal of Geriatric Psychiatry, 16,* 577-584.

Schulberg, H., Coulehan, J., Block, M., Lave, J., Rodriguez, E., Scott, C., Madonia, M., Imber, S., and Perel, J. (1993). Clinical trials of primary care treatments for major depression: Issues in design, recruitment, and treatment. *International Journal of Psychiatric Medicine, 23,* 29-42.

Schulberg, H., McClelland, M., and Gooding, W. (1987). Six-month outcomes for patients with major depressive disorder. *Journal of General Internal Medicine, 2,* 312-317.

Schulberg, H., Pilkonis, P., and Houck, P. (1998). The severity of major depression and choice of treatment in primary care practice. *Journal of Consulting and Clinical Psychology, 66,* 932-938.

Schulberg, H., Raue, P., and Rollman, B. (2002). The effectiveness of psychotherapy in treating depressive disorders in primary care practice: Clinical and cost perspectives. *General Hospital Psychiatry, 24,* 203-212.

Scott, A., and Freeman, C. (1992). Edinburgh primary care depression study: treatment outcome, patient satisfaction, and cost after 16 weeks. *British Medical Journal, 304,* 883-887.

Segal, Z., Kennedy, S., Cohen, L., and the CANMAT Depression Work Group. (2001). Clinical Guidelines For The Treatment of Depressive Disorders. V. Combining psychotherapy and pharmacotherapy. *Canadian Journal of Psychiatry, 46* (Suppl. 1), 59S-62S.

Segal, Z., Whitney, D., Lam, R., and the CANMAT Depression Work Group. (2001). Clinical Guidelines for the Treatment of Depressive Disorders. III. Psychotherapy. *Canadian Journal of Psychiatry, 46* (Suppl. 1), 29S-37S.

Shapiro, D., Barkham, M., Rees, A., Hardy, G., Reynolds, S., and Startup, M. (1994). Effects of treatment duration and severity of depression on the effectiveness of cognitive-behavioral and psychodynamic-interpersonal psychotherapy. *Journal of Consulting and Clinical Psychology, 62,* 522-534.

Sotsky, S., Glass, D., Shea, M., Pilkonis, P., Collins, J., Elkin, I., Watkins, J., Imber, S., Leber, W., Moyer, J., Oliveri, M. (1991). Patient predictors of response to psychotherapy and pharmacotherapy: Findings in the NIMH Treatment of Depression Collaborative Research Program. *American Journal of Psychiatry, 148,* 997-1008.

Spitzer, R., Kroenke, K., and Williams, J. (1999). Validation and utility of a self-report version of PRIME-MD. The PHQ primary care study. *Journal of the American Medical Association, 282,* 1737-1744.

Spitzer, R., Williams, J., Kroenke, K., Linzer, M., deGruy, F., Hahn, S., Brody, D., and Johnson, J. (1994). Utility of a new procedure for diagnosing mental disorders in primary care. The PRIME-MD 1000 study. *Journal of the American Medical Association, 272,* 1749-1756.

Sturm, R., and Wells, K. (1995). How can care for depression become more cost effective? *Journal of the American Medical Association, 273,* 51-58.

Teasdale, J., Fennell, M., Hibbert, G., and Amies, P. (1984). Cognitive therapy for major depressive disorder in primary care. *British Journal of Psychiatry, 144,* 400-406.

Ten Have, T., Coyne, J., Salzer, M., and Katz, I. (2003). Research to improve the quality of care for depression: Alternatives to the simple randomized clinical trial. *General Hospital Psychiatry, 25,* 115-123.

Thase, M., Greenhouse, J., Frank, E., Reynolds, C., Pilkonis, P., Hurley, K., Grochocinski, V., and Kupfer, D. (1997). Treatment of major depression with psychotherapy or psychotherapy-pharmacotherapy combinations. *Archives of General Psychiatry, 54,* 1009-1015.

Tversky, A., and Kahneman, D. (1974). Judgment under uncertainty: Heuristics and biases. *Science, 185,* 1124-1131.

Tversky, A., and Kahneman, D. (1981). The framing of decisions and the psychology of choice. *Science, 30,* 453-458.

Unutzer, J., Katon, W., Callahan, C., Williams, J., Hunkeler, E., Harpole, L., Hoffing, M., Della Penna, R., Noel, P., Lin, E., Arean, P., Hegel, M., Tang, L., Belin, T., Oishi, S., Langston, C. (2002). Collaborative care management of late-life depression in the primary care setting: a randomized controlled trial. *Journal of the American Medical Association, 288,* 2836-2845.

van Schaik, D., Klijn, A., van Hout, H., van Marwijk, H., Beekman, A., de Haan, M., and van Dyck, R. (2004). Patients' preferences in the treatment of depressive disorder in primary care. *General Hospital Psychiatry, 26,* 184-189.

Ward, E., King, M., Lloyd, M., Bower, P., Sibbald, B., Farrelly, S., Gabbay, M., Tarrier, N., and Addington-Hall, J. (2000). Randomised controlled trial of non-directive counselling, cognitive-behaviour therapy, and usual general practitioner care for patients with depression. I: Clinical effectiveness. *British Medical Journal, 321,* 1383-1388.

Waxman, H., Carner, E., and Klein, M. (1984). Underutilization of mental health professionals by community elderly. *Gerontologist, 24,* 23-30.

Westen, D., and Morrison, K. (2001). A multi-dimensional meta-analysis of treatments for depression, panic, and generalized anxiety disorder: An empirical examination of the status of empirically supported therapies. *Journal of Consulting and Clinical Psychology, 69,* 875-899.

Wexler, B., and Cicchetti, D. (1992). The outpatient treatment of depression. Implications of outcome research for clinical practice. *Journal of Nervous and Mental Disease, 180,* 277-286.

White, R., and Walden, M. (2000). Obstacles to a randomised controlled trial of intensive dynamic psychotherapy: an account of the New South Wales Section of Psychotherapy outcomes project. *Australian and New Zealand Journal of Psychiatry, 34,* 271-278.

Zeitlin, D., Katona, C., D'Ath, P., and Katona, P. (1997). Attitudes to depression in primary care attendees: Effects of age and depressive symptoms. *Primary Care Psychiatry, 3,* 17-20.

In: Trends in Depression Research
Editor: Maurice J. Henri, pp. 53-60

ISBN 1-60021-394-4

Chapter 3

MAJOR DEPRESSION, AGE AND ANTIDEPRESSANT UTILIZATION IN THE GENERAL POPULATION

Scott B. Patten*
University of Calgary, Alberta, Canada

ABSTRACT

Major depression has typically been regarded as an under-treated disorder. Most studies have found a high prevalences of major depression in younger age categories, but particularly low rates of antidepressant treatment in these groups. In this study, the frequency of treatment was assessed using data collected from a longitudinal cohort representative of the household population in Canada. Whereas a very low frequency of antidepressant use was found in the under 35 age category in 1994, a rapid increase eliminated this difference by 2000. As of this date, there was no longer any evidence that the under 35 age category was treated less frequently than other age groups.

In recent years, there has been particular concern about the impact of major depression in young people. This represents a change in emphasis from the previous literature. Epidemiological data collected in the 1980s did not typically identify elevated prevalence rates in younger age categories. In the Epidemiological Catchment Area (ECA) studies conducted in the United States, the point prevalence of major depression was highest in the 25-44 year age group [2]. However, more recent studies have often reported the highest prevalence of major depression as occurring in the youngest age categories. In the National Comorbidity Survey, for example, the point prevalence of major depression peaked in the 15-24 year age group for both men and women [3]. Some authors have suggested that a cohort effect may be occurring, with birth cohorts populating the younger age categories being at higher risk of depression [4]. The pattern of peak prevalence in relatively young age groups

* Scott B. Patten, MD, FRCP(C), PhD. Professor, University of Calgary, Health Scholar, Alberta Heritage Foundation for Medical Research. Fellow, Institute of Health Economics. Department of Community Health Sciences, University of Calgary. 3330 Hospital Drive NW, Calgary, Alberta. T2N 4N1 (V) 403-220-8752 (Fax) 403-270-7307. patten@ucalgary.ca, http://www.ucalgary.ca/~patten .

has also been shown in studies conducted outside of the United States [5]. Clearly, the occurrence of major depression among young people is a cause for public health concern.

With the exception of several national initiatives, such as "National Major Depression Screening Day" in the United States [6] and "Defeat Depression" initiative in the United Kingdom [7], the public health response to major depression has mainly involved ensuring access to treatment, and improving the quality of treatment received, see review by Katon [8]. Canadian data from a variety of sources in the 1990s suggested that young people aged 15-24, despite having the highest prevalence of major depression, had the lowest rate of antidepressant treatment [9]. These results are consistent with an international literature showing higher rates of treatment-seeking in older age groups [10]. This raises some important concerns from the point of view of public health: does there need to be more effort directed at the delivery or acceptance of depression treatment among young people? More recently, opposing concerns have been expressed, most notably in the June 2003 report of the UK Committee on Safety of Medicines - that antidepressant medications may trigger suicide attempts, especially in children and adolescents.

It should be acknowledged that the existing literature leaves several questions about the relationship between age, depression and antidepressant use unanswered. First, it is widely suspected that there have been major changes in the rates of antidepressant prescription in the past decade. The pattern of treatment utilization seen in past studies may have been altered in recent years. Second, in the adolescent age group, antidepressant medications are not necessarily a first line treatment for major depression. Practice guidelines, in fact, emphasize the important role of non-pharmacological treatments in this age group [11].

For both of the reasons cited above, it is important to explore changes over time in the use of antidepressants in different age groups, and also to examine the use of other types of treatment in different age groups. Longitudinal data related to the treatment of depressive disorders is often not available, however, a longitudinal health survey conducted in Canada can provide some important information. This longitudinal study is called the National Population Health Survey (NPHS).

The NPHS is a longitudinal study of a Canadian national sample. The sampling frame includes the entire population dwelling in households, with the exception of military bases, Indian reservations and some remote areas. The study was conducted by the national statistical agency, Statistics Canada[1]. Data collection occurred by face-to-face interview. The NPHS sample did not include residents of institutions. The original survey included 17,262 subjects sampled in 1994/95 and follow-up interviews have taken place every two years since then. The NPHS interview asks respondents to produce pill bottles for all medications taken in the preceding two days. Medication names are recorded and coded using Anatomic Therapeutic Classification (ATC) codes [12]. The NPHS employed a brief predictive instrument designed to identify probable episodes of major depression in the year preceding the interview. The instrument, called the Composite International Diagnostic Interview Short Form for Major Depression (CIDI-SFMD), was originally developed by Kessler et al. [13]. Validation studies suggest that the instrument is sensitive, but somewhat non-specific [14,15] for major depressive disorders. The CIDI-SFMD provides a (12 month) period prevalence

[1] However, the analysis presented here was carried out by the author and the opinions expressed should not be regarded as representing the views of Statistics Canada.

estimate. Period prevalence refers to the proportion of the population meeting DSM-IV criteria for major depression at any time in the preceding year.

Annual period prevalence can be a problematic way of evaluating utilization, however, since the NPHS drug exposure data measures current (past 2 days) drug use rather than in the past year. Having an episode at some time within the past year is not necessarily an indication of current treatment need. Clinical guidelines, for example, typically recommend the continued use of antidepressant medications for 6-9 months after recovery. The proportion of subjects with an episode in the preceding year who are currently taking antidepressants may, for this reason, underestimate the actual proportion receiving pharmacological treatment. Also, some episodes may resolve spontaneously or respond to other types of treatment. For these reasons, antidepressant treatment rates calculated from studies like the NPHS should not be interpreted as if they represented a proportion of treatment needs being met. However, the NPHS is uniquely suited to evaluating trends over time, since exactly the same measures were used in each interview of the survey cohort.

The NPHS measures of treatment utilization are not limited to medication use. The interview also included an indicator for consultations with health professionals about mental health, and also recorded the frequency of such consultations. Identifying the proportion of the population with multiple visits to health professionals for reasons related to mental health serves as an indicator of the proportion who may be receiving non-pharmacological treatment for their depression.

The NPHS sampling procedure, like most large scale surveys, included both clustering and unequal selection probabilities. Sampling weights calculated by Statistics Canada were used in all parts of the analysis reported here. The use of sampling weights was essential to account for the design features of the survey. The use of the sampling weights and the bootstrap variance estimation technique ensure valid estimation despite the complex nature of the survey design.

As noted above, the NPHS initially included 17,262 subjects, 14,713 of whom were over the age of 14 in 1994. The latter group was considered eligible for inclusion in this analysis. Although rates of response in the NPHS were very high, some attrition occurred over the course of the study, principally due to death or non-response. There were 9,438 subjects (83.8%) with complete data at each follow-up interval to 2000/01.

During period of time covered by the NPHS there was an increase in the use of antidepressant medications among persons with major depression, but the pattern of change was different across age groups. The antidepressant utilization rates, calculated as the proportion of those with a probable episode of major depression who were taking antidepressant medications at the time of the survey, are presented in Figure 1. In 1994/95 the proportions taking antidepressants were low in all age groups, but particularly in the 15-34 year old age group. In the ensuing six years, the utilization rate increased in all of the age groups, but most dramatically in the youngest age group, so that by 2000/01 the striking differences evident in 1994 no longer existed.

Another feature that is interesting about Figure 1 is the apparent plateau in the 55+ age group. This plateau is difficult to explain in terms of the traditionally accepted view that depression in all age groups is under treated. In principle one would expect the rate of treatment to continue to increase because of such factors as increased awareness, reduced stigma, improved antidepressant medications as long as there is a large reservoir of untreated persons with major depression in the population. The plateau may actually represent a "point of diminishing returns" in the population. When one considers that non-pharmacological treatments for major depression are available, that some episodes resolve spontaneously, and that the use (or continued use) of the medications involves utilitarian decisions about risks and benefits, the occurrence of a plateau may indicate that an appropriate rate of use has been achieved in this age group in the population. The fact that the rate of use has formed a plateau at a lower frequency of use than in younger age groups may reflect the greater vulnerability of older persons, for example, to adverse effects or drug interactions.

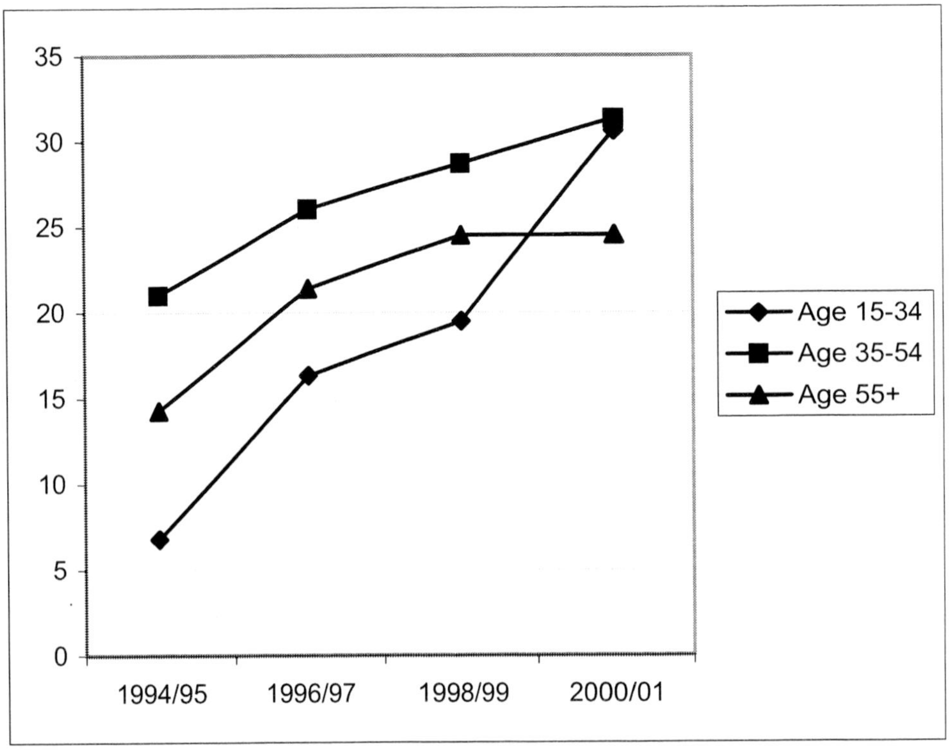

Figure 1. Antidepressant Medication Use (%), Subjects with a Recent Episode of Major Depression

An important use of this kind of data is to inform public health policy. If access to a certain form of health service is impeded in a particular population group, then public health strategies can be implemented to remove whatever barriers exist. This might mean reducing stigma, a social marketing campaign or focused educational efforts. Based on the longitudinal data presented here, it would appear that there is no longer a justification for implementing such efforts with respect to the under 35 age group.

The rapid increase in the use of antidepressants in the 15 - 35 age group could be due to a change in the behavior within the population (e.g. seeking help more often) or a change in the behavior of health professionals (prescribing medications more often). For this reason, it is interesting to determine whether changes in the rate of consultation with health professionals about mental health has been changing. As noted above, this variable was evaluated in the NPHS, see Figure 2.

Figure 2 does not suggest a particularly rapid increase in consultation patterns in the 15 - 35 age group. As such, the rapid increase in antidepressant use that was observed in the

NPHS cannot be accounted for by a change in their rate of consultation with health professionals. The rate of consultation was highest in the 35-54 year age group, lowest in the 55+ age group, and generally assumed an intermediate value in the under 35 group. The most dramatic secular change was an increasing rate of consultation in the 55+ age group. This suggests, therefore, that the rapid increase in antidepressant use observed in the under 35 age group reflects a change in practice on the part of health professionals rather than an altered pattern of help-seeking.

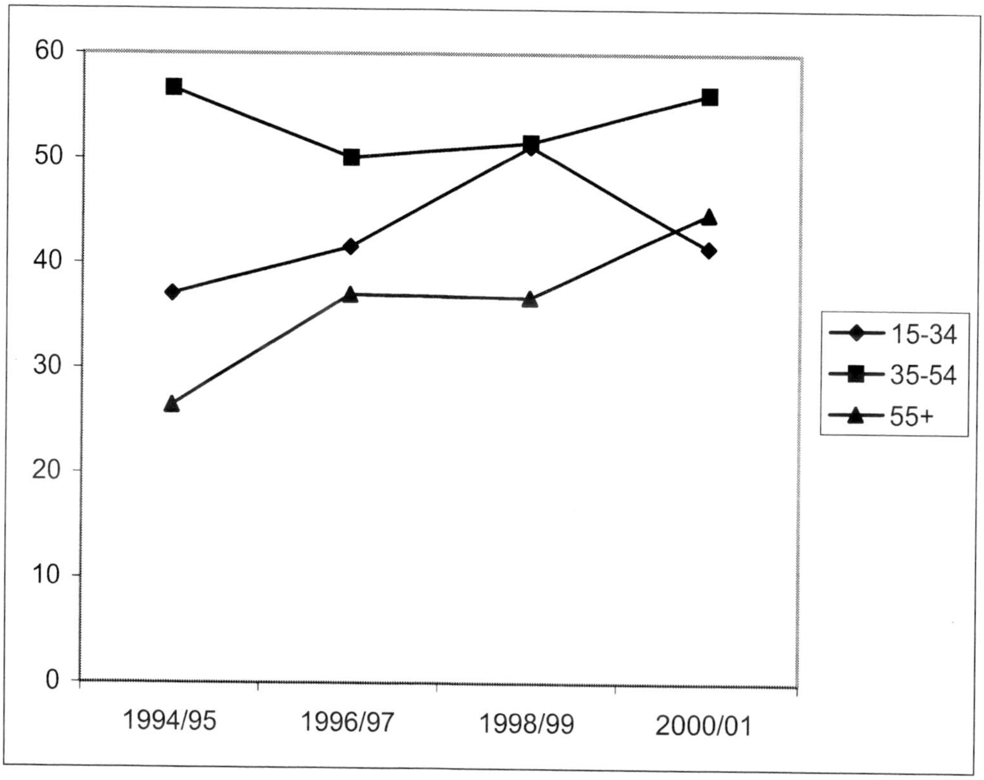

Figure 2. Consultations with Health Professionals About Mental Health, NPHS Respondents with a Probable Recent Major Depressive Episode.

One of the complications in attempting to assess the extent to which treatment needs are being met is that conditions such as major depression can be treated in different ways, and treatment is not restricted to the use of antidepressant medications. The NPHS recorded not only whether each respondent had consulted with a health professional (see above), but also the number of such consultations. Normally, non-pharmacological treatment of major depression would take the form of cognitive or interpersonal psychotherapy, which generally takes approximately 10-12 sessions to complete. In the NPHS dataset, the number of visits was coded between 1 and 6 or more, and the distribution of this variable in persons with major depression in presented in Figure 3.

Figure 3 provides some suggestion that there may be an increase in the proportion of depressed persons who are making enough visits to health professionals regarding their mental health to be receiving non-pharmacological treatment for major depression.

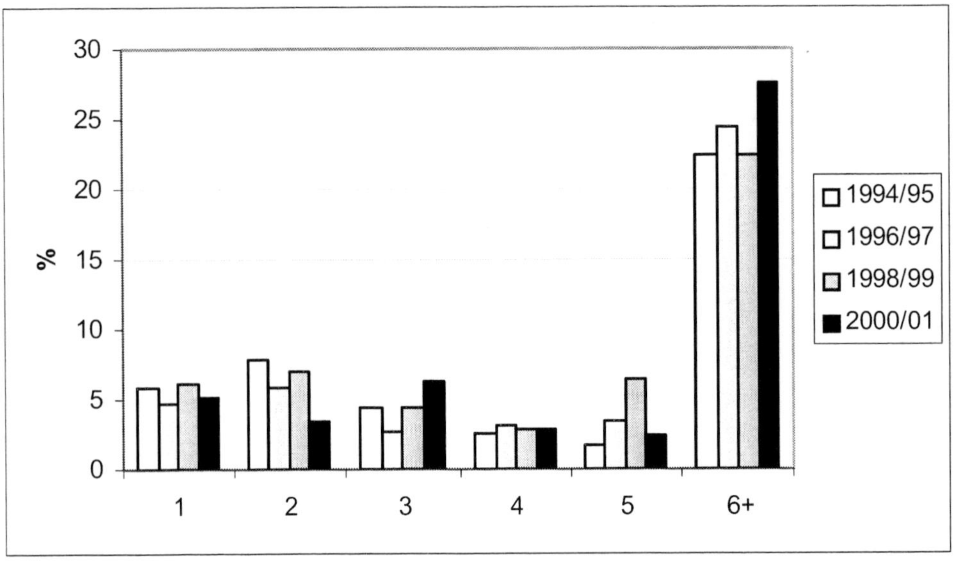

Figure 3. Frequency of Visits to Health Professionals About Mental Health Among Respondents with Probable Recent Episodes of Major Depression.

This data presented here highlights very dramatic shifts in the pharmacoepidemiology of antidepressant use in the Canadian population. Those in the 15 - 35 age group, who were felt to be drastically under treated based on studies conducted in the 1990s, have recorded particularly rapid increases in antidepressant treatment. There is no longer any evidence that this group should be a specific target of public health measures to increase treatment utilization.

That assertion that treatment rates for major depression (which remain in the 30% range in the under 35 age range), do not necessarily indicate drastic under treatment deserves reemphasis. It was noted previously that some of the subjects may have had an episode in the past year that had been effectively treated. For such respondents, antidepressant medications may have been discontinued prior to the date of their NPHS survey interview. Some episodes of major depression are self-limited, and it can therefore not be assumed that everyone meeting DSM-IV criteria for major depression necessarily should be treated. There are also non-pharmacological strategies for treating major depression, so that some persons with major depression who are not taking antidepressants may yet be receiving fully adequate treatment. For all of these reasons, the antidepressant utilization rate, as calculated in the analysis reported here should not be interpreted with reference to a target of 100%.

There is another reason why the traditional way of calculating the antidepressant utilization rate can be expected to underestimate the true rate of antidepressant use. This method of calculation neglects successful use of the medications. If the utilization rate is calculated as the proportion of those with a recent episode of major depression who are taking an antidepressant, then a person who has achieved remission during antidepressant treatment is essentially removed from the calculation, ie. they appear neither in the numerator or the denominator. If those with successful use are added to the numerator and the denominator of the rate, the adjusted utilization rate can be predicted to increase. As such, the neglect of successful use will predictably bias the estimated antidepressant utilization rate downward. Unfortunately, the extent of bias has not yet been determined, but it may be substantial [16].

Another important methodological factor is that of study design. The proportion of persons with major depression who are taking an antidepressant medications is sometimes misinterpreted as the probability that such a medication will be prescribed. In fact, it is better to regard the treated proportion as a prevalence of treatment among those with the illness. The prevalence of treatment is related not only to the chance of getting treatment (analogous to incidence), but also to the duration of treatment (and, in theory, to the relative mortality associated with treatment). In other words, changes in the antidepressant treatment or utilization rate may in fact reflect changes in the duration of treatment. A detailed description of these epidemiological factors, see Rothman [17].

Traditionally, the under-treatment of depression has been viewed as the major public health challenge for major depression. Dramatic changes during the past decade are now beginning to draw this assumption into doubt. Of course, the relatively crude sources of data that are typically collected in large-scale epidemiological studies must be regarded as approximate and somewhat indirect indicators of treatment need. Some episodes of major depression may resolve spontaneously (having no treatment needs), some may be mild or even sub-clinical in severity but yet be associated with pronounced treatment needs because of comorbidity or environmental circumstances. Some studies have attempted to address these issues by collecting very detailed information about mental health needs, and determining the extent to which these are being met in a defined population [18]. However, such approaches are not likely to be effective for purposes of public health surveillance. The epidemiological data presented here suggests that under- treatment may no longer be the overwhelmingly important issue that it was previously. The pattern observed in the 15 - 35 year age group suggests that a particularly dramatic increase in antidepressant use in this age group has erased previously reported inequalities in treatment utilization. On the other hand, data from the 55+ age group suggests a flattening of the trend towards increased in antidepressant use, a plateau effect that may indicate a saturation of treatment needs.

It remains to be seen whether recent concerns about the safety of antidepressants in young adults will have an impact on the pattern of use. Many clinicians believe that the the increase in suicide attempts seen in adolescent antidepressant clinical trials may represent side effects, such as agitation or akathisia, and that these may be offset by longer-term benefits of treatment. The NPHS may be a valuable source of information about long-term trends, since data collection will continue for 20 years, until 2014.

REFERENCES

[1] Murray CJL, Lopez AC. *Global Burden of Disease and Injury*. Boston: Harvard School of Public Health, 1996.

[2] Regier DA, Boyd JH, Burke JD, Myers JK, Kramer M, Robins LN et al. One-month prevalence of mental disorders in the United States. Based on five epidemiological catchment area sites. *Arch Gen Psychiatry* 1988; 45:977-986.

[3] Blazer DG, Kessler RC, McGonagle KA, Swartz MS. The prevalence and distribution of Major Depression in a national community sample: the National Comorbidity Survey. *Am J Psychiatry* 1994; 151:979-986.

[4] Kessler RC, Walters EE. Epidemiology of DSM-III-R major depression and minor depression among adolescents and young adults in the National Comorbidity Survey. *Depression and Anxiety* 2000; 7:3-14.

[5] Offord DR, Boyle MH, Campbell D, Goering P, Lin E, Wong M et al. One year prevalence of psychiatric disorder in Ontarians 15 to 64 years of age. *Can J Psychiatry* 1996; 41:559-563.

[6] Jacobs DG. National depression screening day: educating the public, reaching those in need of treatment, and broadening professional understanding. *Harvard Review of Psychiatry* 1995; 3:156-159.

[7] Priest RG, Vize C, Roberts A, Roberts M, Tylee A. Lay people's attitudes to treatment of depression: results of opinion poll for Defeat Depression Campaign just before its launch. *BMJ* 1996; 313:858-859.

[8] Katon W, Von Korff M, Lin E, Unutzer J, Simon G, Walker E et al. Population-based care of depression: effective disease management strategies to decrease prevalence. *Gen Hosp Psychiatry* 1997; 19:169-178.

[9] Patten SB, Sedmak B, Russell ML. Major depression: prevalence, treatment utilization and age in Canada. *Can J Clin Pharm* 2001; 8:133-138.

[10] Bristow K, Patten SB. Treatment-seeking rates and associated mediating factors among individuals with depression. *Can J Psychiatry* 2002; 47:660-665.

[11] Birmaher B, Brent DA, Benson RS. Summary of the practice parameters for the assessment and treatment of children and adolescents with depressive disorders. J Am Acad Child Adolesc *Psychiatry* 1998; 37:1234-1238.

[12] Statistics Canada. 1998/99 Public use microdata documentation. 2000. Ottawa, Canada, Minister of Supply and Services. Ref Type: Report

[13] Kessler RC, Andrews G, Mroczek D, Ustun B, Wittchen HU. The World Health Organization Composite International Diagnostic Interview Short-Form (CIDI-SF). *International Journal of Methods in Psychiatric Research* 1998; 7:171-185.

[14] Patten SB. Performance of the CIDI Short Form in Clinical and Community Samples. *Chronic Diseases in Canada* 1997; 18:109-112.

[15] Patten SB, Brandon-Christie J, Devji J, Sedmak B. Perfomance of the Composite International Diagnostic Interview Short Form for Major Depression in a Community Sample. *Chron Dis Can* 2000; 21:68-72.

[16] Patten SB, Beck CA. The total proportion of subjects who are using antidepressants. *Am J Psychiatry* 2003; 160(189):190.

[17] Rothman KJ, Greenland S. Measures of Disease Frequency. In: Rothman KJ, Greenland S, editors. *Modern Epidemiology*. Philadelphia: Lippincott-Raven, 1998: 29-64.

[18] Bebbington PE, Marsden L, Brewin CR. The need for psychiatric treatment in the general population: the Camberwell needs for care survey. *Psychol Med* 1997; 27:821-834.

In: Trends in Depression Research
Editor: Maurice J. Henri, pp. 61-86

ISBN 1-60021-394-4

Chapter 4

ANTIDEPRESSANTS IN THE ACUTE TREATMENT OF ADOLESCENT MAJOR DEPRESSION

Mauri Marttunen*

Department of Adolescent Psychiatry, Helsinki University Hospital, Peijas Hospital, Vantaa, Finland

Department of Mental Health and Alcohol Research, National Public Health Institute, Helsinki, Finland

1. INTRODUCTION

Major depressive disorder (MDD) is among the leading causes of morbidity and mortality among adolescents (Aalto-Setälä et al., 2001, Marttunen et al., 1991, Shaffer et al., 1996). Major depression is twice as common in adolescents as in children, with an estimated prevalence around 5 – 8 % (Kessler et al, 2001, Haarasilta et al., 2001). Approximately one third to one half of adolescents treated in psychiatric settings suffer depressive disorders (Aalto-Setälä et al., 1998; Pelkonen et al. 1997).

During an episode of MDD, adolescents demonstrate poor interpersonal functioning in peer and family relationships, and impaired academic performance. An episode of MDD may endanger the development of interpersonal social skills, behavioral control, and the acquisition of academic skills, thus resulting in a delay of social and academic development. Recovery from major depression in clinical samples is often only partial (Emslie et al, 1997), and even after recovery youth may continue to show impairment e.g. in interpersonal relationships and global functioning (Birmaher et al, 1996; Lewinsohn et al, 1994). Adolescent depression tends to run a recurrent course and seems to predict subsequent depressive and other psychiatric disorders in young adulthood (Lewinsohn et al.1999; Aalto-Setälä et al. 2002a; Fergusson and Woodward, 2002). Despite the marked suffering and serious consequences of adolescent MDD, the disorder is underreconized and undertreated (Aalto-Setälä. et al., 2002b, Wittchen et al., 1998).

* e-mail: mauri.marttunen@ktl.fi

This paper reviews the research on the efficacy of antidepressants in adolescent major depression. The focus is in published double-blind placebo-controlled randomized trials and meta-analyses. Supplementary data from unpublished ongoing studies and open trials will be presented.

Published articles were identified through a search in the PubMed database from 1960s through 2002. Reference lists from the main reviews and RCTs were further used as a source of previous studies. RCTs presented in recent congresses providing preliminary results were further searched. Only studies with samples of ten or more subjects using standardized diagnoses of MDD and standardized outcome measures were included.

2. Diagnosis of MDD in Adolescence

According to DSM-IV (APA, 1994), the diagnostic criteria for adolescent MDD are essentially the same as for adults with the exception that in children and adolescents irritable mood may replace depressed mood as a criterion. The disorder must be present for at least two weeks, a minimum of five of nine diagnostic criteria need to be fulfilled, and the disorder has to cause psychosocial impairment or subjective suffering. Comorbid psychiatric disorders may obscure the diagnosis of adolescent MDD. Comorbidity seems to be rather a rule than an exception in adolescent major depression, the most common comorbid disorders being anxiety, disruptive, and substance use disorders (Marttunen and Pelkonen, 1998).

3. Treatment of Adolescent Major Depression

During the past two decades, there has been an increasing interest to develop effective psychosocial and biological treatments for depressed adolescents. Increasing evidence suggests the usefulness of psychotherapeutic interventions in youthful MDD. Opinions vary whether pharmacological interventions alone or combined with psychotherapy should be used as first-line treatments for youth with depressive disorders (Michael and Crowley, 2002; AACAP, 1998). Taken the psychosocial context in which youthful depression occurs, pharmacotherapy should not be applied as the sole treatment of adolescent MDD (AACAP, 1998).

3.1 General Management

The goals of treatment are to relieve symptoms of depression, to shorten the depressive episode, to minimize the adverse effects of psychosocial impairment, and to prevent recurrent episodes of depression (AACAP, 1998). Commonly, a multidisciplinary approach including collaboration with e.g. teachers and school counselors is needed. During pharmacotherapy, a good therapeutic relationship between the clinician and the adolescent as well as his/her family increases compliance with medication. Both the adolescent and family members often need education about depression and its treatment.

3.2 Psychotherapeutic Treatment

Several controlled studies have been published on psychotherapy in adolescents with depressive symptoms and disorders (Harrington et al, 1998). Eight published randomized trials of psychotherapy for adolescents with diagnosed depressive disorders on cognitive-behavioral psychotherapy (CBT) and interpersonal therapy (IPT) are briefly reviewed.

3.2.1 Cognitive-Behavioral Psychotherapy

Lewinsohn and his coworkers (1990) randomized 59 adolescents with depressive disorders to adolescent group CBT, adolescent and parent CBT, or waiting list control group. Youth in both treatment groups improved significantly more than controls with no difference between the two treatment groups. Later the researchers replicated their findings in a sample of 123 depressed adolescents (Clark et al., 1999). Subjects were randomly allocated to similar intervention groups as in the earlier study and waiting list. The two CBT groups did not differ in efficacy but recovery from depression was more common compared with the controls.

Wood et al (1996) compared individual CBT and relaxation training in 53 outpatients with depressive disorders. Subjects receiving CBT gained significant reductions in depressive symptoms, improvement in psychosocial functioning, and remission from depression compared with controls. In a trial by Vostanis et al (1996) 57 clinically referred depressed children and adolescents were randomized either to CBT or a "relatively inactive control treatment" (non-focused intervention, NFI). After treatment, a vast majority of patients no longer had depression, but no significant between-group differences were observed. In a trial by Brent and colleagues (1997) 107 adolescents with MDD were randomized to individual CBT, systemic behavioral family therapy, and nondirective supportive treatment. Subjects receiving CBT responded more rapidly and treatment results were more complete than in the two other treatments. In a small study of eighteen depressed adolescents randomized to cognitive-behavioral social skills training and art and imagery exercises (Reed, 1994) clinicians rated structural learning therapy moderately successful while the control treatment was unsuccessful.

3.2.2 Interpersonal Psychotherapy

Mufson et al (1999) randomized 48 adolescent outpatients with MDD to interpersonal psychotherapy for adolescents (IPT-A) and clinical monitoring in an 8-week trial. A significantly larger proportion of patients receiving IPT-A compared with controls recovered and they also showed greater improvement in social functioning. In another trial (Rossello′ and Bernal, 1999) 71 adolescent outpatients with MDD or dysthymia were randomized to CBT, IPT, and to a waiting list. According to self-reports, both IPT and CBT significantly reduced depressive symptoms when compared with the waiting list condition.

3.2.3 Other Psychotherapies

Although psychodynamic psychotherapy is widely used in clinical practice, no controlled trials on its efficacy in youthful depressive disorders have been published. A retrospective chart review of child and adolescent outpatients who had received either psychoanalysis or intensive psychoanalytic therapy (Target and Fonagy, 1994), found that 40 % of the depressed patients had no diagnosis and were functioning well, and in 62 % reliable improvement in psychosocial functioning was observed at the end of treatment. These findings and clinical experience suggest that also psychodynamic therapy may be of value in treating adolescent depressive disorders.

Taken the relatively high response rates in adolescents receiving "relatively inactive treatments" in controlled psychotherapy trials, Harrington et al, (1998) suggest brief supportive intervention could be used as the first line treatment of youthful depressive disorders.

3.3 Antidepressant Medications in the Treatment of Adolescent Major Depression

Recently, the use of antidepressants in adolescent MDD has substantially increased (Zito and Safer, 2001), yet the number of published double blind randomized placebo-controlled trials (RCT) on the efficacy of antidepressants in the treatment of adolescent MDD is limited.

3.3.1 Tricyclic Antidepressants

In open studies, approximately 50 - 60 % of adolescents with MDD have responded to both TCA and placebo treatment (AACAP, 1998). However, with the exceptión of one trial, published double-blind placebo-controlled trials have failed to show TCAs efficacy compared with placebo in the treatment of adolescent MDD.

Placebo-Controlled Randomized Trials

Of the eight published double-blind placebo-controlled TCA trials included in this review three report on the efficacy of amitriptyline, two of desipramine and one each of nortiptyline, clomipramine and imipramine (Table 1). With the exception of the study by Sallee et al. (1997) reporting on pulse intravenous clomipramine the duration of the trials ranged from six to ten weeks but the patients were not followed up. In four studies study entry criteria included that the subjects were clinically depressed after a placebo washout at the time of randomization. In one of the two studies involving inpatients, the subjects had to be depressed after a "2-day adjustment period" (Kramer and Feiguine, 1981), and in the other it was required that patients meet MDD criteria after discontinuation of psychotropic medication during a four week period (Birmaher et al, 1998). In the study by Kramer and Feiguine (1981) a structured psychiatric rating scale and "global impression of dysphoric symptoms" were used to assess diagnosis of depression, all other studies applied structured diagnostic interviews and explicit diagnostic criteria for MDD, as well as standardized rating instruments for the measurement of outcome. In most studies, outcome was measured using standardized observer-rating scales (HDRS or CDRS) and self-rating scales (CDI/BDI or SCL-90 depression scale) to measure symptoms of depression. Furthermore, in five studies the patients′ global improvement was rated on the CGI, a commonly used instrument in psychopharmacology trials in adults. Psychosocial treatment during the trial was reported in four studies, in the study by Birmaher et al. (1998) also lorazepam was allowed if needed.

The age of the participants ranged 13 through 19 (mean 14.2 - 17.7, Table 2). Subjects were inpatients in two, outpatients in six studies. In most studies, the index MDD episode was of long duration ranging from at least 6 to 14 months. Notably, over 80 % of subjects in the study by Geller at al (1990) had a duration of more than two years. The proportion of melancholic MDD subtype ranged from 32 % through 67 %, 32 – 50 % of patients had suicidal ideation at baseline, and psychiatric comorbidity was common.

The results of the eight trials are summarized in table 3. Seven of them failed to show TCAs efficacy compared with placebo in the treatment of adolescent MDD. The only study (Sallee et al, 1997) reporting a positive finding is not fully comparable with the others. Firstly, clomipramine is the most serotonergic TCA and secondly, it was administered intravenously in a pulse. This study reported significant drug effects over placebo during one week in decline of depressive symptoms and global improvement. The proportion of treatment responders approached significance. Three of the seven clomipramine responders were either free from depressive symptoms or had subclinical symptoms after an eight-week follow-up. Despite the small sample size, according to the authors, the results suggest the efficacy of serotonergic agents in adolescent MDD.

None of the other trials showed TCAs superior over placebo either in defined treatment response or remission rates. Some results, however, suggest some efficacy of the TCAs over placebo. First, in the study by Kramer and Feiguine (1981) one psychologial test (DACL) indicated a significant drug effect. The authors pointed out that the result may have been biased since the placebo group had higher scores on the measure both at baseline and at end of the trial. Second, Kye et al (1996) reported remission of MDD in a higher proportion in the TCA group than in the placebo group (56 % vs 15 %, table 3), with statistical significance approaching significance. Third, in the study by Klein et al (1998), the decrease in depressive symptoms on a self-report measure (SCL-90-depression scale) and the reduction in the number of DSM-III-R diagnostic criteria approached significance favoring the active medication. The comparisons between active medication and placebo on all other measures in the reviewed studies remained nonsignificant.

Meta-Analyses

Meta-analyses of several of the studies included in this reveiw and placebo-controlled trials of TCAs in childhood MDD further suggest the limited efficacy of TCAs in these populations (Thurber et al., 1995; Hazell et al, 1995; 2001; Maneeton and Srisurapanont, 2000). The meta-analysis by Hazell et al (1995) and a recent update of that (Hazell et al, 2001) included 12 and 14 double-blind randomised placebo-controlled studies on the efficacy of tricyclic antidepressants (TCA) in child and adolescent depression. Most studies suggested a larger improvement in favor of the active medication, but in only two (Kramer and Feiguine, 1981; Klein et al., 1998 – see also Table 3) the difference in at least one outcome measure was statistically significant. The autors´ first (Hazell et al. 1995) meta-analysis did not show clinically significant treatment effect for TCAs. However, in the later study (Hazell et al. 2001), subgroup analysis effect size estimates favored TCAs over placebo among adolescents but not among prepubertal children. The authors conclude there is marginal evidence to support the use of TCAs in the treatment of depression in adolescents but not in children.

Table 1. RCTs on tricyclic antidepressants in adolescent MDD: study methodology

Study	Kramer and Feiguine 1981	Geller et. al 1990	Kutcher et.al. 1994	Kye et.al. 1996	Sallee et.al. 1997	Birmaher et.al. 1998	Klein et.al. 1998	Keller et.al. 2001
Agent	amitriptyline	nortriptyline	desipramine	amitriptyline	clomipramine	amitriptyline	desipramine	imipramine
Dose	200mg/d	fixed plasma level	200mg/d	from 5mg/kg/d	single i.v. dose	5mg/kg/d	max 300mg/d	200mg/d
	80±20ng/ml	to 300mg/d	200 mg	max 300mg/d	max 300mg/d			
Duration of trial	6 weeks	8 weeks	6 weeks	8 weeks	1 week (1 dose)	10 weeks	8 weeks	8 weeks
Placebo "washout"								
duration	2 days	2 weeks	1 week	2 weeks	nr	nr	2 weeks	no
n of subjects	20	52	70	nr	nr	29	62	
n randomized	AMI 10	NT 12	DMI 30	AMI 18	CLO 8	AMI 13	DMI 23	IMI 95
	PBO 10	PBO 19	PBO 30	PBO 13	PBO 8	PBO 14	PBO 22	PBO 87
n completers	AMI 10	27	DMI 17	AMI 12	CLO 8	AMI 12	DMI 18	IMI 57
	PBO 10	PBO 25	PBO 10	PBO 8	PBO 9	PBO 18	PBO 66	
Other treatment	daily ward program	nr	nr	nr	no	psychosocial interventions, lorazepam	supportive psychotherapy	supportive management
Diagnostic interview / criteria	PRS	K-SADS	K-SADS	K-SADS	SCID-P	K-SADS, SCID-II	K-SADS	K-SADS
nr	RDC,	DSM-III	DSM-III-R	RDC	DSM-III-R	DSM-III-R	DSM-III-R	DSM-IV
Outcome measures	PRS, DACL	CDRS, CGAS	HDRS, BDI	HDRS, CGI	HDRS, BDI	HDRS, BDI	HDRS, CGI	HDRS, CGI,
	MMPI	SCL-58	K-SADS	CGI	CGI, CGAS	SCL-90, BDI	K-SADS	
	CGAS,SAICA							
Subjects included in efficacy analysis	completers	randomized	completers	randomized	randomized	randomized	completers	randomized with ≥ 1 postbaseline measurement
Follow-up	no	no	no	no	8 weeks	no	no	no

Table 2. RCTs on tricyclic antidepressants in adolescent MDD: subject characteristics

Study	Kramer and Feiguine 1981	Geller et. al. 1990	Kutcher et.al. 1994	Kye et.al. 1996	Sallee et.al. 1997	Birmaher et.al. 1998	Klein et.al. 1998	Keller et.al. 2001
								assessment
Age, mean (range)	14.5 (13-17)	14.2 (12-17)	17.7 (15-19)	14.9 (12-17)	16.2 (14-18)	16.2 (12-18)	15.1 (13-18)	14.9 (12-18)
In- (I) / outpatients (O)	I	O	O	O	O	I	O	O
% females	65	45	70	31	31	70	67	52
Duration (months) of index episode (mean)	at least 6	83 % ≥ 24	nr	nr	6.8	14.3	9.1	14
% first episode	nr	nr	nr	nr	81	nr	64	78
% melancholic subtype	nr	67	nr	32	nr	48	nr	37[1]
% suicidal	50	nr	nr	32	nr	41	40	nr
% current comorbidity any disorder	nr	nr	nr	nr	43.8	nr	nr	IMI 50 PBO 45
anxiety disorders	nr	NT 58.3 PBO 52.6	54	nr	31.3	33.3	31	IMI 26 PBO 20
disruptive disorders	nr	NT 50.0 PBO 36.8	nr	nr	12.5	51.9	7	IMI 26 PBO 20

[1] melancholic or endogeneous

Table 3. RCTs on tricyclic antidepressants in adolescent MDD: main results

Measure	Results	Mean values				Response (%)				Remission (%)			
		time	drug	pbo	p between groups	criteria	drug	pbo	p between groups	criteria	drug	pbo	p between groups
Kramer and Feiguine1981	PRS	baseline end	10.2 5.6	10.3 3.9	ns	moderate or maximum improvement	80	60	ns	…	…	…	…
	DACL	baseline End	16.2 10.3	25.2 22.7	p < 0.001		…	…	…	…	…	…	…
	MMPI	baseline End	77.4 61.4	80.7 67.1	ns		…	…	…	…	…	…	…
Geller et al1990	CDRS	baseline end	51.3 34.7	51.4 37.8	ns	CDRS<25 $\leq$2 DSM III symptoms	8.3	21.1	ns				
	CGAS	baseline end	37.6 54.2	38.6 48.9	ns								
Kutcher et.al1994	HDRS	baseline end	22.6 12.7	23.8 13.4	ns	$\geq$50% decrease	48	35	ns	score < 8	nr	nr	ns (tot 28%)
	BDI	baseline End	nr 13.3	nr 17.2	ns					score < 9	0	0	ns
Kye et al1996	HDRS	baseline end	12.0 8.0	13.2 8.8	ns	$\geq$50% decrease	72	85	ns	score < 6	56	15	ns (<0.09)
	CGI severity	baseline End	3.9 2.2	3.5 3.2	ns (<0.11)								
	K-SADS	baseline End	20.7 15.7	18.7 15.6	ns								
Sallee et al 1997	HDRS	baseline end	22.9 7.9	22.4 13.4	< 0.04	$\geq$50% decrease	88	38	ns (p=0.06)				
	BDI	baseline End	20.4 7.7	24.4 15.0	ns								
	CGI severity	baseline End	5.7 2.5	5.4 4.0	< 0.003								

Table 3. RCTs on tricyclic antidepressants in adolescent MDD: main results (Continued)

Measure	Results	Mean values				Response (%)				Remission (%)			
		time	drug	pbo	p between groups	criteria	drug	pbo	p between groups	criteria	drug	pbo	p between groups
Birmaher et al 1998	HDRS	baseline end	22.9 7.7	21.9 8.6	ns	≥50% decrease	77	79	ns	score <7	69	71	ns
	BDI	baseline End	28.8 10.1	23.1 10.1	ns	≥50% decrease	85	86	ns	score < 9	62	57	ns
	CGI severity	baseline End	4.6 2.8	5.4 3.2	ns								
	CGAS	baseline end	45 64	45 60	ns								
	n of MDD symptoms									<2dg-criteria	38	36	ns
	dg of MDD									No MDD	69	64	ns
Klein et al 1998	HDRS	baseline end	21.4 10.8	21.3 14.6	ns								
	BDI	baseline End	24.6 12.0	21.6 15.9	ns								
	SCL-90-dep	baseline End	1.97 0.91	1.86 1.42	0.05								
	CGAS	baseline end	52 67	50 68	ns								
	CGI improved	end								score 1-2	67	50	ns
	n of MDD symptoms	baseline end	7.2 2.3	6.8 3.9	ns (p=0.07)								
	dg of MDD									No MDD	72	50	ns
Keller et al 2001	HDRS	baseline end	18.1 9.2	18.97 9.9	ns	≥50% decrease / score<9	59	55	ns	score <9	50	46	ns
	K-SADS depr score	baseline End	27.5 17.99	28.8 19.3	ns								
	CGI improved	end								score 1-2	52	48	ns

Table 4. RCTs on SSRIs and other new antidepressants in adolescent MDD: study methodology

	Simeon et al. 1990	Emslie et. al. 1997	Mandoki et.al. 1997	Keller et.al. 2001.	Emslie et.al. 2002
Agent	fluoxetine	fluoxetine	venlafaxine	paroxetine	fluoxetine
Dose	max 60mg/d	20 mg/d	37.5-75 mg/d max	40mg/d	20 mg/d
Duration of trial	7 weeks	8 weeks	6 weeks	8 weeks	9 weeks
Placebo "washout"					
duration	1 week	1 week	1 week	no	1 week
n of subjects	40	106	nr		227
n of randomized subjects	FLUO 15[1]	FLUO 48	VNF 20	PAR 93	FLUO 109
	PBO 15	PBO 48	PBO 20	PBO 87	PBO 110
n of study completers	30	FLUO34	VNF 16	PAR 67	FLUO 90
		PBO 26	PBO 17	PBO 66	PBO 68
Other treatment	nr	nr	weekly behavioral or cognitive psychotherapy	supportive management	nr
Diagnostic interview / criteria	nr	DICA, KSADS	nr	K-SADS-L	DICA
	DSM-III	DSM-III-R	DSM-IV	DSM-IV	DSM-IV
Outcome measures	HDRS,CGI	CDRS-R, CDI,	HDRS, CDRS	HDRS, CGI	CDRS, MADRS,
	CAS, RDS,	BDI, BPRS-C,	CBCL, CDI	K-SADS	HARS,CGI, GAF
	SCL-58	CGI			
Subjects included in efficacy analysis	completers	completers	completers	randomized with≥ 1 postbaseline assessment	randomized with≥ 2 week participation
Follow-up	24 months	no	no	no	no

[1] randomized completers

Table 5. RCTs on SSRIs and other new antidepressants in adolescent MDD: subject characteristics

	Simeon et al 1990	Emslie et. al. 1997	Mandoki et.al. 1997	Keller et.al. 2001	Emslie et.al. 2002
Age, mean (range)	16 (13-18)	12.3 (7-17)	nr	14.9 (12-18)	12.7 (7-17)
		50 % >12	(8-17)	61%≥12	44 % >12
% females	55	46	24	64	49
In- (I) / outpatients (O)	I and O	O	O	O	O
Duration (months) of index episode (mean)	nr	3.3	nr	14	14.2
% first episode	nr	48	nr	80	79
% melancholic subtype	nr	20	nr	35[1]	nr
% suicidal	nr	nr	nr	nr	nr
% current comorbidity					
any disorder	nr	FLUO 85.4[2]	nr	PAR 41	nr
		PBO 77.1[2]		PBO 45	
anxiety disorders	nr	FLUO 66.7[2]	nr	PAR 19	nr
		PBO 45.8[2]		PBO 28	
disruptive disorders	nr	FLUO 27.1[2]	nr	PAR 25	FLUO 18.3
		PBO 33.3[2]		PBO 20	PBO 16.3

[1] melancholic or endogeneous

[2] lifetime comcorbidity

Table 6. RCTs on SSRIs and other new antidepressants in adolescent MDD: main results

	Results	Mean values				Response (%)				Remission (%)			
		time	drug	pbo	p between groups	criteria	drug	pbo	p between groups	criteria	drug	pbo	p between groups
Simeon et al 1990	CGI	end	data not shown, in two thirds CGI-improvement moderate or marked, no significant between-group differences										
		follow-up	data not shown, no significant between-group differences in "global ratings"										
Emslie et al 1997	CDRS-R	baseline end	58.5 38.4	57.6 47.1	0.02					score <29	31	23	ns
	CDI/BDI	baseline end	15.8 9.9	15.3 11.2	ns								
	BPRS-C	baseline end	47.3 38.9	46.2 41.0	ns								
	CGAS	baseline end	48 64	48 60	ns								
	CGI improved	end								score 1-2	56	33	0.02
Mandoki et al 1997		end	data not shown, no significant between-group differences on any outcome measure										
Keller et al 2001	HDRS	baseline end	18.98 8.2	18.97 9.9	ns	≥ 50% decrease / score < 9	67	59	ns	score <9	63	46	0.02
	K-SADS depr score	baseline end	28.3 16.6	28.8 19.3	ns (p=0.07)								
	CGI improved	end								score 1-2	66	48	0.02
Emslie et al 2002	CDRS-R	baseline end	57.1 35.1	55.1 40.2	<0.001	≥ 50% decrease	34	17	0.007	score <29	41	20	<0.01

Table 6. RCTs on SSRIs and other new antidepressants in adolescent MDD: main results (Continued)

	Results	Mean values				Response (%)				Remission (%)			
		time	drug	pbo	p between groups	criteria	drug	pbo	p between groups	criteria	drug	pbo	p between groups
	MADRS	baseline end	21.6 11.2	21.5 13.9	0.023								
	HARS	baseline End	10.2 5.4	11.0 7.4	ns								
	GAF	baseline end	53.3 64.8	54.6 63.9	ns								
	CGI severity	baseline end	4.5 2.9	4.4 3.4	<0.001								

AMI = amitriptyline, CMI = clomipramine, DMI = desipramine, FLUO = fluoxetine NT = nortriptyline, PAR = paroxetine, PBO = placebo, VNF = venlafaxine

Nr = not reported

BDI = Beck Depression Inventory (Beck et.al., 1961); BPRS-C = Brief Psychiatric Rating Scale for Children (Overall and Pfefferbaum, 1982); CAS = Covi anxiety scale (Covi and Lipman, 1984); CDI=Children´s depression inventory (Kovacs, 1985); CDRS = Children´s depression rating scale (Poznanski et.al., 1979); CGAS = Children´s Global Assessment Scale (Shaffer et.al., 1983); CGI = Clinical Global Impression (NIMH, 1985); DACL = Depression Adjective Check List (Kramer and Feiguine, 1981); DICA= Diagnostic Interview for Children and Adolescents (Welner et.al., 1987); DSM-III, DSM-III-R, DSM-IV = versions of the Diagnostic and statistical manual of mental disorders (APA, 1980; 1987; 1994); GAF=Global Assessment of Functioning Scale of DSM-IV (APA, 1994); HDRS = Hamilton Depression Rating Scale (Hamilton, 1960); HARS = Hamilton Anxiety Rating Scale (Hamilton, 1959); K-SADS = Children´s Schedule for Affective Disorders and Schizophrenia (Chambers et.al., 1985); MADRS = Montgomery-Asberg Depression Rating Scale (Montgomery and Asberg, 1979); MMPI = Minnesota Multiphasic Personality Inventory (Marks et.al., 1974); PRS = Psychiatric Rating Scale (Kramer and Feiguine, 1981); RDC = Research Diagnostic Criteria (Spitzer et.al., 1977); RDS = Raskin Depression Scale (Covi and Lipman, 1984); SCID-P = Structured Clinical Interview for DSM-III-R - Patient Version 1.0 (Spitzer et.al., 1990); SAICA = Social Adjustment Inventory for Children and Adolescents (John, et al, 1987); SCL-58 = Hopkins Symptom Checklist (Derogatis et.al., 1974), SCL-90 = Symptom Checklist-90 (Derogatis et al, 1973).

Adverse Effects

The most common adverse effects of TCAs in adolescents are the same as reported in adults. Due to the anticolinergic effects they commonly cause dry mouth, blurred vision, constipation and urinary retention. Also increased heart rate and mild prolongation of intracardiac conduction are relatively common (Findling et al., 1999). As also other antidepressants, the TCAs may cause seizures and mania. The most disconcerting side-effects are the effects on intracardiac conduction potentially leading to dysrythmias and heart block, and the high lethality of TCAs in overdose (Kutcher, 1997).

3.3.2 Selective Serotonine Reuptake Inhibitors and other New Antidepressants

Several double-blind randomized placebo-controlled studies on the efficacy of selective serotonine reuptake inhibitors (SSRI) and other new antidepressants in child and adolescent depression are under way (Martin et al, 2000) but only five have been published thus far (Table 4). Four studies report on the efficacy of SSRIs – three of fluoxetine and one of paroxetine – and one on the efficacy of venlafaxine, an agent that primarily inhibits both serotonin and noradrenaline reuptake at the synaptic cleft. In the following, each of these studies will be reviewed.

Placebo-Controlled Randomized Trials of the SSRIs

In the first published double-blind trial Simeon et al. (1990) studied a sample of 40 out- and inpatient adolesents with DSM-III major depression who had to have a HDRS score of 20 or higher. After a one-week single-blind placebo treatment, 30 adolescents were randomized to fluoxetine and placebo groups. Fluoxetine was titrated to a dose of 60 mg per day, the treatment continued for seven weeks. Outcome was measured using the HDRS, the CGI, the Raskin Depression Scale (RDS), the Covi Anxiety Scale (CAS), and the 58-item Hopkins Symptom Checklist (SCL-58).

By three weeks of treatment, a significant improvement was seen in both study groups. Approximately two thirds of the patients showed marked or moderate clinical global improvement. Although no statistically significant between-group differences were found, all outcome variables (HDRS, CGI, RDS, CAS) except the sleep disturbance factor of the HDRS indicated greater improvement in the fluoxetine than in the placebo group. After an average of 24 months, 32 patients were interviewed and outcome measured using HDRS, CAS, SCL-58, a DSM-III symptom checklist for major depressive disorder, and an adaptive functioning scale. At follow-up, according to global ratings, 63 % of the patients were doing well, 31 % were evaluated as being depressed. During the follow-up, 59 % had received treatment, and 28 % were still in treatment. The high placebo response and the small sample size may partly explain the negative finding. Unfortunately, the limited reporting of study methodology and results hampers a more detailed reviewing of the study.

Emslie et al. (1997) compared the efficacy of fluoxetine with placebo in a sample of 96 children and adolescent outpatients suffering from DSM-III-R MDD and having a CDRS-R score greater than 40 after a three-week assessment and one-week single-blind placebo run-in. The diagnoses were assessed using the DICA and K-SADS interviews. The patients received fluoxetine 20 mg / day for eight weeks. The primary outcome measures were the CGI and the CDRS-R, secondary measures were BPRS-C, CDI for children, BDI for adolescents, and the CGAS.

Based on the CGI scale rating "very much or much improved", a significantly larger proportion (56 %) of patients receiving fluoxetine responded to treatment compared with the placebo group (33 %) (Table 6). Also a weekly intention-to-treat analysis with the last observation carried forward (LOCF-analysis) of CDRS-R scores as a continuous variable, fluoxetine was found superior to placebo. The difference favoring fluoxetine emerged after five weeks of treatment. Age or sex did not affect the results. Despite these encouraging findings, it should be noted that only 31 % of patients in the fluoxetine group and 23 % in the placebo group achieved complete remission. Furthermore, the secondary outcome measures showed no between-goup differences.

In a naturalistic one-year follow-up of 87 patients participating the trial, Emslie et al. (1998) found that 85 % recovered (defined as $\leq$2 symptoms of MDD for at least two months). Recovery appeared to be associated with younger age, lower severity of depressive symptoms at baseline, higher family functioning, and fewer comorbid diagnoses. Of those who recovered, 39 % had a recurrence during the follow-up period, with 55 % of recurrences occurring within six months. Apparently due to the brief follow-up and the small sample size, no clear predictors of recurrence were found.

A recent multicenter eight-week trial by Keller and colleagues (2001) compared paroxetine (20 - 40 mg / day) with placebo and imipramine (200 – 300 mg / day) with placebo in 275 adolescents with DSM-IV MDD ascertained with K-SADS-L interviews. After a screening phase of 1 – 2 weeks with no placebo administration, the patients had to fulfill the diagnostic criteria for MDD, to have a score of at least 12 on the 17-item HDRS, and a score of less than 60 on the CGAS. Ninety-three patients were randomized to receive paroxetine, 95 imipramine, and 87 placebo. The primary outcome measures were response defined as a HDRS score of less than 9 or a 50 % or greater reduction in HDRS scores, and change from baseline in HDRS total score. Secondary outcome measures were change in the depressed mood item of the HDRS, change in the depression item of the K-SADS-L, CGI improvement scores, and change in the nine-item depression subscale of the K-SADS-L.

The response to imipramine was not significantly different from that to placebo on any of the depression-related measures (Table 3). On the primary outcome measures at endpoint a statistically significantly larger proportion of patients in the paroxetine group than in the placebo group showed a treatment response (66 % vs 48 %) but there was no between-goup difference in the change form baseline HDRS total scores (Table 6). Of the other depression-related variables, paroxetine was superior compared with placebo on the HDRS depressed mood item (p=0.001), K-SADS-L depressed mood item (p=0.05), much or very much improved on the CGI (p=0.02). The difference trended toward significance on two measures, change in the depression subscale of the K-SADS-L (p=0.07) and mean CGI score (p=0.09). Compared with placebo, a significantly larger proportion of subjects in the paroxetine group achieved remission from MDD (HRSD total score $\leq$ 8) at endpoint (63 % vs 46 %).

Emslie et al (2002) conducted a multicenter trial comparing the efficacy of fluoxetine (20 mg / day) and placebo in 122 children and 97 adolescents suffering from DSM-IV MDD. The patients were recruited from study site outpatient populations, and using newspaper and radio advertising aiming at collecting a study population with a wide range of severity of MDD. The diagnoses were assessed in three separate DICA or MAGIC (which incorporates DICA) interviews during a two-week evaluation period (Table 4). In all, 420 subjects were screened, after the two-week evaluation period and a one-week placebo run-in 109 subjects were assigned to fluoxetine, 110 to placebo. The patients had to fulfil the diagnostic criteria for

MDD, to have a CDRS-R score of more than 40, and a CGI score of 4 or more. Randomization was stratified by gender and age category.

The primary outcome measures were response and remission. Response was defined as a decreasee of 30 % or greater in the CDRS-R total score form baseline to last visit and remission as an endpoint CDRS-R total score of less than 29. Secondary measures included changes in CDRS-R sub-scores and CGI-severity scores from baseline to endpoint. In intention to treat analyses with LOCF of response and remission including patients treated for at least two weeks, a significantly larger proportion of patients in the fluoxetine group met the criteria for remission (41.3 % vs 19.8 %). Using the predefined criteria for response, the difference between fluoxetine and placebo approached significance (p= 0.093). However, when other definitions (e.g. the widely used definintion of a decrease of 50 % or more in total score) were used, the difference was statistically significant favoring fluoxetine (Table 6). Compared with placebo, fluoxetine treatment was associated with significantly greater reduction in CDRS-R scores after one week of treatment and for the remainder of the trial. Gender, age category or family history of depression did not affect the result. Significantly more of the fluoxetine treated patients than those on placebo were rated as much or very much improved in the CGI (52.3 % vs 36.8 %, p=0.028). Somewhat surprisingly, no significant between-group differences were observed in reduction of anxiety or in improvement of psychosocial functioning.

Adverse Effects

The SSRIs have been found generally well tolerated. Approximately 10 – 20 % of adolescent patients may be expected to experience adverse effects, most commonly headache, nausea, reduced appetite, dizziness, initial insomnia and weight gain (Kutcher, 1997). Induction of manic symptoms or irritability have been reasons for discontinuation of medication in the reported trials. Recently, the Medicines and Healthcare Products Regulatory Agency (MHRA) in the UK reported increased risk for suicidality in children and adolescents using paroxetine, and advised not to give this agent to patients under 18 years (Waechter, 2003). Until published, these results need to be considered as preliminary.

Summary

The duration of the trials ranged from seven to nine weeks, the patients were followed up in two studies (Simeon et al, 1990; Emslie et al, 1998). Three studies required that the subjects were clinically depressed after a placebo washout at the time of randomization, in one study (Keller et al, 2001) persistence of symptoms was determined during a 7-14-day screening period. Three studies applied structured diagnostic interviews and explicit diagnostic criteria for MDD, one a "DSM-III symptom checklist for MDD" (Simeon et al, 1990). All the studies applied DSM-criteria for MDD and used standardized instruments for the measurement of outcome. In one study the patients received psychosocial treatment during the trial. The subjects′ age ranged 7 through 18, the mean age ranging from 12.3 to 16.0 (Table 5). Two studies included also prepubertal children, however, approximately half of the subjects in these studies were adolescents. Simeon et al. (1990) studied mixed in- and outpatients, subjects were outpatients in the other studies. Three studies reported the duration of the index MDD episode, in two it was approximately 14 months, in one three months. Two studies reported the proportion of melancholic MDD subtype which ranged from 20 %

through 35 %. Comorbid anxiety and disruptive disorders were common. None of the studies reported the subjects´ suicidal ideation.

Unpublished Placebo-Controlled RCTs of the SSRIs

In a randomized double-blind, placebo-controlled, flexible dose study, the efficacy of citalopram was compared with placebo in the treatment of 83 7-11-year-old children and 91 12-17-year-old adolescents with DSM-IV major depression confirmed using the K-SADS interview (Wagner et al, 2001). Citalopram was administered for eight weeks with a dose of 20 – 40 mg / day. The primary outcome measure was the CDRS-R, response was defined as a CDRS-R score $\leq$ 28. In comparison with placebo, the decrease in the mean CDRS-R total scores was statistically significantly grater in the citalopram group, as was the proportion of responders. Another large randomized double-blind, placebo-controlled 10-week trial of sertraline (50 – 200 mg per day) in 376 children and adolescents aged 6 – 17 years suffering major depression found sertraline to be more efficacious than placebo (Wagner et al, 2002).

There are also negative trials of SSRIs in youthful major depression. One recent unpublished 12-week trial of citalopram with a daily dose of 10 – 40 mg in 233 clinic referred 13 – 18-year-old outpatients with MDD found a response rate of approximately 60 % of patients both in citalopram and placebo groups with no statistically significant between-group differences (A-L von Knorring, personal communication). Another unpublished 12-week trial (Milin et al, 1999) of 286 adolescents (age 13-18 years) with unipolar major depression found a response rate of 60.5 % for paroxetine administered with a dose of 20 – 40 mg / day and 58.2 for placebo. No overall statistically significant differences were found but, among patients aged over 16 years the proportion of responders was higher in the paroxetine group. Publication is needed for detailed evaluation of these negative studies.

Studies Directly Comparing SSRIs with TCAs

While the above reviewed studies have compared new antidepressants with placebo, they have not compared them with TCAs. In a multicenter, double-blind trial, Braconnier et al. (2003) compared paroxetine with clomipramine in a sample of 121 12-20-year-old adolescent outpatients with DSM-IV major depression having a MADRS score of 24 or greater. No structured diagnostic interviews were applied. In all, 136 subjects were screened, and after a one week period 63 patients were randomized to receive paroxetine 20 – 40 mg / day and 58 subjects clomipramine 150 mg / day for eight weeks. Concurrent treatment had to be avoided during the trial. The primary outcome measures were the CGI improvement and the MADRS, secondary measures were the SCL-58, the GAF, and the CDI for subjects aged 15 year and younger.

In intention-to-treat analyses on the CGI scale rating "very much or much improved", no differences were found between the groups (paroxetine 58.2 % vs clomipramine 59.3 %). Based on a 50 % or larger decrease in the MADRS score as the definition of response, the statistical difference approached significance in favor of paroxetine (paroxetine 65.1 % vs clomipramine 48.3 %, p=0.062). No between-group differences were found in changes in the GAF or the SCL-58. When only those 79 subjects who received at least 3 weeks of treatment were compared, a statistically significantly larger proportion (34 of 41, 82.9 %) of those receiving paroxetine than in the clomipramine group (22 of 38, 57.9 %) responded to treatment (p=0.01). Based on the findings on the primary outcome measures, the authors concluded paroxetine and clompramine are equally efficacious in adolescent MDD.

Another study compared fluoxetine with imipramine-treated historical controls in adolescent MDD according to RDC-criteria among 13 to 17-year-old consecutively admitted adolescent inpatients (Strober et al, 1999). Fifty-two subjects during an eight-year period between 1988 and 1995 with a HDRS score 16 or greater and a CGI score of 3 or greater five days following admission were entered into a standardized open-label protocol to receive fluoxetine (mean dose 33.2 $\pm$ 7.6 mg / day) for six weeks and a variety of psychosocial interventions at the ward. These patients were compared with 28 historical controls comprising consecutively admitted adolescents to the same inpatient service between 1984 and 1988 who had received imipramine (mean dose 217 $\pm$ 52 mg / day). Despite the nonrandom assignment of the two patient cohorts, the groups did not differ significantly in major socioeconomic or clinical characteristics.

Change in the total score in the HDRS from baseline to six weeks, the percentage decrease in HDRS score from baseline, and the CGI score at last assessment were used as the primary outcome measures. In intention-to-treat analyses, compared with imipramine-treated patients, the mean change in HDRS score was significantly greater in the fluoxetine group (change in score: fluoxetine –13.2 vs imipramine – 10.2, $p<0.002$) as was also the mean percentage decrease in HDRS score (fluoxetine 54.3 % vs imipramine 41.4 %, $p<0.003$). Mean CGI scores at completion were lower in the fluoxetine group (fluoxetine 2.5 $\pm$ 1.0 vs imipramine 3.4 $\pm$ 1.0 $p<0.001$). When treatment response was defined as $\geq$ 50 % decrease in HDRS total score from baseline no statistically significant between-group difference was observed (fluoxetine 53.8 % vs imipramine 39.3 %). However, using "much or very much improved" in the CGI as the criterion for treatment response, the result was in favor of fluoxetine (fluoxetine 48.1 % vs imipramine 17.9 %, $p=0.009$). Notably, only few patients in either group (fluoxetine 7.7 %, imipramine 7.1 %) met criteria for full remission defined as a HDRS score of seven or less at study exit. In spite of the nonrandomized nature of the study, the results give further support to the use of SSRIs rather than TCAs as first line medications in youthful MDD.

3.3.3 Other Antidepressants

Only one published double-blind randomised placebo-controlled trial has studied the efficacy of new second-generation antidepressants other than the SSRIs in youthful major depression. Mandoki and coworkers (1997) randomized 40 child and adolescent outpatients with DSM-IV MDD for six weeks to a combination of weekly cognitive-behavioral therapy and either venlafaxine or placebo (Tables 4 – 6). The way diagnostic data was obtained was not specified. After randomization there was a one-week washout for patients already on medication. Thereafter, the dose of venlafaxine was titrated during the first week to 37.5 mg / day in children aged 8 to 12 years, in adolescents aged 13 to 17 years to 75 mg / day. Outcome measures were the CDRS for children, the HDRS for adolescents, the CBCL, and the CDI. Weekly cognitive-behavioral therapy was given concurrently with pharmacotherapy. Thirty-three patients completed the trial. Over time, patients in both treatment groups improved significantly on the HDRS, the CDRS, the CBCL but no statistically significant group differences were found. Notably, no significant improvement on the CDI was observed. Possible explanations of the negative finding are small sample size, low dosage of venlafaxine, and concomitant active psychotherapy. Another small study of moclobemide in the treatment of major depression in young adolescents (Avci et al, 1999) showed inconclusive results.

Additionally, several nonblind reports on the newer antidepressants have been published (for a review, see e.g. Findling et al, 1999). These medications have fewer side-effects, only modest cardiovascular effects, and are less toxic in overdose than the TCAs.

3.4 Continuation and Maintenance Treatment

Although most adolescents respond to acute treatment of MDD, approximately 40 % fail to respond, recovery from depression is commonly is only partial (Birmaher et. al, 2000). Adolescent MDD tends to run a recurring course with reported recurrence rates of over 50 % to almost 75 % over a period three to eight years (Emslie and Mayes, 2001). Only limited data exists on the successfulness of continuation or maintenance treatment. One study of continuation CBT after acute treatment of adolescent major depression found booster sessions with a frequency of one to two times a month prevented relapses compared with historical controls receiving only acute treatment (Kroll et al, 1996). Another study reported on continuation group CBT with a frequency of four times a year compared with only one yearly follow-up session (Clarke et al, 1999). After one year more subjects still depressed after acute treatment in the former group had recovered but after two years, no difference was found.

One study by Emslie et al (2001) found that, after responding to fluoxetine in the acute treatment phase, young patients continuing on fluoxetine had a lower rate of relapse than those switched to placebo for 19 weeks. In addition, time to relapse was longer among those remaining on fluoxetine.

4. Discussion

Studies on the effectiveness of SSRIs are limited in number but seem to support their use as first line antidepressant medication in youthful depression. They are generally better tolerated, and less toxic in overdose than the TCAs. The evidence suggests that TCAs should not be used as first line medications due to the lack of effectiveness in youthful depression, their toxicity in overdoses, and the risk of serious adverse events. It has been suggested that neurodevelopmental factors explain the lack of response of adolescent MDD to TCAs and response to the SSRIs. Preliminary evidence suggests e.g. that the noradrenergic neurotransmitter system may not be fully developed until young adulthood while the serotonergic system matures relatively early (Carrey et al, 2002; Kaufman et al, 2002).

When considering the generalizability of the reported findings to ordinary clinical settings selection of subjects to the trials should be kept in mind. For example, subjects with the most severe comorbid conditions seen in clinical practice, such as conduct disorders and substance abuse, were excluded as were also subjects with severe suicidal tendencies. It is plausible to assume these youth need additional or different treatments. Particularly data on the psychopharmacological treatment of suicidal depressed adolescents is lacking (Pelkonen and Marttunen, 2003).

A clear shortcoming of the early studies reviewed is the small sample sizes. The detection of a 33 % difference between the antidepressant and placebo response with a power of 0.80 and at a significance level of 0.05 would require a total of about 120 subjects (Kye and Ryan,

1995). Obviously, many of the reviewed trials have been underpowered. The issue of sample size seems particularly relevant taken the high response rate to placebo in adolescents (17 - 85 %) in the reviewed trials. However, even the large trial by Keller et al (2001) and the three meta-analyses reported negative findings regarding the TCAs. Another issue is the small number of published trials and participants, as only 412 patients participated the reviewed TCA studies and 209 received active medication. The respective numbers for the SSRI studies were 525 and 265.

Other methodological factors possibly affecting the results are heterogeneity of study samples, dose of medication, duration of the trials, instrumentation, concomitant other treatment, and definition of treatment response and recovery.

Two of the reviewed studies involved inpatients, one mixed in- and outpatients, the others outpatients. The patients in the study by Geller et al (1990) seem to have suffered from particulalry severe and comorbid MDD, and Birmaher et al (1998) recruited inpatients referred to a state hospital for long-time hospitalization after they had failed to respond to several previous inpatient interventions. On the other hand, study subjects were recruited from clinical sites and by advertisements in the study by Emslie et al (2002) possibly leading to heterogeneity in baseline characteristics and outcome between clinic-referred and advertisement-referred subjects. The baseline scores on the reported measures (Tables 3, 6) show variation in symptom and global severity between trials. Also phase of the depressive illness, whether first-episode or recurrent MDD as well as differing profile of psychiatric comorbidity may have affected the results. Exclusion of subjects with possible bipolar genotype using family-history of bipolarity as an exclusion criterion has been done only in the later studies. It seems that dosing of medication may have been inadequate in some trials but at least the later studies have monitored plasma levels.

The duration of most of the reviewed trials have ranged from 6 to 8 weeks, while some evidence suggest that to achieve full response medication may need to be continued up to 10 weeks (Ambrosini, 2000).

Uncontrolled concomitant other treatments during the trials have probably blurred the effects of active medication. The effect of other treatment may be particularly difficult to assess when studying inpatients since many daily activities, personal interactions, psychosocial and behavioral interventions rarely can be controlled satisfactorily. Finally, reporting, instrumentation, definition of treatment response and recovery vary hampering comparisons between trials. The use and reporting of both self-report scales (e.g. CDI, BDI) and observer rating scales (e.g. HRSD, CDRS) as well as global assessments (e.g. GAS, C-GAS, CGI) is likely to give a full picture of response and recovery and enhance comparisons between trials.

5. Implications

Accumulating evidence shows that both certain psychosocial and psychopharmacological treatments are efficacious in the adolescent MDD. Obviously, more research on the efficacy of both specific psychotherapies and SSRIs and other new antidepressants is needed. Some patients may benefit more from psychosocial, others from psychopharmacological treatment while some patients may need combined treatments. Other issues requiring additional research are the efficacy of continuation and maintenance treatment in preventing recurrence of adolescent MDD and the management of treatment resistant youthful depression (Emslie and Mayes, 2001). Two ongoing studies will address the relative efficacy of psychosocial and psychopharmacological treatments and their combination as well as maintence treatment of adolescent MDD. The Treatment of Adolescent Depression Study (TADS) evaluates the short- and long-term effects of four treatments for adolescent MDD: fluoxetine, cognitive-behavioral therapy, their combination, and acutely, placebo in over 400 12-17-year-old adolescents (TADS Study team, 2003). Treatment of SSRI-resistant Depression in Adolescents (TORDIA) adolescents who have not responded to a SSRI will be randomized to one of four treatments: an alternate SSRI, venlafaxine, an alternate SSRI combined with cognitive-behavioral therapy and venlafaxine plus cognitive-behavioral therapy. Finally, effectiveness studies are needed to find out how results of efficacy studies generalize to routine clinical practice (Kazdin, 2000).

REFERENCES

Aalto-Setälä T, Haarasilta L, Marttunen M. Major depressive disorder in adolescence: prevalence, comorbidity and treatment utilization. *Psychiatr Fenn* 1998;29:12-28.

Aalto-Setälä T, Marttunen M, Poikolainen K, Tuulio-Henriksson A, Lönnqvist J. One-month prevalence of depression and other DSM-IV disorders among young adults. *Psychol Med* 2001;31:791-801.

Aalto-Setälä T, Marttunen M, Tuulio-Henriksson A, Poikolainen K, Lönnqvist J. Depressive symptoms in adolescence predict early adulthood depressive disroders and maladjustment. *Am J Psychiatry* 2002a;159:1235-1237.

Aalto-Setälä T, Marttunen M, Tuulio-Henriksson A, Poikolainen K, Lönnqvist J. Psychiatric treatment seeking and psychosocial impairment among young adults with depression. *J Affect Disord* 2002b;70:35-47.

Ambrosini PJ. A review of pharmacotherapy of major depression in children and adolescents. *Psychiatric Services* 2000;51:627-633.

American Academy of Child and Adolescent Psychiatry. Preactice prameters for the assessment and treatment of children and adolescents with depressive disorders. *J Am Acad Child Adolesc Psychiatry* 1998;37(10 Supplement):63S-83S.

American Psychiatric Association: *Diagnostic and statistical manual of mental disorders.* Fourth edition. APA, Washington, DC, 1994.

American Psychiatric Association: *Diagnostic and statistical manual of mental disorders.* Third edition. APA, Washington, DC, 1980.

American Psychiatric Association: *Diagnostic and statistical manual of mental disorders.* Third edition - Revised. APA, Washington, DC, 1987.

Avci A, Dileer RS, Kibar M, Sezgin F. Comparison of moclobemide and placebo in young adolescents with major depressive disorder. *Ann Med Sci* 1999;8:31-40.

Beck AT, Ward CH, Mendelson M, ym: An inventory for measuring depression. *Arch Gen Psychiatry* 1961;4:561-571.

Birmaher B, Brent DA, Kolko D et al. Clinical outcome after short-term psychotherapy for adolescents with major depressive disorder. *Arch Gen Psychiatry* 2000;57:29-36.

Birmaher B, Ryan ND, Williamson DE, Brent DA, Kaufman J, Dahl R, Perel J, Nelson B. Childhood and adolescent depression: A review of the past 10 years. Part I. *J Am Acad Child Adolesc Psychiatry* 1996;35:1427-1439.

Birmaher B, Waterman GS, Ryan N, Perel J, McNabb J, Balach L, Beaudry MB, Nasr FN, Karambelkar J, Elterich G, Quintana H, Williamson DE, Rao U. Randomized, controlled trial of amitriptyline versus placebo for adolescents with "treatment-resistant" major depression. *J Am Acad Child Adolesc Psychiatry* 1998;37:527-535.

Braconnier A, Le Coent R, Cohen D. Paroxetine versus clomipramine in adolescents with severe major depression: a double-blind randomized, multicenter trial. *J Am Acad Child Adolesc Psychiatry* 2003;42:22-29.

Brent DA, Holder D, Kolko D, et al. A clinical psychotherapy trial for adolescent depression comparing cognitive, family, and supportive therapy. *Arc Gen Psychiatry* 1997; 54: 877-85

Carrey NJ, Dursun S, Clements R, Renton K, Waschbusch D, MacMaster F. Noradrenergic and serotonoergic neuroendocrine responses oiun prepubertal, peripubertal, and postpubertal rates pretreated with desimpraminen and sertraline. *J Am Acad Child Adolesc Psychiatry* 2002;41:999-1006.

Chambers WJ, Puig-Antich J, Hirsh M ym. The assessment of affective disorders in children and adolescents by semistructured interview. *Arch Gen Psychiatry* 1985;42:696-703.

Clarke GN, Rohde P, Lewinsohn PM, et al. Cognitive-behavioral treatment of adolescent depression: efficacy of acute group treatment and booster sessions. *J Am Acad Child Adolesc Psychiatry* 1999;38:272-9

Clarke GN, Rohde P, Lewinsohn PM, Hops H, Seeley JR. Cognitive-behavioral treatment of adolescent depression: efficacy of acute group treatment and booster sessions. *J Am Acad Child Adolesc Psychiatry* 1999;38:272-9.

Covi L, Lipman RS. Primary depression or primary anxiety? A possible approach to a diagnostic dilemma. *Clin Neuropharmacol* 1984;7:924-925.

Derogatis LR, Lipman RS, Covi L. SCL-90: an outpatient psychiatric rating scale. *Psychopharmacol Bull* 1973;9:13-28.

Derogatis LR, Lipman RS, Rickels K, Uhlemhuth EH, Covi L. The Hopkins Symptom Checklist (HSCL): A self report symptom inventory. *Behav Sci* 1974;19:1-15.

Emslie G, Rush AJ, Weinberg AW, Kowatch RA, Hughes CW, Carmody T, Rintelmann J. A double-blind, randomized placebo-controlled trial of fluoxetine in children and adolescents with depression. *Arch Gen Psychiatry* 1997;54:1031-1037.

Emslie GJ, Heiligenstein JH, Hoog SL, Findling RL, Wagner KD, Ernest DE et al. Fluoxetine for maintenance of recovery from depression in children and adolescents: a placebo-controlled, randomized clinical trial. Paper presented at the 154th Annual Meeting of the American Psychiatric Association, New Orleans, LA, May 5-10, 2001.

Emslie GJ, Heiligenstein JH, Wagner KD, Hoog SL, Ernest DE, Brown E, Nilsson M, Jacobson JG. Fluoxetine for acute treatment of depression in children and adolescents: a placebo-controlled, randomized clinical trial. *J Am Acad Child Adolesc Psychiatry* 2002;41:1205-1215.

Emslie GJ, Mayes TL. Mood disorders in children and adolescents: psychopharmacological treatment. *Biol Psychiatry* 2001;49:1082-1090.

Emslie GJ, Rush AJ, Weinberg AW, Kowatch RA, Carmody T, Mayes TL. Fluoxetine in child and adolescent depression: acute and maintenance treatment. *Depression and Anxiety* 1998;7:32-39.

Fergusson DM, Woodward LJ. Mental health, educational, and social role outcomes of adolescents with depression. *Arch Gen Psychiatry* 2002;59:225-231.

Findling RL, Reed MD, Blumer JL. Pharmacological treatment of depression in children and adolescents. *Paediatr Drugs* 1999;1:161-82.

Geller B, Cooper TB, Graham DL, Marsteller FA, Bryant DM. Double-blind placebo-controlled study of nortriptyline in depressed adolescents using a "fixed plasma level" design. *Psychopharmacol Bull* 1990;26:85-90.

Haarasilta L, Marttunen M, Kaprio J, Aro H. The 12-month prevalence and characteristics of major depressive episode in a representative nationwide sample of adolescents and young adults. *Psychol Med* 2001;31:1169-1179.

Hamilton M. A rating scale for depression. *J Neurol Neurosurg Psychiatry* 1960;23:56-62.

Hamilton MA. The assessment of anxiety states by rating. *Br J Med Psychol* 1959;32:50-55.

Harrington R, Whittaker J, Shoebridge P, Campbell F. Systematic review of efficacy of cognitive behaviour therapies in childhood and adolescent depressive disorder. *B M J* 1998;316:1559-1563.

Hazell P, O'Connell D, Heathcote D, et al. Tricyclic drugs for depression in children and adolescents (Review). Cochrane database of systematic reviews 2001;1.

Hazell P, O'Connell D, Heathcote D, Robertson J, Henry D. Efficacy of tricyclic drugs in treating child and adolescent depression: a meta-analysis. *BMJ* 1995;310:897-901.

John K, Gammon GD, Prusoff BA, Warner V. The Social Adjustment Inventory for Children and Adolescents (SAICA): Testing of a new semi-structured interview (SAICA). *J Am Acad Child Adolesc Psychiatry* 1987;26:898-911.

Kaufman J, Martin A, King RA, Charney D. Are child-, adolescent-, and adult-onset depression one and the same disorder? *Biol Psychiatry* 2002;49:980-1001.

Kazdin AE. Developing a research agenda for child and adolescent psychotherapy. *Arch Gen Psychiatry* 2000;57:829-35.

Keller MB, Ryan ND, Strober M, et al. Efficacy of paroxetine in the treatment of adolescent major depression: a randomized, controlled trial. *J Am Acad Child Adolesc Psychiatry* 2001;40:762-72.

Kessler RC, Avenevoli S, Ries Merikangas K. Mood disorders in children and adolescents: an epidemiologic perspective. *Biol Psychiatry* 2001;49:1002-1014.

Klein RG, Manuzza S, Koplewicz HS, Tancer NK, Shah MJ, Liang V, Davies M. Adolescent depression: controlled desipramine treatment and atypical features. *Depr Anx* 1998;7:15-31.

Kovacs M. The Children's Depression Inventory (CDI). *Psychopharmacol Bull,* 1985;21:995-998.

Kramer AD, Feiguine RJ. Clinical effects of amitriptyline in adolescent depression. A pilot study. *J Am Acad Child Psychiatry* 1981;20:636-644.

Kroll L, Harrington, R, Jayson D, Fraser J, Gowers S: Pilot study of continuation cognivie-behavioral therapy for major depression in adolescent psychiatric patients. *J Am Acad Child Adolesc Psychiatry* 1996;35:1156-1161.

Kutcher S, Boulos C, Ward B, Marton P, Simeon J, Ferguson HB, Szalai J, Katic M, Roberts N, Dubois C, Reed K. Response to desipramine treament in adolescent depression: a fixed- dose, placebo-controlled trial. *J Am Acad Child Adolesc Psychiatry* 1994;33:686-694.

Kutcher S. Practitioner review: the pharmacotherapy of adolescent depression. *J Child Psychol Psychiatry* 1997;38:755-767.

Kye CH, Ryan ND. Pharmacologic treatment of child and adolescent depression. *Child Adolesc Clin North Am* 1995;4:261-281.

Kye CH, Waterman GS, Ryan ND, Birmaher B, Williamson DE, Iyengar S, Dachille S. A randomized, controlled trial of amitriptyline in the acute treament of adolescent major depression. *J Am Acad Child Adolesc Psychiatry* 1996;35:1139-1144.

Lewinsohn PM, Clarke GN, Hops H, et al. Cognitive-behavioral treatment for depressed adolescents. *Behav Ther* 1990;21:385-401

Lewinsohn PM, Clarke GN, Seeley JR, Rohde P. Major depression in community adolescents: age at onset, episode duration, and time to recurrence. *J Am Acad Child Adolesc Psychiatry* 1994;33:809-818.

Lewinsohn PM, Rohde P, Klein DN, Deeley JR. Natural course of adolescent major depressive disorder: I. Continuity into young adulthood. *J Am Acad Child Adolesc Psychiatry* 1999;38:56-63.

Mandoki MW, Tapia MR, Tapia MA, et al. Venlafaxine in the treatment of children and adolescents with major depression. *Psychopharmacol Bull* 1997;33:149-54.

Maneeton N, Srisurapanont M. Tricyclic antidepressants for depressive disorders in children and adolescents: a meta-anlysis of randomized-controlled trials. *J Med Assoc Thai* 2000;83:1367-1374.

Marks P, Seeman W, Haller D. *Actual use of the MMPI with adolescents and adults.* Baltimore, Md: Oxford University Press, 1974.

Martin A, Kaufman J, Charney D. Pharmacotherapy of early-onset depression. *Child Adolesc Psychiatr Clin North Am* 2000;9:135-157.

Marttunen M, Aro H, Henriksson M, Lönnqvist J. Mental disorders in adolescent suicide. DSM-III-R axes I and II in suicides among 13 to 19 year olds in Finland. *Arch Gen Psychiatry* 1991;48:834-839.

Marttunen M, Pelkonen M. Phenomenology of adolescent depression. *Psychiatr Fenn* 1998;29:29-39.

Michael KD, Crowley SL. How effective are treatments for child and adolescent depression? A meta-analytic review. *Clin Psychol Rev* 2002;22:247-269.

Milin R, Simeon J, Spenst W. Double-blind study of paroxetine in adolescents with unipolar major depression. *Poster presented at the annual meeting of American Academy of Child and Adolescent Psychiatry.* Los Angeles, CA, October 1999; NR-67.

Montgomery SA, Asberg M. A new depression scale designed to be sensitive to change. Br J Psychiatry 1979;134;382-389.

Mufson L, Weissman MM, Moreau D, et al. Efficacy of interpersonal psychotherapy for depressed adolescents. *Arch Gen Psychiatry* 1999;56:573-579.

National Institute of Mental Health, Special Feature. Rating scales and assessment instruments for use in pediatric psychopharmacology research. *Psychopharmacol Bull* 1985;21:839-844.

Overall JE, Pfefferbaum B. The Brief Psychiatry Rating Scale for Children. *Psychopharmacol Bull* 1982;18:10-16.

Pelkonen M, Marttunen M, Pulkkinen E, ym. Psychosocial functioning in adolescent psychiatric patients: A prospective study on the change of psychosocial functioning among severely and moderately impaired adolescent psychiatric outpatients. *Acta Psychiatr Scand* 1997;96:217-224.

Pelkonen M, Marttunen M. Child and adolescent suicide: epidemiology, risk factors, and approaches to prevention. *Paediatric Drugs* 2003;5:243-265.

Poznanski EO, Cook SC, Carrol BJ. A depression rating scale for children. *Pediatrics* 1979;64:442-450.

Reed MK. Social skill s training to reduce depression in adolescents. *Adolescence* 1994;29:293-302.

Rossello´ J, Bernal G. The efficacy of cognitive-behavioral and interpersonal treatments for depression in Puerto Rican adolescent. *J Cons Clin Psychol* 1999;67:734-45

Sallee FR, Vridavanam NS, Deas-Nesmith D, Carson SW, Sethuraman G. Pulse intravenous clomipramine for depressed adolescents: double-blind, controlled trial. *Am J Psychiatry* 1997;154:668-673.

Shaffer D, Gould M, Brasic J et al., A children´s global assessment scale (CGAS). *Arch Gen Psychiatry* 1983;40:1228-1231.

Shaffer D, Gould MS, Fisher P, et al. Psychiatric diagnosis in child and adolescent suicide. *Arch Gen Psychiatry* 1996;53:339-48.

Simeon J, Dinicola VF, Ferguson HB, Copping W. Adolescent depression: a placebo-controlled fluoxetine treatment study and follow-up. *Prog Neuropsychopharmacol Biol Psychiatry* 1990;14:791-795.

Spitzer RL, Endicott J, Robins E. *Research Diagnostic Criteria (RDC) for a selected group of functional disorders, 3. painos*. New York: Biometrics Research 1977.

Spitzer RL, Williams JBW, Gibbon M, First MB. *Structured clinical interview for DSM-III-R - patient version 1.0 (SCID-P)*. Washington DC, American Psychiatric Press, 1990.

Strober M, DeAntonio M, Schmidt-Lackner S, et al. The pharmacotherapy of depressive illness in adolescents: an open-label comparison of fluoxetine with imipramine- treated historical controls. *J Clin Psychiatry* 1999;60:164-169.

Target M, Fonagy P. Efficacy of psychoanalysis for children with emotional disorders. *J Am Acad Child Adolesc Psychiatry* 1994;33:361-71.

The Treatment for Adolescents With Depression Study Team. Treatment for adolescents with depression study (TADS): rationale, design, and methods. *J Am Acad Child Adolesc Psychiatry* 2003;42:531-542.

Thurber S, Ensign J, Punnett AF, Welter K. A meta-analysis of antidepressant outcome studies that involved children and adolescents. *J Clin Psychol* 1995;51:340-345.

Waechter F. Paroxetine must not be given to patients under 18. (News.) BMJ 2003;326:1282.

Wagner KD, Ambrosini PJ, Donnelly CL et al. Sertraline treatment of major depression in children and adolescents. Presented at: Annual meeting of the American Psychiatric Association; May 18-23, 2002; Philadelphia, Pa.

Wagner KD, Robb AS, Findling R, Tiseo PJ. Citalopram treatment of pediatric depression: results of a placebo-controlled trial. Poster presented at the annual meeting of The American College of Neuropsychopharmacology. Waikoloa Village, Hawaii, December 9-13, 2001.

Welner Z, Reich W, Herjanic B, ym. Reliability, validity, and parent-child agreement studies of the diagnostic interview for children and adolescents. *J Am Acad Child Adolesc Psychiatry* 1987;26:649-653.

Wittchen H-U, Nelson CB, Lachner G. Prevalence of mental disorders and psychosocial impairments in adolescents and young adults. *Psychol Med* 1998;28:109-126.

Wood A, Harrington R, Moore A. Controlled trial of a brief cognitive-behavioural intervention in adolescent patients with depressive disorders. *J Child Psychol Psychiatry* 1996;37:737-46.

Vostanis P, Feehan C, Grattan E, Bickerton W-L. Treatment for children and adolescents with depression: lessons from a controlled trial. *Clin Child Psychol Psychiatry* 1996;1:199-212.

Zito JM, Safer DJ. Services and prevention: pharmacoepidemiology of antidepressant use. *Biol Psychiatry*. 2001 Jun 15;49:1121-1127.

In: Trends in Depression Research
Editor: Maurice J. Henri, pp. 87-112

ISBN 1-60021-394-4

Chapter 5

MANAGING TREATMENT-RESISTANT DEPRESSION: FOCUSING ON INCREASING SEROTONERGIC TRANSMISSION

Ali Saffet Gonul[1,*]***, Kerem Doksat***[2]***,***
Çagdas Eker[1] ***and Ozlem Donat Eker***[1]
[1]Ege University School of Medicine, Department of Psychiatry, Affective Disorders Unit and Ege University Center for Brain Research, Izmir, Turkey
[2]Istanbul University Cerrahpasa School of Medicine Department of Psychiatry, Director of Affective Disorders Unit Istanbul, Turkey

ABSTRACT

Among the more challenging problems in the treatment of major depressive disorder is the lack of adequate response to adequate monotherapy. Only partial or no response to antidepressant treatment is observed in as many as 29% to 46% of depressed patients. For those patients, three treatment strategies are the main options for the clinicians; switching to another antidepressant, augmenting with other psychotropic agents, or combining antidepressants. In many of these strategies, the aim is to increase serotonergic transmission without increasing side effects. Augmentation and combination strategies may produce a more rapid response than switching, not only because of neuropharmacological potentiation, but also because the time lost discontinuing one drug and starting another is avoiding.

Recent studies showed that venlafaxine, which has a dual-inhibition effect on serotonin and noradrenalin reuptake might be a good alternative for depressed patients who did not show any improvement with other antidepressants, especially serotonin reuptake inhibitors (SSRIs). However, there are limited data about the augmentation or combination strategies for treatment resistant patients who showed partial or no response to venlafaxine. Our previous experiences give us an idea that adding an SSRI to venlafaxine might help patients who did not respond to previous venlafaxine treatment. In this study, 38 patients who were on 225 mg/day venlafaxine for 8 weeks and still not responding to venlafaxine were ordinarily assigned to into two groups, venlafaxine up to 375 mgday or 50-100 mg/day sertraline add on venlafaxine 225 mg/day. At the second week, a significant difference on HAM-D scores was emerged between the groups. However, at the end of the study (eight week) there was no significant difference between the groups. Eight (42.1 %) of 19 patients taking high-dose venlafaxine and ten (52.6 %) of patients taking sertraline-venlafaxine combination had responded to treatments. However, the difference was not significant. Remission was observed in 4 patients (21.1 %) in high-dose venlafaxine group and 7 patients (36.8 %) in sertraline add-on venlafaxine group. The difference between the groups was significant (p=0.02, Fisher's exact test). Drop-out rates were similar but one patient from the combination group showed mild symptoms of serotonergic syndrome which were ceased with the termination of treatment.

Adding a SSRI to an ongoing venlafaxine treatment of treatment resistant unipolar patients might have benefits in faster onset of action and higher rates of remission rates compared to high-dose venlafaxine. On the other hand, the cost-benefit ratio of this combination should be kept in mind as there was no clear superiority of combination treatment observed at the end of eight week.

Keywords: Antidepressants, Major Depressive Disorder, Serotonin Reuptake Inhibitors, Serotonin, Treatment Resistant Depression

1. INTRODUCTION

Major depressive disorder (MDD) is one of the most prevalent and disabling psychiatric disease. The prevalence rates are approximately 2%-3% in men and 5%-9% in women, with a lifetime risk for developing an episode 5%-12% and 10%-25%, respectively (American Psychiatric Association 2000). "The Global Burden of Diseases Study" of World Health Organization predicts that it would be the second most disability causing disease in 2020 (Greden 2001) and the age of first depressive episode is steadily decreasing by time (Klerman and Weissman 1989). Thus, the diagnosis, treatment and following-up the patients are the crucial issues for psychiatrist and primary care doctors but understanding its pathophysiology and finding better and effective treatments is also another fundamental matter for researchers.

Generally, depression is thought to have a positive outcome. One of the main reasons of this thought is antidepressant clinical trials' results are showing optimistic response rates from 60% - 80%. However, these favorable statistics have some discouraging elements. For example, most pharmaceutical trials define response as a 50% or a greater improvement in depression ratings (Prien et al 1991), usually Hamilton Depression Rating Scale for Depression (HAM-D) scores (Hamilton 1960). Although scores on such measurement clearly indicate an improvement, they do not necessarily define a

* Correspondence concerning this article should be addressed to Dr. Ali Saffet Gonul Ege University School of Medicine Psychiatry Department Affective Disorder Unit 35100 Bornova Izmir, Turkey. Tel & Fax: +90 232 336 8804; e-mail: saffet@med.ege.edu.tr.

remission. Rigorously defined remission (a reduction of symptom scores and improvement of global functioning to levels that are virtually indistinguishable from those of people who are not depressed; lower than 8 for HAM-D or lower than 10 for Montgomery-Asberg Depression Rating Scale (MADRS)) appears to occur in a substantially smaller percentage of patients (Frank et al 1991). Even in studies which have the antidepressant response as a major outcome, 29% to 46% of depressed patients show only partial and no response to antidepressants (Fava and Davidson 1996), and even among responders to antidepressant treatment, residual symptoms are common and have been shown to be associated with greater likelihood of relapsing and perhaps having a poorer prognosis (Fava et al 1994, Rush and Trivedi 1995, Nierenberg et al 1999). Unfortunately, comparing to many good studies showing efficacy of antidepressants in placebo-controlled trails of outpatients or inpatients with major depressive disorder, there are only a few controlled clinical trials among patients with treatment resistant depression or among patients who have partially benefited from antidepressant treatment. Most of the time, clinicians' decisions are guided by anecdotal reports, case serious and relatively small uncontrolled clinical trials.

2. Defining Treatment-Resistant Depression (TRD)

Both the terms treatment-resistant depression (TRD) and treatment-refractory depression are frequently used interchangeably to identify the patients with depression that does not respond to initial antidepressant treatment although they have been defined in different ways and there is no clear consensus among researchers. In the literature, the patient population described as TRD varies from study to study. At times, the term refers to patients who failed achieve to remission in a single short trial of medication, whereas other studies define treatment-resistant patients as those who have failed to respond to multiple lengthy trails of different classes of antidepressants. In general, patients with TRD are viewed as those who have failed to respond to adequate trails of two antidepressants of different classes (Thase and Rush 1995, Ananth et al 1998, Nelson et al 1997). Thase and Rush (1997) have proposed a descriptive classification that borrows heavily from the method used by oncologists to stage the clinical progression of malignancies. As summarized in table 1, this approach stages the patients' degree of resistance on the basis of the number and type of prior adequate treatment trials. Selection of alternate treatment strategies may then fallow logically from this hierarchical classification by moving from simpler to progressively more complex strategies. However, no evidence based data from controlled trails and the decrement in prescribing of tricyclic antidepressants (TCAs) and monoamine oxidase inhibitors (MAOIs) makes the classification less useful for everyday clinical practice.

In clinical practice, patients were considered treatment-resistant if multiple treatments have failed. During an initial assessment, it is difficult to determine treatment status without though medication history that includes information on tolerability (approximately 10-20% of patients can not tolerate the side effects of antidepressant treatment) or whether previous clinicians maximized medication doses. However, it is inappropriate to ascribe treatment resistance until multiple treatment options have been pursued. Often patients are not totally resistant to treatment, but require a more complicated course of treatment with a longer duration. It is therefore important to apply an adequate sequence of treatment trails prior to diagnosing a patient as having TRD. Additionally, these patients often have inadequate follow-up (Ford 2000), particularly during the initial stages of treatment (Lin et al 1995). The result is the desired outcome (full symptomatic remission and return to premorbid levels of functioning) are often not achieved.

Table 1. Staging Criteria for Treatment-Resistant Depression

Stage I:	Failure of at least one adequate trial of one major class of antidepressants
Stage II:	Failure of at least two adequate trials of at least two distinctly different class of antidepressants
Stage III:	Stage II resistance plus failure of an adequate trail of a TCA
Stage IV:	Stage III resistance plus failure of an adequate trail of a MAOI
Stage V:	Stage IV resistance plus failure of a course of bilateral ECT

TCA: Tricyclic antidepressant; MAOI: Monoamino oxidase inhibitor; ECT: Electroconvulsive therapy.

It is estimated that fewer than 50% of patients in treatment receive at least moderate dose of medication (Keller et al 1986). Patients either may be left at lower dose due to intolerance of higher doses and/or in an effort to minimize the side effects, or inadequately evaluated to optimize treatment outcomes. Since the prevalent use of new antidepressants like serotonin reuptake inhibitors (SSRIs) and serotonin-noradrenalin reuptake inhibitors (SNRIs), fewer patients leave their drug due to intolerance or adverse effects (Steffens et al 1997). One other advantage of SSRIs is their flat dose-response curve. The initial dose of SSRIs is generally enough for many patients for both acute and maintenance antidepressant activity (Preskorn et al 2004). Thus dosage titration is less needed. However, not all patients respond similarly to a medication at a given dose and some patients may benefit from higher doses, and some of the nonresponders to antidepressant treatment may also improve with an extension of the treatment trial. The initial symptomatic response of depressed patient to medication may be detected as early as the first week, but is often delayed by several weeks. An adequate trial of an antidepressant medication has been traditionally defined as treatments with therapeutic dosages of a drug for a total of 6 to 8 weeks (American Psychiatric Association 2000). However, full response and functional restoration often take longer. It is not unusual for full benefit to be delayed until 12 weeks of treatment, especially patients with chronic depression (Quitkin et al 1996). In a double blind randomized trial comparing sertraline with imipramine in 635 chronically depressed outpatients, 21% of patients who achieved a therapeutic response at week 12 had not done so at week 8. Like patients with chronic depression (Koran et al. 2001, Trivedi and Kleiber 2001), patients classified, as treatment refractory may need a medication trial of 12-16 weeks to achieve a full response. This idea is supported by a study conducted by Licht and Qvitzau (2002) in which, 295 patients were identified as nonresponders from a group 1629 patients with major depression who had received 6 weeks of treatment with 100 mg/day sertraline. These 295 nonresponder patients were randomly assigned to double-blind treatment for another 5 weeks with 100 mg/day sertraline and placebo, 200 mg/day sertraline and placebo or 100 mg/day sertraline and 30 mg/day mianserin. The patients who stayed on 100 mg/day of sertraline and placebo had a similar response rate (70%) to patients who received combination of sertraline and mianserin and had a better rate of response than who received 200 mg/day sertraline and placebo. This study illustrated that longer duration of treatment on the initial dose was just effective as an augmentation strategy, and, in fact the effectiveness of the augmentation could be explained by the longer duration, rather than addition of mianserin.

One factor which keeps the patients in depression is patients' non-adherence to pharmacotherapy. Drug trials for the treatment of depression report a 10%-30% rate of nonadherence, and it is thought that nonadherence is much grater in everyday clinical practice (Depression Guideline Panel 1993). It was showed that 28% of patients discontinued taking antidepressants in the first month of therapy and that 44% discontinued their antidepressants by the third month (Lin et al 1995). It is also reported that up to 60% of patients in primary care had discontinued their antidepressant medications prior to completion of 6 months recommended pharmacotherapy (Katon et al 1992). These studies clearly emphases the importance of assessing the treatment adherence before reaching the diagnosis of TRD.

The other significant contributing factor is comorbitidy. Comorbid psychiatric disorders are common in patients with depressive symptoms and may increase the likehood of treatment resistance (Kornstein and Schneider 2001). If these disorders are missed or inadequately treated, patients can easily be diagnosed as TRD. For example up to 40% of patients diagnosed as panic disorder have also a diagnosis of major depression. These patients tend to be more severely depressed and slower to respond to treatment. They are more likely to have residual symptoms and have increased rates of relapse and response (Fawcett 1997, Kornstein and Schneider 2001). Up to 40% of patients with bipolar disorder are initially diagnosed as major depressive disorder (Ghaemi et al 1999) and it is well known that bipolar depression is more resistant to antidepressant treatment compared to recurrent major depression. General medical conditions (like Cushing or Addison disease, diabetes, hypothyroidism etc) or their treatment may also cause or worsen the symptoms of depression and may contribute to TRD. The acute and chronic effects of substance abuse or withdrawal may cause or worsen the depression and increase the likehood of noncompliance (Thase and Rush 1997).

As a conclution, we suggest that depression not responding antidepressants from 2 different classes for at least 8 weeks should be defined as TRD. However, the issues of adherence of treatment, doses of antidepressants, co-morbity of both mental and general medical situations should be clarified before reaching this definition.

3. Treating Treatment-Resistant Depressed Patients

Depressed patients who do not respond adequately to an optimal trial of antidepressant may be treated in a number of different ways. They may be 1) switched to another antidepressant from the same class or from another class, 2) treated with electroconvulsive therapy (ECT), or 3) kept the initial ineffective/partially effective antidepressant and increase it's effectiveness by the addition of various psychoactive compounds. Once, the practice of using multiple medications for treatment of a single psychiatric disorder was anathema. However, evidences from studies adding lithium or thyroid hormone on antidepressants let this idea changed. Today, a number of new alternatives have been looked for to augment the effect of initial antidepressants. Basically, *augmentation* can be described as strategies involve adding a second pharmacologic agent that is not generally used as an antidepressant but may enhance the effect of antidepressants. On the other hand, *combination therapy* is adding another antidepressant, typically from a different class, to enhance the effects. They may have an advantage over switching on achieving a more rapid response not only because of neuropharmacological potentiation, but also because the time lost discontinuing one drug and starting another is avoided. The addition of a second agent also helps maintain any improvement that occurred with the first drug. Continuing the first medication means the patient avoids possible discontinuation symptoms and demoralizing aspects of the "giving up" on the first medication. This appears to explain why augmentation and combination strategies are especially popular in partial responders.

Interventions intended to provide complimentary clinical effects, such as the addition of a benzodiazepine to help control anxiety or insomnia, do not really augment the mechanism of action of the primary antidepressant treatment. Therefore, it is suggested that these kinds of strategies should be referred as *adjuvant therapy*. The use of a second psychotropic medication to reverse treatment-emergent side effects like sexual side effects could be viewed as yet another type of adjunctive therapy.

3.1. Augmentation Strategies

A wide range of medication has been suggested as effective augmentation agents. Many of these agents have not been studies in controlled trials. Few but well controlled studies showed that lithium augmentation has positive effects in acute and long term treatment of resistant patients, especially those on tricyclic antidepressants (TCAs) (Bauer et al 2003). It is proposed that lithium's ability to increase presynaptic transmission of serotonin would potentiate TCA-induced post-synaptic serotonin supersensitivity, which would result in enhanced serotonin transmission (de Montingy et al 1983). Indeed, there is consistent evidence from animal studies that lithium enhances serotonergic responsiveness by actions on both turnover and release (Müller-Oerlinghausen 1985, Price et al, 1990, de Montingy 1994). It is clearly showed that lithium administration augments serotonin release in the rats' dorsal hippocampus and enhance serotonin synthesis (Broderick et al 1982). Further, short-term administration of lithium also augmented the efficacy of electrically stimulating ascending serotonin pathway that suppresses firing of postsynaptic neurons in rats' dorsal hippocampus (Blier and de Montingny 1985). It was demonstrated that long-term TCA treatment induced a selective increase in the responsiveness to serotonin in rats' dorsal hippocampus (de Montingny and Aghajanian 1978), and this was later shown to be mediated by postsynaptic 5-HT1A receptors (Chaput et al 1991).

Additional evidence for a true augmentation effect derived from animal studies showed that, in contrast to lithium alone, lithium added to antidepressant treatment with an SSRI (citalopram) potentiated presynaptic serotonergic functions in rats (Okamoto et al 1996). Subchronic lithium added to chronic citolopram therapy, using microdialysis techniques, further elevated basal levels of serotonin in ventral hippocampus (Wegener et al 2003).

Human neuroendocrine challenge tests have been studied repeatedly in depressed patients during lithium augmentation therapy. The pharmacological challenge test used most frequently to asses central serotonin function is the prolactin response to intravenous L-tryptophan (Price et al 1990). Cowen and his associates (1991) found that administering lithium increased the prolactin response to L-tryptophan after both 4 days and 4 weeks of treatment in patients receiving TCAs. These results provide evidence that lithium may facilitate serotonin neurotransmission. However, the magnitude of prolactin increase did not correlate with the clinical outcome. In another study (McCance-Katz et al 1992), it was showed that primary antidepressant medication did not increase prolactin response but that lithium augmentation significantly increased prolactin response, compared to placebo pretreatment and antidepressant treatment alone.

Although initial reports favored lithium effect in a very short time, others have showed that 4-6 weeks of time period might be necessary for the positive effects of lithium. It is highly probable that lithium have some other effects on neurons rather than just increasing serotonin transmission. Recent reports showed that lithium have a neuroprotective effects on neurons. Current evidences illustrate that neuroprotective effects of lithium might be independent from its serotonin releasing effect and is due to its inhibition of glycogen synthase kinase 3 (GS3K) and markedly increase the levels of neuroprotective proteins called bcl-2 and brain-derived neurotrophic factor (BDNF) (Manji et al 2001, Bhat el al 2004, Williams et al 2004). The inhibition of GS3K starts a cascade preventing destruction of tubules, which is thought to be a cause of neuronal degeneration and atrophy of grey-matter in mood disorders. Beyond these neuroprotective effects, it has been recently showed that lithium also exerts regenerative effects on axons of retinal ganglion cells, enhances hippocampal neurogenesis, and protects neurons proapopitotic stimuli (Chen et al 2000, Phiel et al 2003). Thus, lithium is a good example for a drug, which has different effects on neuron via different mechanisms.

The usefulness of thyroid augmentation for the treatment of a partial responder or no response to antidepressants has been assessed repeatedly over past two decades in controlled trials, culminating in the positive meta-analysis by Altshuler et al (2001). The effects of thyroid hormone application to experimentally induced hypothyroidism and euthyroid animals include an increase in cortical serotonin concentration and a desensitization of autoinhibitory 5-HT1A receptors in the raphe area, resulting in disinhibition of cortical and hippocampal serotonin release (Heal et al 1988, Sandrini et al 1996). Further evidence for an interaction between thyroid status and the serotonin system derives from studies that have demonstrated a significant blunted cortisol and prolactin response to the serotonin agonist d-fenfluramine in hypothyroid patients (Cleare et al 1995, Gur et al 1999). This blunted response to d-fenfluramine stimulation normalized after the thyroid hormone replacement therapy suggesting reduced central serotonin functioning in hypothyroidism. Thyroid hormone also appears to play an important role in regulating central noradrenergic function. It was also found that T3 may function as a cotransmitter with norepinephrine in the adrenergic nervous system (Gordon et al 1999). Few pre-clinical studies addressed the issue of neuroprotective effects of thyroid hormone on neurons (Koibuchi et al 1999, Vaidya et al 2001).

Atypical antipsychotics have been studied primarily for use in psychotic depression, schizoaffective disorder, and depressive symptoms in patients with schizophrenia (Rothchild 1996). Affective symptom improvement in these disorders has prompted some investigators to look at atypical antipsychotics as adjunctive agents in treatment resistant major depression. In a double-blind, placebo controlled trial (Shelton et al 2001) it was showed that olanzapine plus fluoxetine was a superior combination to either agent alone. However, it should be noted that while there were significant differences between combination treatment and fluoxetine monotherapy in patient scores on the MADRS scale, no differences were found in the HAM-

D scores between the groups. The Augmentation with RISperidone in Resistant Depression (ARISe-RD) study is a placebo-controlled relapse prevention study currently underway in patients who had achieved remission with citolopram and adjunctive risperidone after a non-response to the SSRI alone (Rapaport et al 2003). Adjunctive risperidone was associated with significant improvements as early as day 4, and remission was achieved by 52% of patients at endpoint. Although there are no controlled study done with other atypical antipsychotics, results from open-labeled and case series promotes that they will be an alternative as an augmentation strategy in treatment resistant depression (Barbee et al 2004, Papakostas et al 2004). It is interesting that in pre-clinical studies, it was demonstrated that risperidone and olanzapine have 5-HT2A antagonist effect, which may enhance the action of serotonin, and thus may augment the therapeutic effects of an SSRI. In rats, atypical antipsychotics and SSRIs were found to have synergistic effects on the release of norepinephrine and dopamine (Zhang et al 2000). Recent studies showed that atypical antipsychotics may also have neuroprotective effects on neuron and may increase neurogenesis in hippocampus (Kodama et al 2004). In a study done by Donat-Eker et al (2004) showed that olanzapine-fluoxetine combination may have more neuroprotective effect in amygdale in stressed rats compared to either treatment alone.

There are other augmenting strategies like addition of pindolol, buspirone or tryptophan to current antidepressants. It is thought that increasing monoaminergic transmission (mainly serotonin) is the main hallway to treat depression in those strategies. By blocking somatodendritic 5-HT1A receptors, pindolol enhances the presynaptic release of serotonin (Hoffman and Lefkowitz 1990). This property was for the foundation for the number of augmentation trials of pindolol to either enhance or speed the response to SSRIs. Although the results of open-label studies (Blier and Bergeron 1995, Maes et al 1996) support the effectiveness of pindolol as an augmentation agent, double-blind, placebo-controlled studies have produced mixed results (Berman et al 1997, 1999, Moreno et al 1997, Perez et al 1999, Perry et al 2004). Buspirone, another agent for augmentation acts as a partial 5-HT1A receptor agonist both auto receptors and postsynaptic receptors. It is thought that buspirone activity on postsynaptic receptors mimics serotonin (Susman 1995). There is also evidence that buspirone may potentiate the clinical effects of SSRIs by markedly facilitating elevation of both dopamine and noradrenalin in the frontal cortex (Taylor et al 1985). Four open-label studies of buspirone augmentation have reported positive results (Bakish 1991, Jacobsen 1991, Joffe and Schuler 1993, Dimitriou and Dimitriou 1998). All four studies involved the addition of buspirone to current SSRI therapy and rates of response were usually greater than 50% by week 3, with most patients sustaining the response after 3 months. However, two randomized placebo-controlled studies (Landen et al 1998, Appelberg et al 2001) were not able detect a difference between the buspirone plus SSRI group and the placebo plus SSRI group in patients with TRD. In one of the study (Appelberg et al 2001), those patients who had a initial MADRS scores more than 30 showed a significant reduction in symptoms of their depression compared to those of placebo group. The question of "might buspirone be more effective in heavily depressed patients as an augmentation agent" should be clarified with further studies.

It would not be wrong to reach a conclusion that, all the augmentation agents mentioned above, in way or another have a capability of increasing serotonergic transmission in TRD patients. Some of them like lithium, atypical antipsychotics also act as a neuroprotective agent and increase neurogenesis. It also should be kept in mind that serotonin activates the cascade systems that synthesizing the neurotrophic factors, thus playing an important factor for both neuronal plasticity and neurogenesis (Sodhi and Sanders-Bush 2004).

3.2. Combining Antidepressants

Combining antidepressants for patients with TRD was first described in the early 1960s with monoamine oxidase inhibitors and tricyclic antidepressants. However, clinicians were often reluctant to combine antidepressants because it is thought that these antidepressants had a similar action (e.g. combining two tricyclic or two SSRIs) or potential hazardous interaction (e.g. tricyclic and monoamine oxidase inhibitors). Other possible disadvantages of the combination of antidepressants are nonadherence of such a complex regimen and increased cost of treatment. In spite of their unpopularity especially in the last decade, some but mostly uncontrolled trials have positive results.

Bupropion (sustained-release formulation, 100-150 mg once or twice a day) combined with SSRIs is one of the most practical augmentation strategy chosen by psychiatrist (Fredman et al 2000). However, only a few open label trials examining the combination (Bodkin et al 1997; Kennedy 2002). Clinical lore suggests that bupropion may be helpful as add-on in patients whose anergic symptoms do not respond adequately to treatment with SSRIs, via increasing dopamine and noradrenaline in the synaptic cleft. Another popular combination strategy is combining mirtazapine, a dual-action antidepressant that increase both serotonergic and noradrenergic activity by blocking the α2-adrenergic autoreceptors and heteroreceptors and the serotonergic 5-HT2 and 5-HT3 receptors, with SSRIs. A recent study by Debonnel et al. (2000) showed significantly a higher response rate to the combination of paroxetine and mirtazapine than monotherapy with either drug and a 64% response rate after switching to combination therapy for patients not responding to monotherapy. One of the main reason makes the mirtazapine plus SSRI combination popular is the mirtazpine's positive effects on SSRIs' side effects like sexual dysfunction or nausea. The main disadvantages of this strategy are the weight gain and sedation that have been reported with its use (Carperter et al 1999).

Combinations of SSRIs with TCAs were one the best studied strategy in the area of TRD. However, TCA levels build up as the action of the SSRI interferes with its clearance, and there is risk for cardiac toxicity. The biggest concern for a pharmacokinetic interaction between TCAs and SSRIs is with hepatic cytochrome enzyme system CYP 1A2 (fluvoxamine) and CYP 2D6 (paroxetine and fluoxetine) inhibitors and the TCAs that are metabolized by those enzyme systems (imipramine, clomipramine, and amitriptyline). Even though these disadvantages, several open studies support the effectiveness of combination of SSRIs and TCAs (Nelson et al 1991, Seth et al 1992). One controlled study (Nelson et al 2004) found the combination therapy (desipramine plus fluoxetine) was more effective than each treatment alone especially when the remission was taken as a primary outcome. In another controlled study Fava et al (1994, 2002), failed to find advantage for the combination of desipramine and fluoxetine combination. The dose of desipramine (varied from 25-50 mg/day) used in last studies might have been too low compared to previous study (mean 98 mg/day). Thus, one might conclude from these studies that during combined treatment with SSRI and desipramine, a therapeutic dose and plasma levels are required. There have also been anecdotal reports and open trials suggesting efficacy of combining SSRIs with reboxetine (Rubio et al 2003).

The main idea behind the combination treatments is to increase both serotonergic and noradrenergic (possible dopaminergic) transmission which might be necessary in treating depression especially TRD patients. It is thought that this can be achieved with antidepressants which have different mechanism of action. To our knowledge, there is no study focusing on the neurotrophic effects of antidepressant combinations on neurons and glial cells.

Antidepressants like venlafaxine (VLF) and duloxetine have a capability of inhibiting both serotonin and noradrenalin reuptake pump like clomipramine and other TCAs like amitriptilline and imipramine (Bymaster et al 2001). Unlike tertiary amine TCAs, they have low affinity for most other neural receptors and do not inhibit sodium fast channels, making them relatively safe in overdose. A review by Thase et al (2001) confirmed that, at doses of 150 mg/day or higher, VLF therapy was associated with a 10% advantage in remission rates when compared with SSRIs. This finding is parallel to the result of an earlier meta-analysis comparing TCAs and SSRIs (Anderson 1998). Thus, VLF has received a considerable attention for those patients who had been on different antidepressant treatment but did not respond to it. Indeed, the results of different studies indicate that 40-55% of patients with treatment-resistant depression stages I to IV would respond to 8 weeks or more of treatment with VLF in doses of 150 to 375 mg/day (Nierenberg et al 1994, de Montingny et al 1999, Mitchell et al 2000, Poierer and Boyer 1999). On the hand, 45-60% of patients did not respond to VLF treatment, and when those patients who had responded but not remitted were included, this number is increased up to 70%. Only a few researchers specifically address the issue of the next step in the VLF treatment in resistant patients. Initial reports showed that lithium augmentation to VLF or VLF combination with tricyclic antidepressant or bupropion might be effective in treatment-resistant patients (Gomez and Perramon 2000, Hoencamp et al 2000, Kennedy et al 2000).

4. A Novel Combination VLF Plus SSRI

Our group reported 4 cases of treatment-resistant depressed patients who had remission with VLF-SSRI combination (Gonul et al 2003). Each of the patients had a partial response to VLF treatment and did not improve with further dosage increment of VLF. However, addition of SSRI improved their depression. We speculated that adding SSRI to VLF might increase the serotonin reuptake inhibition that might further improvement in symptoms by increasing serotonergic transmission. This speculation based on two evidences; first VLF has a lower serotonin reuptake inhibition potential compared to SSRIs (Sanchez and Hyttel 1999) and second, a study showed that lithium augmentation which is known to increase serotonergic transmission led to a further decrease in depressive symptoms in patients treated with VLF (Hoencamp et al 2000).

We designed another study for further testing the effectiveness of VLF-SSRI combination in TRD patients. In this study we added sertraline to the treatment protocol of patients who had VLF 225 mg/day for 8 weeks and had not responded to previous antidepressant treatment including recent VLF treatment. The control group was kept on VLF monothreaphy and based on clinician decision patients had VLF up to 375 mg/day. For keeping the pharmacokinetic interaction minimum, sertraline which has minor effect of CYP 2D6 and no effect on CYP 1A2, was chosen for the combination.

4.1. Subjects

Patients involved in this study were recruited from Ege University School of Medicine Department of Psychiatry Outpatient Clinic. Patients who were diagnosed as major depressive disorder defined as DSM-IV by a psychiatrist and not responding to initial SSRI treatment for 8 weeks of were switched to VLF XR. The minimum therapeutic doses for SSRIs were defined as 20 mg/day for fluoxetine (mean: 28 ± 13 mg/day), 100 mg/day for sertraline (mean: 115 ± 55 mg/day), 20 mg/day for paroxetine (mean: 26 ± 18 mg/day), and 20 mg/day for citalopram (mean: 30 ± 10 mg/day). VLF XR 75 mg/day was started and the dose was increase according to clinical response up to 225 mg/day. Patients who were on 225 mg/day VLF XR for 8 weeks (not more than 10 weeks) and not responding (decrement of Hamilton Depression Scale more than 50% prior to treatment) to VLF XR were invited to the study. We made research diagnosis of major depressive disorder by The Mini-International Neuropsychiatric Interview (M.I.N.I.) and depressive symptoms were rated using 17-item Hamilton Depression Scale (HAM-D). Clinical status was secondarily assessed by using the Clinical Global Impression (CGI) severity scale.

The following patients groups were excluded: pregnant women or women of child bearing potential who were not using medically accepted contraception; patients with serous or unstable medical illness, patients with a history of seizure disorder or any other organic mental disorder; patients with a history of substance use disorder, delusional disorder, bipolar disorder, schizophrenia, antisocial personality disorder, mood congruent or incongruent psychotic features, clinical and laboratory evidence of hypothyroidism. We also exclude the patients with a history of multiple adverse drug reaction or allergy and patients who had VLF XR more than 225 mg/day and not responded to the treatment.

4.2. Study Drugs

During recruitment, all patients had HAM-D scores greater than 18 and had been on 225 mg/day VLF XR for at least 8 weeks (mean duration: 62 days, range: 57-67 days). Patients were ordinarily assigned to into two groups; in the first group, VLF XR was increased up to 375 mg/day depending on tolerability and side effects of the VLF XR and in the second group, 50-100 mg/day sertraline were added on VLF XR 225 mg/day. The patients were seen by the investigators every week during the 8 weeks of the study period.

4.3. Data Analyses

Efficacy and safety analyses were conducted on all patients who completed at least 1 week of treatment. Analyses were based on last observation carried forward. Proportions of responders and nonresponders in each group were compared by chi-square or Fischer exact tests. HAM-D scores, which are in means and standard deviations, were analyzed with Mann-Whitney U test (between the groups) and Wilcoxon signed ranks test) (within the group). All statistical teats were two tailed with an alpha level of 0.05.

5. RESULTS

Characteristics of patients taking high dose VLF or sertraline add-on VLF are summarized in table 2. The completion rates were same in two groups (15 patients in each group, 78%). Mean dose of VLF XR was 359.2 ± 31.4 mg/day in the first group and the patients in the second group received mean dose of 63.16 ± 19.3 mg/day sertraline in addition to 225 mg/day VLF XR.

Baseline HAM-D scores were not statistically different between the groups (U=151 p>0.05). At the second week, a significant difference on HAM-D scores was emerged between the patients who were on sertraline add-on VLF treatment and patients on high dose VLF (for week 2, U=75 p=0.02; for week 4, U=111.1 p=0.04) (figure 1). However, at the sixth week this difference was vanished (U=121 p=0.08, non-significant). At the end of the study (eight week) there was no significant difference between the groups (U=127 p=0.11). Mean HAM-D scores of patients decreased significantly decreased in both groups compared to baseline values (W=3.7 p<0.01 for high-dose VLF group, W=3.8 p<0.01 for sertraline add-on VLF group; Wilcoxon signed ranks test). A reduction of 50% or more from baseline HAM-D was evident among eight (42.1 %) of 19 patients taking high-dose VLF and ten (52.6 %) of patients taking sertraline-VLF combination. However, this difference was not significant (p=0.2, Fisher's exact test). Remission defined as a HAM-D score of 8 or less, occurred 4 patients (21.1 %) in high-dose VLF group and 7 patients (36.8 %) in sertraline add-on VLF group. The difference between the groups was significant (p=0.02, Fisher's exact test).

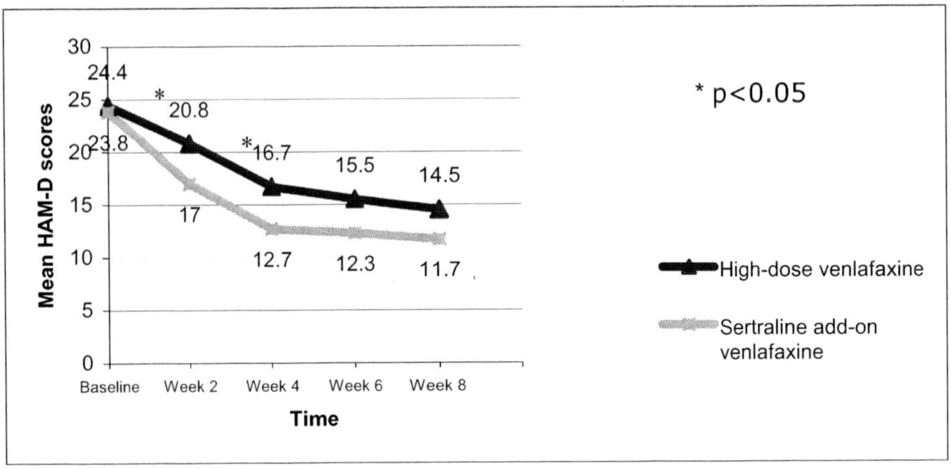

Figure 1. At the second week, a significant difference on HAM-D scores was emerged between the patients who were on sertraline add-on VLF XR treatment and patients on high dose VLF XR. At the sixth week this difference had vanished. At the end of the study (eight week) there was no significant difference between the groups (see text for statistical details).

Four patients from each group dropped out prematurely from the study. From the high-dose VLF group, one patient had a high blood pressure (160/120) despite antihypertensive drugs (amilodipin, catapres) and two patients were lost to follow up. One patient from each group drew their consent from the study. One patient from sertraline add-on VLF group showed mild symptoms of serotonergic syndrome and his drugs were ceased by the researchers. From the combination group one patient had severe nausea after sertraline addition and another patient became manic.

Table 2. Characteristics of 38 Depressed Patients with Major Depressive Disorder Assigned to Treatment With High-Dose Venlafaxine or Sertraline Add-On Venlafaxine

Characteristics	High-Dose Venlafaxine Group (N=19)	Sertraline Add-On Venlafaxine Group (N=19)	Comparison
Sex			
Male	5	4	X^2=0.14 df=1
Female	14	15	p > 0.05
Age (years) (Mean ± SD)	43.21 ± 7.21	44.15 ± 6.79	U=168 p > 0.05
DSM-IV Diagnosis			
MDD, single episode	4	5	X^2=0.14 df=1
MDD, relapsing	15 (78%)	14 (73%)	p > 0.05
Duration of recent episode (Mean ± SD weeks)	80 ± 88 (Range: 28-150)	68 ± 98 (Range: 32-170)	U=132 p > 0.05
Number of previous episode (Mean ± SD)	3.1 ± 3.3	3.2 ± 3.5	U=150 p > 0.05
HAM-D			
Baseline	24.5 ± 2.3 [a]	23.8 ± 3.1 [b]	U=151 p > 0.05
End-point	14.5 ± 6.5 [a']	11.7 ± 6.2 [b']	U=127 p > 0.05
Response rate	8 (42.1%)	10 (52.6%)	p=0.2, Fisher's exact test
Remission rate	4 (21.1%)	7 (36.8%)	p=0.02, Fisher's exact test

a-a' and b-b': Significantly different (see text for the statistical details).

6. Discussion

Algorithms related to treatment of major depressive disorder recommend serotonin-noradrenalin uptake inhibitors as a first line treatment as well as for those patients who did not respond to initial SSRI treatment (Texas Medication Algorithm Project (TMAP), Sequenced Treatment Alternatives to Relieve Depression (STAR*D)). These recommendations depend on evidences from different trials support the idea of switching to VLF in patients who did not respond to initial SSRI treatment (Saiz-Ruiz et al 2003). A survey done on antidepressant prescribing practices in the TRD showed that switching to VLF was preferred by nearly 40% of clinician that had agreed to participate the research. Most patients with major depression may be effectively treated with VLF 75-225 mg/day, and patients with more severe depression or TRD may need up to 375 mg (Nierenberg et al 1994). However, incased dosages also associates with higher incidence of side-effects and drop-out rates (Rudolph et al 1998) and for doses above 200 mg/day, regular blood pressure monitoring is strongly recommended by the health authorities. Thus, in case of patients with a history of resistance to SSRIs and not responding to 225 mg/day of venlafaxine, clinicians should give a new decision of increasing the dose of VLF or switching to another antidepressant. Augmentation and combination strategies are the two other options for continuing the pharmacotherapy. New evidences certainly would help clinicians to give the right decision.

In this trial, we compared high-dose VLF treatment strategy to another strategy, venlafaxine-SSRI combination which, we have observed promising results previously in patients who partially respond to VLF treatment (Gonul et al 2003).

The results of this study showed that both treatment strategies had a similar effect on TRD patients when the response rate (52.1% for the combination group vs. 42.1% for the high-dose VLF group) accepted as the main outcome of the study. However, when the remission was taken into account, patients treated with venlafaxine-SSRI combination had a significantly better rate of remission compared to high-dose VLF group (36.8% vs. 21.1%; respectively). Patients on combination therapy had also a faster response rate compared to high-dose group.

More than 70% of patients included in this study had a history of depression with multiple episodes and mean duration of the recent episode is more than 1 year. Neither of the patients had less than one trial of SSRI before VLF treatment. Two of the patients in each group had responded ECT in their previous episodes; of note they did not respond to either treatment in this trial. Thus, it would not be incorrect to state that patients selected for this study were highly resistant to antidepressant treatment. Additionally, five of the patients had a treatment of TCAs for their recent episodes but could not reach to recommended dose due to side effects. It is interesting to note that 4 of 5 patients with a past psychiatric history of dysthmia responded to treatment in the combination group compared to 1 of 4 patients with the same diagnosis in the high-dose VLF group in our study.

To our knowledge, there are 4 double-blind controlled study, which allow high dose VLF in patients with TRD (Nierenberg et al 1994, de Montigny et al 1999, Mitchell et al 2000, Poierer and Boyer 1999). Only, Michell et al (2000) specifically reported the response rate as 40.5% of patients receiving 300 mg/day which was the maximum VLF dosage for the study. Our finding of 42.1% respond rate in high-dose VLF group is parallel to the previous finding. However, it should be emphasized that compared to Mitchell et al study; our patients have higher doses of VLF (359.2 ± 31.4 mg/day vs 300 mg/day) in a longer time period. There are few reports focusing on very high dose VLF (375-600 mg/day) treatment in depressed patients. Mybaya (2002) reported that 4 of the 5 patients with TRD responded very high-dose VLF (450-600 mg/day) in 24 weeks of time on the other hand, Harrison et al (2004) did not report a better efficacy data for the very high-dose VLF treatment (mean: 437 mg/day, range: 375-600 mg/day) compared to standard dose VLF treatment (mean: 195 mg/day, range: 75-300 mg/day).

Few studies address the issue of augmentation or combination treatment in patients who had been already on VLF treatment. Hoencamp et al (2000) augment VLF with lithium in 23 depressed patients who had already been on 225 mg/day VLF for 7 weeks. Sociodemographic variables and previous treatments of patients in that study were very close to those of patients in our study. After 6 weeks of lithium augmentation 35% of patients responded to treatment with only 2 (9%) of them were in remission. Even though these rates were lower than what we have observed in this study, it would be wrong to reach a conclusion that high-dose VLF or VLF-SSRI combination are more effective than lithium augmentation before conducting a direct comparison trial between each treatment strategy. In another report Gomez et al (2000) added VLF to treatment of their patients who had already been on TCAs and they observed high rate of response (82%) and remission (64%) rate. But, in last study, the homogeneity of depression was not conserved.

6.1. The Effect of VLF on Monoamines

The capacity of VLF for inhibiting the serotonin and noradrenalin reuptake pumps and its effect of extracellular serotonin and noradrenalin levels were particularly studied in many studies. The results of these studies are complex and sometimes confusing. The reasons for this confusion are not clear, but may be due to differences in routes of administration of the drugs, brain regions examined and microdialysis techniques. The most replicated finding is the potency of VLF and it's metabolite ODV for inhibiting the serotonin reuptake pump are lower than those of SSRIs' (Koch et al 2003, Beique et 1998) and can be classified as moderate. Interestingly, the capacity for inhibiting noradrenalin reuptake pump is about 30-fold lower compared to that of serotonin reuptake pump. During moderate doses (15 mg/kg), VLF increases only serotonin levels in the rat brain. However, 40 mg/kg of VLF robustly and about equally increases extracellular concentration of serotonin and noradrenalin up to the peak levels (Koch et al 2003, Felton et al 2003). Nonetheless, the peak level of serotonin is not more than those induced by SSRIs (Felton et al 2003). It was also showed that not lower doses but higher doses of VLF can desensitize the 5-HT1A autoreceptors and presynaptic 5-HT1B receptors (Beique et al 2000). This process which is also associated with SSRIs and it is known to be necessary for antidepressant response and regular serotonin release from presynaptic membranes (Blier et al 1998).

The venlafaxine–induced increase in noradrenalin is surprising since it has low affinity for noradrenalin reuptake pump in vitro and potency in vivo; possibly suggesting some additional pharmacological effect is involved in increasing the extracellular noradrenalin in the brain. Increased serotonergic transmission might be enough for increasing extracellular levels of noradrenalin depending on the findings of David et al (2003) who observed high levels of noradrenalin with potent serotonin reuptake inhibitors citalopram and paroxetine; although opposite results were also been reported (Bymaster et al 2002). Moreover, the regulation of monoamine release involves interplay of complex brain circuitries including interaction at various cell bodies and receptors (Ichikawa et al 2001, Pudovkina et al 2002,).

6.2. Can SSRI Additon Bring an Additional Effect to those of Venlafaxine?

The pharmacokinetic interaction might be one of the answers. The usual final pharmacokinetic interaction is such an "added-drug" situation is an increase in the blood levels of the first drug, in this case VLF. VLF is extensively metabolized by the hepatic cytochrome P450 (CYP) enzyme system, mainly CYP2D6 isoenzyme. CYP2D6 is subject to genetic polymorphism and metabolism of VLF varies between the patients. However, the total amount of active compounds (VLF and ODV) was similar in CYP2D6-poor and CYP2D6-extensive metaboliser (data on file, Wyeth-Ayerst Laboratories, GMR 26711), which suggest that dose adjustment is unnecessary when VLF is administered with a CYP2D6 inhibitors. This might not be the all story, because VLF and its metabolites are chiral compounds (the R enantiomer is more selective for noradrenalin and the S enantiomer is more selective for serotonin), and there is evidence of concentration dependent stereoselective metabolism (Otton et al 1996, Montogomery 1993, Muth et al 1991). Thus, the patients who have a diminished CYP2D6 capacity with any reason (genetic polymorphism or a drug like fluoxetine) might have stereoisomeric profile similar to those of patients taking much higher doses of VLF. For this study, sertraline was chosen as the combination drug because it is a poor inhibitor of CYP enzymes. Thus, it is unlikely to explain the efficacy of combination treatment used in this study by only pharmacokinetic interaction. However, definitive conclusion can only be reached after the measuring each antidepressants' and their metabolites' plasma levels. The lack of plasma levels of VLF and sertraline is absolutely a limitation of this study.

Although it is well known that there is no efficacy difference between SSRIs in controlled trials, recent reports clearly showed that patients who are nonresponsive to one SSRI might response to another SSRI (Zarate et al 1996, Thase et al 2001, 2002). This might be explained by differences of their reuptake potencies and receptor binding affinity. Thus, minor differences between antidepressants or differences created by dosages might be important during the response to a specific antidepressant in an individual patient. Genetic polymorphisms of the receptors and the reuptake pumps together with the metabolism rate of a specific drug might play a significant role in determining these minor differences (Serreti et al 2004, Joyce 2003). Moreover, Stain-Malmgren et al (2001) showed that depressed patients with multiple episodes or had a chronic form of the disease have a different serotonin indices. These patients showed no correlation between plasma drug concentration and serotonin reuptake inhibition which indicates that the sensitivity of the uptake mechanism may become more resistant to pharmacological modulation over time especially in patients who faced many antidepressants. This last finding might explain why more intervention like lithium augmentation or what we had in this study by adding SSRI to VLF is needed for increasing serotonin transmission in TRD patients.

One other explanation for the efficacy of SSRI-VLF combination depends on their pharmacodynamic interaction. As we noted earlier, VLF has a lower binding capacity to serotonin reuptake pump compared to SSRIs. This suggests that addition of a SSRI which has higher binding capacity might release more VLF from serotonin pump sites and have them a chance to go and inhibit noradrenalin reuptake pump more efficiently. In no doubt that this speculation should be tested in animal models.

6.3. Safety and Adverse Effects

Discontinuation rates in VLF research studies have varied from 8 % (de Montigny et al 1994) to 21% (Mehtonen *et al.*, 2000), but are usually around 11% (Thase, 1997). Twenty-two percent drop-out rate of this trial is in the higher limit compared to those of previous trials. One of our patients from high-dose VLF group had a problem of high blood pressure and another patient from the combination group showed early signs of serotonin syndrome which were restlessness, myoclonus, hyperreflexia, diaphoresis, and mild tremor. Serotonin syndrome due to VLF combination with fluoxetine has been previously reported (Bhatara et al 1998). Fluoxetine is a potent inhibitor of CYP2D6 which is the main metabolizer of venlafaxine. Thus, pharmacokinetic interaction between VLF and fluoxetine might be complex and this complex interaction might promote serotonin syndrome in the reported case. However, it should be kept in mind that antidepressants like citalopram and sertraline which has no or minor pharmacokinetic with VLF may also cause serotonin syndrome as we had one in this study.

6.4. Limitations

This study has many limitations. First, this is an open-labeled study and both the researchers and the patients knew the antidepressants that were prescribed. Second, there was no placebo arm. Thus, we can not know what would be the response rate if patients had been kept on VLF XR 225 mg/day for another 8 weeks. Extended treatment might increase the response rate up to 20% among the patients who have chronic or treatment-resistant depression. Third, absence of lithium augmentation arm in this study prevents us comparing the VLF-SSRI combination to the best studied strategy in TRD. This comparison is needed if VLF-SSRI combination is going to be an alternative strategy in TRD. Fourth and the most important limitation of this study is not detaching the blood levels of the antidepressants used in the study. Due to technical limitations we could not achieved these measurements.

7. CONCLUSION

The results of this study suggest that the venlafaxine-sertraline combination is an effective treatment strategy for treatment-resistant depressive patients. It has a faster onset of action and achieved a better remission rate compared to high-dose VLF treatment. This combination might be an alternative to treatment-resistant depressed patients who have already been on VLF but can not go for higher doses due to side effects of VLF like hypertension. However, safety issue on serotonin syndrome should always be kept in mind.

References

Altshuler, LL; Bauer, M; Frye, MA; Gitlin, MJ; Mintz, J; Szuba, MP; Leight, KL; Whybrow, PC. Does thyroid supplementation accelerate tricyclic antidepressant response? A review and meta-analysis of the literature. *Am J Psychiatry* 2001, 158(10), 1617-1622.

American Psychiatric Association. Practice guideline for major depressive disorder in adults. *Am J Psychiatry* 2000, (suppl 4),1-45.

Ananth, J. Treatment-resistant depression. *Psychother Psychosom* 1998, 67, 61-70.

Anderson, IM. Selective serotonin reuptake inhibitors versus tricyclic antidepressants: a meta-analysis of efficacy and tolerability. *J Affect Disord* 2000, 58(1), 19-36.

Appelberg, BG; Syvalahti, EK; Koskinen, TE; Mehtonen, OP; Muhonen, TT; Naukkarinen, HH. Patients with severe depression may benefit from buspirone augmentation of selective serotonin reuptake inhibitors: results from a placebo-controlled, randomized, double-blind, placebo wash-in study. *J Clin Psychiatry* 2001, 62(6), 448-452.

Bakish, D. Fluoxetine potentiation by buspirone: three case histories. *Can J Psychiatry*. 1991, 36(10),749-750.

Barbee, JG; Conrad, EJ; Jamhour, NJ. The effectiveness of olanzapine; risperidone; quetiapine; and ziprasidone as augmentation agents in treatment-resistant major depressive disorder. *J Clin Psychiatry*. 2004, 65(7), 975-981.

Bauer, M; Adli, M; Baethge, C; Berghofer, A; Sasse, J; Heinz, A; Bschor, T. Lithium augmentation therapy in refractory depression: clinical evidence and neurobiological mechanisms. *Can J Psychiatry* 2003, 48(7), 440-448.

Beique, J; de Montigny, C; Blier, P; Debonnel, G. Effects of sustained administration of the serotonin and norepinephrine reuptake inhibitor venlafaxine: II. In vitro studies in the rat. *Neuropharmacology* 2000, 39(10),1813-1822.

Beique, JC; de Montigny, C; Blier, P; Debonnel, G. Blockade of 5-hydroxytryptamine and noradrenaline uptake by venlafaxine: a comparative study with paroxetine and desipramine. *Br J Pharmacol* 1998, 125(3), 526-532.

Berman, RM; Anand, A; Cappiello, A; Miller, HL; Hu, XS; Oren, DA; Charney, DS. The use of pindolol with fluoxetine in the treatment of major depression: final results from a double-blind; placebo-controlled trial. *Biol Psychiatry* 1999, 45(9), 1170-1177.

Berman, RM; Darnell, AM; Miller, HL; Anand, A; Charney, DS. Effect of pindolol in hastening response to fluoxetine in the treatment of major depression: a double-blind; placebo-controlled trial. *Am J Psychiatry* 1997, 154(1), 37-43.

Bhat, RV; Budd, Haeberlein, SL; Avila, J. Glycogen synthase kinase 3: a drug target for CNS therapies. *J Neurochem* 2004, 89(6), 1313-1317.

Bhatara, VS; Magnus, RD; Paul, KL; Preskorn, SH. Serotonin syndrome induced by venlafaxine and fluoxetine: a case study in polypharmacy and potential pharmacodynamic and pharmacokinetic mechanisms. *Ann Pharmacother* 1998, 32(4), 432-436.

Blier, P; Bergeron, R. Early onset of therapeutic action in depression and greater efficacy of antidepressant treatments: are they related? *Int Clin Psychopharmacol* 1997, 12 Suppl 3, S21-28.

Blier, P; Bergeron, R. Effectiveness of pindolol with selected antidepressant drugs in the treatment of major depression. *J Clin Psychopharmacol* 1995, 15(3), 217-222.

Blier, P; De Montigny, C. Short-term lithium administration enhances serotonergic neurotransmission: electrophysiological evidence in the rat CNS. *Eur J Pharmacol* 1985, 113(1), 69-77.

Blier, P; Pineyro, G; el Mansari, M; Bergeron, R; de Montigny C. Role of somatodendritic 5-HT autoreceptors in modulating 5-HT neurotransmission. *Ann N Y Acad Sci* 1998, 861, 204-216.

Bodkin, JA; Lasser, RA; Wines, JD Jr; Gardner, DM; Baldessarini, RJ. Combining serotonin reuptake inhibitors and bupropion in partial responders to antidepressant monotherapy. *J Clin Psychiatry* 1997, 58(4), 137-145.

Broderick, P & Lynch, V. Behavioral and biochemical changes induced by lithium and L-tryptophan in muridical rats. *Neuropsychopharmacol* 1982, 21, 671-679.

Bymaster, FP; Dreshfield-Ahmad, LJ; Threlkeld, PG; Shaw, JL; Thompson, L; Nelson, DL; Hemrick-Luecke, SK; Wong, DT. Comparative affinity of duloxetine and venlafaxine for serotonin and norepinephrine transporters in vitro and in vivo; human serotonin receptor subtypes; and other neuronal receptors. *Neuropsychopharmacology* 2001, 25(6), 871-880.

Bymaster, FP; Zhang, W; Carter, PA; Shaw, J; Chernet, E; Phebus, L; Wong, DT; Perry, KW. Fluoxetine; but not other selective serotonin uptake inhibitors; increases norepinephrine and dopamine extracellular levels in prefrontal cortex. *Psychopharmacology (Berl)* 2002, 160(4), 353-361.

Carpenter, LL; Yasmin, S; Price, LH. A double-blind; placebo-controlled study of antidepressant augmentation with mirtazapine. *Biol Psychiatry* 2002, 51(2), 183-188.

Chaput, Y; de Montigny, C; Blier, P. Presynaptic and postsynaptic modifications of the serotonin system by long-term administration of antidepressant treatments. An in vivo electrophysiologic study in the rat. *Neuropsychopharmacology* 1991, 5(4), 219-229.

Chen, G; Rajkowska, G; Du, F; Seraji-Bozorgzad, N; Manji, HK. Enhancement of hippocampal neurogenesis by lithium. *J Neurochem* 2000, 75(4), 1729-1734.

Cleare, AJ; McGregor, A; O'Keane, V. Neuroendocrine evidence for an association between hypothyroidism; reduced central 5-HT activity and depression. *Clin Endocrinol (Oxf.* 1995, 43(6), 713-719.

Cowen, PJ; McCance, SL; Ware, CJ; Cohen, PR; Chalmers, JS; ier, DL. Lithium in tricyclic-resistant depression. Correlation of increased brain 5-HT function with clinical outcome. *Br J Psychiatry* 1991, 159, 341-346.

David, DJ; Bourin, M; Jego, G; Przybylski, C; Jolliet, P; Gardier, AM. Effects of acute treatment with paroxetine; citalopram and venlafaxine in vivo on noradrenaline and serotonin outflow: a microdialysis study in Swiss mice. *Br J Pharmacol* 2003, 140(6), 1128-1136.

de Montigny C; Cournoyer G; Morissette R; Langlois R; Caille G. Lithium carbonate addition in tricyclic antidepressant-resistant unipolar depression. Correlations with the neurobiologic actions of tricyclic antidepressant drugs and lithium ion on the serotonin system. *Arch Gen Psychiatry* 1983, 40(12), 1327-1334.

de Montigny, C & Aghaian, GK. Tricyclic antidepressants: long-term treatment increases responsivity of rat forebrain neurons to serotonin. *Science* 1978, 202(4374), 1303-1306.

de Montigny, C & Blier P. Effects of antidepressant treatments on 5-HT neurotransmission: electrophysiological and clinical studies. *Adv Biochem Psychopharmacol* 1984, 39, 223-239.

de Montigny, C. Lithium addition in treatment-resistant depression. *Int Clin Psychopharmacol* 1994, 9 Suppl 2, 31-35.

de Montigny, C; Silverstone, PH; Debonnel, G; Blier, P; Bakish, D. Venlafaxine in treatment-resistant major depression: a Canadian multicenter; open-label trial. *J Clin Psychopharmacol* 1999, 19(5),401-406.

DeBattista, C; Solvason, HB; Poirier, J; Kendrick, E; Schatzberg, AF. A prospective trial of bupropion SR augmentation of partial and non-responders to serotonergic antidepressants. *J Clin Psychopharmacol* 2003, 23(1), 27-30.

Deonnel, G; Gobbi, G; Turcotte, J. The alpha-2 antagonist mirtazapine combined with SSRI paroxetineinduces a greater antidepressant response : a double blind controlled study. 39th American College of Neuropsychopharmacology; 10-14; 2000; San Juan; Puerto Rico.

Depression Guideline Panel (1993) Clinical Practice Guideline. Depression in primary care: Volume 2: Treatment of major depression. U.S. Department of Health and Human Services-Agency for health Care Policy Research; Publication No.93-0551.

Dewan, MJ; Anand, VS. Evaluating the tolerability of the newer antidepressants. *J Nerv Ment Dis* 1999, 187(2), 96-101.

Dimitriou, EC; Dimitriou, CE. Buspirone augmentation of antidepressant therapy. *J Clin Psychopharmacol.* 1998, 18(6), 465-469.

Donat, O; Gozen, O; Gonul, AS; Koylu, E; Eker, C; Akdeniz, F; Vahip, S; Pogun, S. The effects of chronic fluoxetine, olanzapine or olanzapine-fluoxetine combination treatment on the expression of brain derived neurotrophic factor levels in chronically stressed rats. 17th ECNP Congress, Stockholm, Sweden, October 9-13, 2004

Fava, M; Alpert, J; Nierenberg, A; Lagomasino, I; Sonawalla, S; Tedlow, J; Worthington, J; Baer, L; Rosenbaum, JF. Double-blind study of high-dose fluoxetine versus lithium or desipramine augmentation of fluoxetine in partial responders and nonresponders to fluoxetine. *J Clin Psychopharmacol* 2002, 22(4), 379-387.

Fava, M; Bless, E; Otto, MW; Pava, JA; Rosenbaum, JF. Dysfunctional attitudes in major depression. Changes with pharmacotherapy. *J Nerv Ment Dis* 1994, 182(1), 45-49.

Fava, M; Davidson, KG (1996) Definition and epidemiology of treatment resistant depression. *Psychtr Clin North Am* 1996, 19, 179-200.

Fava, M; Rosenbaum, JF; McGrath, PJ; Stewart, JW; Amsterdam, JD; Quitkin, FM. Lithium and tricyclic augmentation of fluoxetine treatment for resistant major depression: a double-blind; controlled study. *Am J Psychiatry* 1994, 151(9), 1372-1374.

Fawcett, J. The detection and consequences of anxiety in clinical depression. *J Clin Psychiatry* 1997; 58 Suppl 8, 35-40.

Felton, TM; Kang, TB; Hjorth, S; Auerbach, SB. Effects of selective serotonin and serotonin/noradrenaline reuptake inhibitors on extracellular serotonin in rat diencephalon and frontal cortex. *Naunyn Schmiedebergs Arch Pharmacol* 2003, 367(3), 297-305.

Ford, DE. Managing patients with depression: is primary care up to the challenge? *J Gen Intern Med* 2000, 15(5), 344-345.

Frank, E; Prien, RF; Jarrett, RB; Keller, MB; Kupfer, DJ; Lavori, PW; Rush, AJ; Weissman, MM.Conceptualization and rationale for consensus definitions of terms in major depressive disorder. Remission; recovery; relapse; and recurrence. *Arch Gen Psychiatry* 1991, 48(9), 851-855.

Fredman, SJ; Fava, M; Kienke, AS. Partial response; nonresponse and relapse with serotonin reuptake inhibitors in major depression: a survey of current "next-step" practice. *J Clin Psychiatry* 2000, 61, 403-408.

Ghaemi, SN; Sachs, GS; Chiou, AM; Pandurangi, AK; Goodwin, K. Is bipolar disorder still underdiagnosed? Are antidepressants over utilized? *J Affect Disord* 1999, 52(1-3), 135-144.

Gomez, JM & Perramon, C. Combined treatment with venlafaxine and tricyclic antidepressants in depressant patients who had partial response to clomipramine or imipramine: initial findings. *J Clin Psychiatry* 2000, 61, 285-289.

Gonul, AS; Akdeniz, F; Donat, O; Vahip, S. Selective serotonin reuptake inhibitors combined with venlafaxine in depressed patients who had partial response to venlafaxine: four cases. Prog Neuropsychopharmacol *Biol Psychiatry* 2003, 27(5), 889-891.

Gordon, JT; Kaminski, DM; Rozanov, CB; Dratman, MB. Evidence that 3;3';5-triiodothyronine is concentrated in and delivered from the locus coeruleus to its noradrenergic targets via anterograde axonal transport. *Neuroscience* 1999, 93(3), 943-954.

Greden, JF. The burden of disease for treatment-resistant depression. *J Clin Psychiatry* 2001, 62 Suppl 16, 26-31.

Gur, E; Lerer, B; Newman, ME. Chronic clomipramine and triiodothyronine increase serotonin levels in rat frontal cortex in vivo: relationship to serotonin autoreceptor activity. *J Pharmacol Exp Ther*. 1999, 288(1), 81-87.

Hamilton, M. A rating scale for depression. *J Neurol Neurosurgery Psychiatry* 1960, 23, 56-62.

Harrison, CL; Ferrier, N; Young, AH. Tolerability of high-dose venlafaxine in depressed patients. *J Psychopharmacol* 2004, 18(2), 200-204.

Harvey, AT; Rudolph, RL; Preskorn, SH. Evidence of the dual mechanisms of action of venlafaxine. *Arch Gen Psychiatry* 2000, 57(5), 503-509.

Heal, DJ; Smith, SL. The effects of acute and repeated administration of T3 to mice on 5-HT1 and 5-HT2 function in the brain and its influence on the actions of repeated electroconvulsive shock. *Neuropharmacology* 1988, 27(12), 1239-1248.

Hoencamp, E; Haffmans, J; Dijken, WA; Huijbrechts, IP. Lithium augmentation of venlafaxine: an open-label trial. *J Clin Psychopharmacol* 2000, 20(5), 538-543.

Hoffman, BB; Lefkowics, RJ; (1990): Adrenergic receptor antagonists. In:Gilman AG, Rall TW, Nies AS, Taylor P, editors. *The Pharmacological Basis of Therapeutics*, 8th ed. New York Pergamon Press, pp 221-243.

Ichikawa, J; Ishii, H; Bonaccorso, S; Fowler, WL; O'Laughlin, IA; Meltzer, HY. 5-HT(2A) and D(2) receptor blockade increases cortical DA release via 5-HT(1A) receptor activation: a possible mechanism of atypical antipsychotic-induced cortical dopamine release. *J Neurochem* 2001, 76(5), 1521-1531.

Jacbsen, FM. Possible augmentation effect of antidepressant response of buspirone. *J Clin Psychiatry* 1991, 52, 217-230.

Joffe, RT; Schuller, DR. An open study of buspirone augmentation of serotonin reuptake inhibitors in refractory depression. *J Clin Psychiatry* 1993, 54(7), 269-271.

Joyce, PR; Mulder, RT; Luty, SE; McKenzie JM; Miller AL; Rogers GR; Kennedy MA. Age-dependent antidepressant pharmacogenomics: polymorphisms of the serotonin transporter and G protein beta3 subunit as predictors of response to fluoxetine and nortriptyline. *Int J Neuropsychopharmacol* 2003, 6(4), 339-346.

Katon, W; von Korff, M; Lin, E; Bush, T; Ormel, J. Adequacy and duration of antidepressant treatment in primary care. *Med Care* 1992, 30(1), 67-76.

Keller, MB; Lavori, PW; Rice, J; Coryell, W; Hirschfeld, RM The persistent risk of chronicity in recurrent episodes of nonbipolar major depressive disorder: a prospective follow-up. *Am J Psychiatry* 1986, 143(1), 24-28.

Kennedy, SH; McCann, SM; Masellis, M; McIntyre, RS; Raskin, J; McKay, G; Baker, GB. Combining bupropion SR with venlafaxine; paroxetine; or fluoxetine: a preliminary report on pharmacokinetic; therapeutic; and sexual dysfunction effects. *J Clin Psychiatry* 2002, 63(3), 181-186.

Klerman GL & Weissman MM. Increasing rates of depression. JAMA 1989, 261, 2229-2235.

Koch, S; Hemrick-Luecke, SK; Thompson, LK; Evans, DC; Threlkeld, PG; Nelson, DL; Perry, KW; Bymaster, FP. Comparison of effects of dual transporter inhibitors on monoamine transporters and extracellular levels in rats. *Neuropharmacology* 2003, 45(7), 935-944.

Kodama, M; Fujioka, T; Duman, RS. Chronic olanzapine or fluoxetine administration increases cell proliferation in hippocampus and prefrontal cortex of adult rat. *Biol Psychiatry* 2004, 15;56(8), 570-80.

Koibuchi, N; Fukuda, H; Chin, WW. Promoter-specific regulation of the brain-derived neurotropic factor gene by thyroid hormone in the developing rat cerebellum. *Endocrinology* 1999, 140(9), 3955-3961.

Koran, LM; Gelenberg, AJ; Kornstein, SG; Howland, RH; Friedman, RA; DeBattista, C; Klein, D; Kocsis, JH; Schatzberg, AF; Thase, ME; Rush, AJ; Hirschfeld, RM; LaVange, LM; Keller, MB. Sertraline versus imipramine to prevent relapse in chronic depression. *J Affect Disord* 2001, 65(1), 27-36.

Korstein SG & Schneider RK. Clinical features of treatment-resistant depression. *J Clin Psychiatry* 62 (Suppl 16), 18-25.

Landen, M; Bjorling, G; Agren, H; Fahlen, T. A randomized; double-blind; placebo-controlled trial of buspirone in combination with an SSRI in patients with treatment-refractory depression. *J Clin Psychiatry* 1998, 59(12), 664-668.

Licht, RW; Qvitzau, S. Treatment strategies in patients with major depression not responding to first-line sertraline treatment. A randomised study of extended duration of treatment; dose increase or mianserin augmentation. *Psychopharmacology (Berl)* 2002, 161(2), 143-151.

Lin, EH; Von Korff, M; Katon, W; Bush, T; Simon, GE; Walker, E; Robinson, P. The role of the primary care physician in patients' adherence to antidepressant therapy. *Med Care* 1995, 33(1), 67-74.

Maes, M; Vandoolaeghe, E; Desnyder, R. Efficacy of treatment with trazodone in combination with pindolol or fluoxetine in major depression. *J Affect Disord* 1996, 41(3), 201-210.

Manji, HK; Moore, GJ; Chen, G. Bipolar disorder: leads from the molecular and cellular mechanisms of action of mood stabilizers. *Br J Psychiatry* Suppl. 2001, 41, s107-19.

Maragnoli, ME; Fumagalli, F; Gennarelli, M; Racagni, G; Riva, MA. Fluoxetine and olanzapine have synergistic effects in the modulation of fibroblast growth factor 2 expression within the rat brain. *Biol Psychiatry* 2004, 55(11), 1095-1102.

Mbaya, P. Safety and efficacy of high dose of venlafaxine XL in treatment resistant major depression. *Hum Psychopharmacol* 2002, 17(7), 335-339.

McCance-Katz, E; Price, LH; Charney, DS; Heninger, GR. Serotonergic function during lithium augmentation of refractory depression. *Psychopharmacology (Berl)* 1992, 108(1-2), 93-97.

Mehtonen, OP; Sogaard, J; Roponen, P; Behnke, K. Randomized; double-blind comparison of venlafaxine and sertraline in outpatients with major depressive disorder. Venlafaxine 631 Study Group. *J Clin Psychiatry* 2000, 61(2), 95-100.

Mitchell, PB; Schweitzer, I; Burrows, G; Johnson, G; Polonowita, A. Efficacy of venlafaxine and predictors of response in a prospective open-label study of patients with treatment-resistant major depression. *J Clin Psychopharmacol* 2000, 20(4), 483-487.

Montgomery, SA. Venlafaxine: a new dimension in antidepressant pharmacotherapy. *J Clin Psychiatry* 1993, 54, 119-126.

Moreno, FA; Gelenberg, AJ; Bachar, K; Delgado, PL. Pindolol augmentation of treatment-resistant depressed patients. *J Clin Psychiatry* 1997, 58,437-439.

Muller-Oerlinghausen, B. Lithium long-term treatment--does it act via serotonin? *Pharmacopsychiatry*. 1985 ;18(2),214-7.

Murphy, GM Jr; Hollander, SB; Rodrigues, HE; Kremer, C; Schatzberg, AF. Effects of the serotonin transporter gene promoter polymorphism on mirtazapine and paroxetine efficacy and adverse events in geriatric major depression. *Arch Gen Psychiatry* 2004, 61(11),1163-1169.

Muth, EA; Moyer, JA; Haskins, JT; Andree, TH; Husbands, GEM. Biochemical; neurophysiological; and behavioral effects of Wy-45;233 and other identified metabolites of the antidepressant venlafaxine. *Drug Dev Res* 1991, 23,191-199.

Nelson JC; Mazure CM; Bowers MB Jr; Jatlow PI. A preliminary; open study of the combination of fluoxetine and desipramine for rapid treatment of major depression. *Arch Gen Psychiatry* 1991, 48(4), 303-307.

Nelson, JC. Treatment of refractory depression. *Depres Anxiety* 1997, 5,165-174.

Nelson, JC; Mazure, CM; Jatlow, PI; Bowers, MB Jr; Price, LH. Combining norepinephrine and serotonin reuptake inhibition mechanisms for treatment of depression: a double-blind; randomized study. *Biol Psychiatry* 2004, 55(3), 296-300.

Nierenberg, AA; Feighner, JP; Rudolph, R; Cole, JO; Sullivan, J. Venlafaxine for treatment-resistant unipolar depression. *J Clin Psychopharmacol* 1994, 14(6), 419-423.

Nierenberg, AA; Keefe, BR; Leslie, VC; Alpert, JE; Pava, JA; Worthington, JJ 3rd; Rosenbaum, JF; Fava, M. Residual symptoms in depressed patients who respond acutely to fluoxetine. *J Clin Psychiatry* 1999, 60(4), 221-225.

Okamoto, Y; Motohasi, N; Hayakawa, H; Muraoka, M; Yamawaki, S. Addition of lithium to chronic antidepressant treatment potentiates presynaptic serotonergic function without changes in serotonergic receptors in the rat cerebral cortex. *Neuropsychobiology* 1996; 33(1), 17-20.

Otton, SV; Ball, SE; Cheung, SW; Inaba, T; Rudolph, RL; Sellers, EM. Venlafaxine oxidation in vitro is catalysed by CYP2D6. *Br J Clin Pharmacol* 1996, 41, 149-156.

Papakostas, GI; Petersen, TJ; Nierenberg, AA; Murakami, JL; Alpert, JE; Rosenbaum, JF; Fava, M. Ziprasidone augmentation of selective serotonin reuptake inhibitors (SSRIs) for SSRI-resistant major depressive disorder. *J Clin Psychiatry* 2004, 65(2), 217-221.

Perez, V; Soler, J; Puigdemont, D; Alvarez, E; Artigas, F. A double-blind; randomized; placebo-controlled trial of pindolol augmentation in depressive patients resistant to serotonin reuptake inhibitors. Grup de Recerca en Trastorns Afectius. *Arch Gen Psychiatry* 1999, 56(4), 375-379.

Perry, EB; Berman, RM; Sanacora, G; Anand, A; Lynch-Colonese, K; Charney, DS. Pindolol augmentation in depressed patients resistant to selective serotonin reuptake inhibitors: a double-blind; randomized; controlled trial. *J Clin Psychiatry* 2004, 65(2), 238-243.

Phiel, CJ; Wilson, CA; Lee, VM; Klein, PS. GSK-3alpha regulates production of Alzheimer's disease amyloid-beta peptides. *Nature* 2003, 423(6938), 435-439.

Pirraglia, PA; Stafford, RS; Singer, DE. Trends in Prescribing of Selective Serotonin Reuptake Inhibitors and Other Newer Antidepressant Agents in Adult Primary Care. Prim Care Companion J *Clin Psychiatry* 2003, 5(4), 153-157.

Poirier, MF; Boyer, P. Venlafaxine and paroxetine in treatment-resistant depression. Double-blind; randomised comparison. *Br J Psychiatry* 1999, 175, 12-16.

Preskorn, SH; Ross, R; Stanga, SY. Selective serotonin reuptake inhibitors. In:Preskorn SH; Feighner JP; Stanga CY; Ross Ruth; Editors. *Antidepressant: Past; Present and Future.* New York: Springer-Verlag Berlin Heidelberg; 2004; 241-262.

Price, LH; Charney, DS; Delgado, PL; Goodman, WK; Krystal, JH; Woods, SW; Heninger, GR. Clinical data on the role of serotonin in the mechanism(s) of action of antidepressant drugs. *J Clin Psychiatry* 1990, 51 Suppl, 44-50.

Prien, RF; Carpenter, LL; Kupfer, DJ. The definition and operational criteria for treatment outcome of major depressive disorder. A review of the current research literature. *Arch Gen Psychiatry* 1991, 48(9), 796-800.

Pudovkina, OL; Cremers, TI; Westerink, BH. The interaction between the locus coeruleus and dorsal raphe nucleus studied with dual-probe microdialysis. *Eur J Pharmacol* 2002, 445(1-2), 37-42.

Quitkin FM; McGrath PJ; Stewart JW; Ocepek-Welikson K; Taylor BP; Nunes E; Deliyannides D; Agosti V; Donovan SJ; Petkova E; Klein DF. Chronological milestones to guide drug change. When should clinicians switch antidepressants? *Arch Gen Psychiatry* 1996, 53(9), 785-792.

Rapaport, M; Canuso, C; Loescher, A; Lasser, R; Gharabawi, G. Prelimanary results from the ARISe-RD (Risperidon Augmentation in Resistant Depression) trial. 156th APA Annual Meeting, San Fransisco, CA, 17-22, 2003.

Rothschild, AJ. Management of psychotic treatment-resistant patients. Psychiatr Clin North Am 1996, 19, 237-251.

Rubio, G; San, L; Lopez-Munoz, F; Garcia-Garcia, P; Alamo, C. Combination therapy with reboxetine for major depression patients who are partial or nonresponders to serotonin selective reuptake inhibitors] *Actas Esp Psiquiatr* 2003, 31(6), 315-324.

Rudolph, RL; Fabre, LF; Feighner, JP; Rickels, K; Entsuah, R; Derivan, AT. A randomized; placebo-controlled; dose-response trial of venlafaxine hydrochloride in the treatment of major depression. *J Clin Psychiatry* 1998, 59(3), 116-122.

Rush, AJ & Trivedi, MI. Treating depression to remission. *Psychiatric Annals* 1995, 25, 704-709.

Saiz-Ruiz, J; Ibanez, A; Diaz-Marsa, M; Arias, F; Padin, J; Martin-Carrasco, M; Montes, JM; Ferrando, L; Carrasco, JL; Martin-Ballesteros, E; Jorda, L; Chamorro, L. Efficacy of venlafaxine in major depression resistant to selective serotonin reuptake inhibitors. *Prog Neuropsychopharmacol Biol Psychiatry* 2002, 26(6), 1129-1134

Sanchez, C; Hyttel, J. Comparison of the effects of antidepressants and their metabolites on reuptake of biogenic amines and on receptor binding. *Cell Mol Neurobiol* 1999, 19(4), 467-489.

Sandrini, M; Vitale, G; Vergoni, AV; Ottani, A; Bertolini, A. Effect of acute and chronic treatment with triiodothyronine on serotonin levels and serotonergic receptor subtypes in the rat brain. *Life Sci* 1996, 58(18), 1551-1559.

Sequenced Treatment Alternatives to Relieve Depression (STAR*D). 2004 November 1st. Available from: http://www.edc.gsph.pitt.edu/stard.html

Serretti, A; Zanardi, R; Franchini, L; Artioli, P; Dotoli, D; Pirovano, A; Smeraldi, E. Pharmacogenetics of selective serotonin reuptake inhibitor response: a 6-month follow-up. *Pharmacogenetics* 2004, 14(9), 607-613.

Seth, R; Jennings, AL; Bindman, J. Combination treatment wit noradrenalin and serotonin reuptake inhibitors in resistant depression. *Br J Psychiatry* 1992, 161, 562-565.

Sheehan, DV; Lecrubier, Y; Sheehan, KH; Amorim, P; avs, J; Weiller, E; Hergueta, T; Baker, R; Dunbar GC. The Mini-International Neuropsychiatric Interview (M.I.N.I.): the development and validation of a structured diagnostic psychiatric interview for DSM-IV and ICD-10. *J Clin Psychiatry* 1998, 59 Suppl 20, 22-33

Shelton, RC; Tollefson, GD; Tohen, M; Stah,l S; Gannon, KS; Jacobs, TG; Buras, WR; Bymaster, FP; Zhang W; Spencer KA; Feldman PD; Meltzer HY. A novel augmentation strategy for treating resistant major depression. *Am J Psychiatry* 2001, 158(1), 131-134.

Sodhi, MS & Sanders-Bush, E. Serotonin and brain development. *Int Rev Neurobiol* 2004, 59, 111-174.

Stain-Malmgren, R; Khoury, AE; Aberg-Wistedt, A; Tham, A. Serotonergic function in major depression and effect of sertraline and paroxetine treatment. *Int Clin Psychopharmacol* 2001, 16(2), 93-101.

Steffens, DC; Krishnan, KR; Helms, MJ. Are SSRIs better than TCAs? Comparison of SSRIs and TCAs: a meta-analysis. *Depress Anxiety* 1997, 6(1), 10-18.

Sussman, N. Anxiolytic antidepressant augmentation. *J Clin Psychiatry* 1998, 59 (suppl 5), 437-439.

Taylor, DP; Eison, MS; Riblet, LA. Pharmacological and clinical effects of buspirone. *Pharmacol Biohem Behav 1985*, 23,687-694.

Texas Medication Algorithm Project (TMAP). 2004 November 1st. Available from: http://www.mhmr.state.tx.us7centraloffice/medicaldirector/tmaptoc.html

Thase ME & Rush AJ. When at first you don't succeed: sequential strategies for antidepressant nonresponders. *J Clin Psychiatry* 1997; 58 (suppl 13),23-29.

Thase, ME & Rush, AJ. Treatment resistant depression. In Bloom FE; Kupfer GJ; Eds. *Psychopharmacology :The Fourth Generation of Progress*. New York; NY: Raven Press; 1995,1081-1097.

Thase, ME; Entsuah, AR; Rudolph, RL. Remission rates during treatment with venlafaxine or selective serotonin reuptake inhibitors. *Br J Psychiatry* 2001, 178, 234-241.

Thase, ME; Feighner, JP; Lydiard, RB. Citalopram treatment of fluoxetine nonresponders. *J Clin Psychiatry* 2001, 62(9), 683-687.

Thase, ME; Ferguson, JM; Lydiard, RB; Wilcox, CS. Citalopram treatment of paroxetine-intolerant depressed patients. *Depress Anxiety* 2002, 16(3),128-133.

Thase, ME; Friedman, ES; Howland, RH. Venlafaxine and treatment-resistant depression. *Depress Anxiety* 2000, 12 Suppl 1, 55-62.

Trivedi, MH & Kleiber, BA. Using treatment algorithms for the effective management of treatment-resistant depression. *J Clin Psychiatry* 2001, 62 Suppl 18, 25-29.

Vaidya, VA; Castro, ME; Pei, Q; Sprakes, ME; Grahame-Smith, DG. Influence of thyroid hormone on 5-HT(1A) and 5-HT(2A) receptor-mediated regulation of hippocampal BDNF mRNA expression. *Neuropharmacology* 2001, 40(1), 48-56.

Wegener, G; Bandpey, Z; Heiberg, IL; Mork, A; Rosenberg, R. Increased extracellular serotonin level in rat hippocampus induced by chronic citalopram is augmented by subchronic lithium: neurochemical and behavioral studies in the rat. *Psychopharmacology (Berl)* 2003,166(2),188-194.

Williams, R; Ryves, WJ; Dalton, EC; Eickholt, B; Shaltiel, G; Agam, G; Harwood, AJ. A molecular cell biology of lithium. *Biochem Soc Trans* 2004, 32(Pt 5), 799-802.

Zarate, CA; Kando, JC; Tohen, M; Weiss, MK; Cole, JO. Does intolerance or lack of response with fluoxetine predict the same will happen with sertraline? *J Clin Psychiatry* 1996, 57(2), 67-71.

Zhang, W; Perry, KW; Wong, DT; Potts, BD; Bao, J; Tollefson, GD; Bymaster, FP. Synergistic effects of olanzapine and other antipsychotic agents in combination with fluoxetine on norepinephrine and dopamine release in rat prefrontal cortex. *Neuropsychopharmacology* 2000, 23(3), 250-262.

In: Trends in Depression Research
Editor: Maurice J. Henri, pp. 113-124

ISBN 1-60021-394-4

Chapter 6

SUPPORT RECIPROCITY AND DEPRESSION AMONG CHILDREN

Hirokazu Taniguchi** and Mitsuhiro Ura
Hiroshima University, Higashi-Hiroshima, Japan

ABSTRACT

This study examined the relationship between support reciprocity in relationships with both parents and friends and depression among elementary school, middle school, and high school students, taking specific account of the quality of parent-child relationships. The participants were 340 first-year high school students, 312 second- and third-year middle school students, and 317 sixth-year elementary school students. Consistent with predictions, it was shown that support reciprocity in friendships correlated significantly with lower depression only among high school students. Moreover, it was found that for high school students who perceived their parents as caring and affectionate, support reciprocity in friendships related significantly to lower depression but not for those who perceived their parents as distant and dismissive.

INTRODUCTION

Many studies have found that reciprocity of social support is associated with mental health (e.g., Acitelli and Antonucci, 1994; Antonucci, Fuhrer, and Jackson, 1990; Antonucci and Jackson, 1990; Buunk, Doosje, Jans, and Hopstaken, 1993; Hachiya, 1990; Jones and Vaughan, 1990; Jung, 1990; Levitt, Guacci, and Weber, 1992; Rook, 1987; van Tilburg, 1992). For example, Jung (1990) examined the relationship between three aspects of social support: receiving, giving, and reciprocity, and college students' symptoms of distress, and found that support reciprocity among family members had a strong connection with lower

* Correspondence concerning this article should be addressed to Hirokazu Taniguchi, Faculty of Education, Okayama University, Tsushimanaka, Okayama 700-8530, Japan. E-mail: hirokazu@cc.okayama-u.ac.jp.

distress levels. Buunk et al. (1993) also found that perceived support reciprocity in relationships with colleagues as well as with superiors was accompanied by the lowest negative affect experienced at work in a sample of employees.

Reciprocity or equality is the dominant principle of distributive justice in relationships between close friends (Deutsch, 1975; Nagata, 1987; Shaver and Buhrmester, 1983). Therefore, it seems that in such relationships, reciprocity of support is strongly associated with mental health. In fact, Rook (1987) found that support reciprocity with friends rather than with children was strongly related to less loneliness among older women. Ingersoll-Dayton and Antonucci (1988) also found that in relationships with friends, nonreciprocity of sick care was strongly associated with middle-aged and older adults' negative affect. According to these findings, this study examined whether in friendships, support reciprocity is strongly related to mental health than in parent-child relationships.

In addition, we examined differences in the effect of support reciprocity in friendships on depression among three developmental periods: preadolescence (elementary school students), early adolescence (middle school students), and middle adolescence (high school students). Kusumi and Kano (1986), in a study of adolescents, found that concerns of reciprocity in friendships may become more important as students grow older. In this study, therefore, we predicted that support reciprocity in friendships would be strongly related to depression among high school students but not among elementary school and middle school students.

Furthermore, we examined whether the quality of parent-child relationships has an influence on the relation between support reciprocity in friendships and depression. Attachment theorists have argued that children's experiences with their parents form the basis for their internal working models of the self and others (Bowlby, 1969). Children with secure, caring attachments to their parents tend to develop working models of themselves as being valued and worthy, and of significant others as being reliable and trustworthy. In contrast, children with insecure, distant attachments to their parents tend to develop working models of themselves as being unlovable and incompetent, and of significant others as being unreliable and undependable. These working models have a significant impact on patterns of support receiving and support giving in later adult relationships (Main, Kaplan, and Cassidy, 1985). Simpson, Rholes, and Nelligan (1992) examined whether and how internal working models moderate support receiving and support giving in romantic couples. They found that secure persons were likely to receive more support from their partners when they felt distressed or anxious and to offer more support when they sensed their partners require it. This evidence indicates that support reciprocity may be more characteristic of secure persons' intimate relationships than insecure persons'. Based on this reasoning and the prediction mentioned above concerning differences in the effect of support reciprocity among three age groups, it is predicted that support reciprocity in friendships would be strongly associated with depression among high school students with secure, caring attachments to their parents but not among those who with insecure, distant attachments to their parents. Because parents' attitudes and behavior toward the children influence children's experiences with their parents (B.R. Sarason, Pierce, Bannerman, and I.G. Sarason, 1993), we compared the effect of support reciprocity on depression among high school students, according to ratings of their parents' child rearing attitudes.

In summary, we examined elementary school, middle school, and high school students to consider the relation between depression and support reciprocity in relationships with both parents and friends, taking specific account of the quality of parent-child relationships. Our hypotheses are as follows.

- Hypothesis 1: In a friendship, support reciprocity will correlate more strongly with lower depression than in a parent-child relationship.
- Hypothesis 2: Support reciprocity in a friendship will relate strongly to lower depression among high school students but not among elementary school and middle school students.
- Hypothesis 3: For high school students who perceived their parents as caring and affectionate, support reciprocity in a friendship will correlate strongly with lower depression but not for those who perceived their parents as distant and dismissive.

METHOD

Participants and Procedure

The participants were 340 first-year high school students (175 boys and 165 girls), 312 second- and third-year middle school students (182 boys and 130 girls), and 317 sixth-year elementary school students (165 boys and 152 girls). The average ages of the high school students, middle school students, and elementary school students were 16.0, 14.0, and 11.2 years, respectively. A questionnaire package was distributed by homeroom teachers during a long homeroom period or after school. Students completed the questionnaire package at their own pace.

Measures

Support Receiving in a Friendship

A six-item scale was used to assess support receiving in a friendship. The items on this scale were adapted from the Scale of Expectancy for Social Support for Middle School Students (Okayasu, Shimada, and Sakano, 1993) for measuring support receiving in elementary school, middle school, and high school students. Participants were asked to choose their best close friend and to complete the items on the basis of how often their friend had given support to them in the past several months. Answers could range from *never* (1) to *very often* (4). Sample items include "When you fail to do something, the person helps you," "When you are worried about something, the person advises you what to do," and "When you are depressed, the person notices right away that you are not in good condition and cheers you up."

Support Giving in a Friendship

We rewrote six items on the support receiving scale so that each of the items could imply support given to a friend and be used to assess the actual support given to a friend. Participants were asked to choose the same friend whom they chose in rating support receiving and to complete the items based on how often they had given support to their friend in the past several months. Answers could range from *never* (1) to *very often* (4). Sample items include "When your friend fails to do something, you help him," "When your friend is worried about something, you advise him what to do," and "When your friend is depressed, you notice right away that he is not in good condition and cheer him up."

Support Receiving in a Parent-child Relationship

This scale comprised the same six items as the support receiving in a friendship scale contained. Participants were asked to choose one of their parents, mother or father, and to complete the items on the basis of how often that parent had given support to them in the past several months. The participants who have neither of their parents were asked to choose a foster parent, for instance, their grandmother or grandfather.

Support Giving in a Parent-child Relationship

Six items were newly developed to assess the amount of support given to a parent. The items were generated on the basis of free-descriptions in a pilot study to tap the support children can give to a parent. Examples of the items are "You help your parent with the housework," "You give your parent a present on his or her birthday or a memorial day," and "You grant the request of your parent, for example, giving him or her a massage." Participants were asked to choose the same parent or foster parent whom they chose in rating support receiving and to complete the items based on how often they had given support to their parent or foster parent in the past several months. Answers could range from *never* (1) to *very often* (4).

Depression

Depression was assessed with Sakurai's (1989) 17-item Hopelessness Scale for Children. Hopelessness has been identified as the most important element of depression (Beck, 1972). Examples of the items are "I might as well give up, because I can't make things better for myself," "All I can see ahead of me are bad things, not good things," and "I don't think I will have any real fun when I grow up." Participants were asked to respond "yes" or "no" to each item on the basis of whether each item was true for themselves. The direction of responses for an answer indicating depression varied with items. When the answer indicated depression, a score of one was given. Scores were added up across items. The higher scores indicated higher depression. The coefficient alpha was .68 for high school students, .71 for middle school students, and .72 for elementary school students, all of which are higher than the coefficient alpha reported by Sakurai (1989).

Child Rearing Attitudes

Parents' child rearing attitudes among high school students were assessed with a shortened and translated Japanese version of the Care Subscale of the Parental Bonding Instrument (Parker, Tupling, and Brown, 1979). This subset of 10-items assessed the extent to which each parent was affectionate and sympathetic or distant and neglectful. Sample items include "Spoke to me with a warm and friendly voice," "Appeared to understand my problems and worries," and "Could make me feel better when I was upset." Participants were asked to respond to the items on the basis of the extent to which each item was true for attitudes and behavior that their mother (or foster parent in case of participants with no mother) had shown towards them. Answers could range from *not at all true* (1) to *very true* (4). Scores were summed up across items. The coefficient alpha was .83.

RESULTS

Support Receiving and Giving

Support in a Friendship

To examine the construct validity of support receiving and support giving in a friendship, a factor analysis with varimax rotation and a fixed number of two factors was carried out with all the support receiving and the support giving items. For high school students, all of the support receiving items loaded higher than .40 on the first factor and all of the support giving items loaded higher than .40 on the second factor. The factor solution supported the conceptual independence of the two variables completely. For middle school students, the result of a factor analysis was identical with that for high school students. For elementary school students, one item of the support receiving scale loaded higher on the giving factor than on the receiving factor and one item of the support giving scale loaded higher on the receiving factor than on the giving factor. Therefore, we omitted these two items and conducted another factor analysis. All the four items of the support receiving scale loaded on the receiving factor and all the four items of support giving scale loaded on the giving factor. In the following analyses, we used two factor scores extracted by the final factor analyses as the support receiving score and the support giving score, respectively.

Support in a Parent-child Relationship

A factor analysis was conducted with all the support receiving and support giving items in the same way that it was done with the friendship support items. For high school students, one of the support giving items loaded higher than .40 on both factors and we omitted it. For middle school students and elementary school students, one item on the support giving scale loaded higher on the receiving factor than on the giving factor. We accordingly left out this item. The results of the final factor analyses indicated the adequate conceptual independence of the two scales. In the following analyses, we used two factor scores extracted by the final factor analyses as the support receiving score and the support giving score, respectively.

Support Reciprocity and its Influence on Depression

Support Reciprocity in a Parent-child Relationship

To examine whether support reciprocity in a parent-child relationship has an influence on depression, hierarchical multiple regression analyses were conducted. In the analyses, as predictors of depression, support receiving was entered as the first step, support giving as the second step, and the interaction of support receiving and giving as the third step. The results of the regression analyses are shown in the upper portion of Table 1. For all students, the increment of R^2 induced by including the third interactional step was not significant. These results suggest that support reciprocity in a parent-child relationship has no effect on depression.

Table 1. Summary of Hierarchical Multiple Regression Predictions of Depression by Support Receiving and Support Giving among Elementary School, Middle School, and High School Students

Variable	Elementary		Middle		High	
	β	ΔR^2	β	ΔR^2	β	ΔR^2
			Parent			
Receiving (R)	-.322**	.104**	-.182**	.033**	-.154**	.024**
Giving (G)	-.220**	.049**	-.140*	.021**	-.127*	.016*
R × G	.001	.000	.040	.002	-.065	.004
			Friend			
Receiving (R)	-.172**	.030**	-.062	.005	-.107*	.012*
Giving (G)	-.246**	.059**	-.194**	.034**	-.199**	.029**
R × G	-.011	.000	-.036	.001	-.136*	.017*

*$p < .05$. **$p < .01$.

Support Reciprocity in a Friendship

To examine whether support reciprocity in a friendship has an influence on depression, hierarchical multiple regression analyses were carried out in the same way that they were done with support reciprocity in a parent-child relationship. The results of the regression analyses are shown in the lower portion of Table 1. Only for high school students was the increment of R^2 induced by including the third interactional step significant, $F(1, 336) = 6.24, p < .05$.

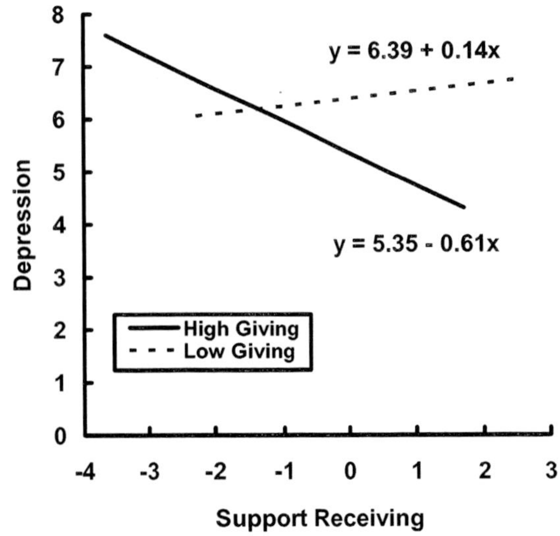

Figure 1. Relationship of support receiving in a friendship with depression at high and low levels of support giving among high school students.

To examine the interaction effect of support receiving and support giving, we divided high school students into two groups according to the average of the support giving score, that is, high support giving group and low support giving group, and conducted linear regression analyses with support receiving as the independent variable and depression as the dependent variable. The results are shown in Figure 1. In the high support giving group, support receiving correlated negatively and significantly with depression, $F\,(1,\ 171) = 11.99$, $p < .01$. This result suggests that high school students who gave to and received more support from their friend reported the lowest degrees of depression.

To investigate the effect of support reciprocity on depression more directly, first, we computed a support reciprocity score by subtracting the support giving score from the support receiving score. A score close to zero represents that support receiving and support giving are equal, a positive score represents that they receive more support than they give, and a negative score represents that they give more than they receive. Second, to test for a curvilinear relationship between support reciprocity and depression, we carried out a regression analysis with the squared value of support reciprocity as the independent variable and depression as the dependent variable. The result is shown in Figure 2. The regression was significant, $F\,(1,\ 338) = 3.98$, $p < .05$. This result indicates that depression was lowest when support receiving and support giving were equal.

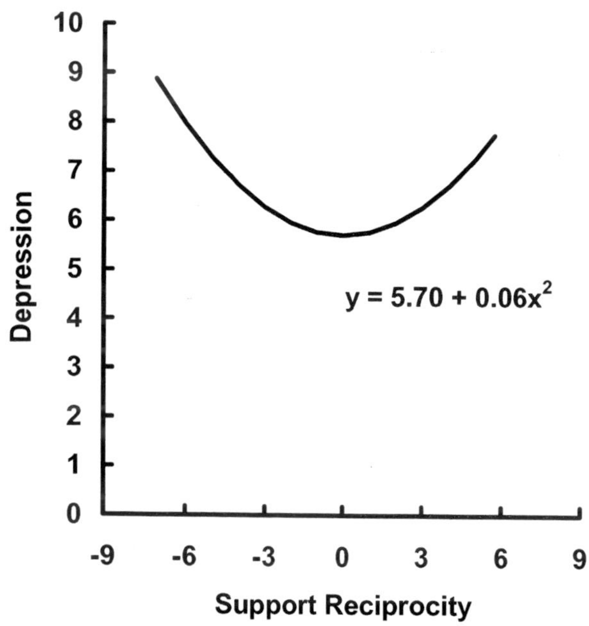

Figure 2. Relationship of support reciprocity in a friendship with depression among high school students.

These findings and the results from the examination of a parent-child friendship were in support of hypothesis 1: that in a friendship, support reciprocity will correlate more strongly with lower depression than in a parent-child relationship. Moreover, these findings supported hypothesis 2: that support reciprocity in a friendship will relate strongly to lower depression among high school students but not among elementary school and middle school students.

The Quality of a Parent-Child Relationship and Support Reciprocity among High School Students and its Influence on Depression

To examine whether the effect of support reciprocity among high school students on depression varies with the quality of a parent-child relationship, we divided high school students into two groups according to the average of the parental care score: high parental care group and low parental care group. In each group, hierarchical multiple regression analyses were conducted. In the analyses, as predictors of depression, support receiving was entered as the first step, support giving as the second step, and the interaction of support receiving and support giving as the third step. The results of the regression analyses are shown in Table 2. Only in the high parental care group was the increment of R^2 induced by including the third interactional step significant, $F\,(1, 165) = 3.90, p < .05$.

Table 2. Summary of Hierarchical Multiple Regression Predictions of Depression in High and Low Parental Care Groups among High School Students

Variable	Parental care			
	Low		High	
	β	ΔR^2	β	ΔR^2
Receiving (R)	-.079	.010	-.089	.003
Giving (G)	-.172	.010	-.202**	.049**
R × G	-.130	.012	-.150*	.022*

* $p < .05$. ** $p < .01$.

To examine the interaction effect, first, we divided the students in the high parental care group into two groups according to the average of support giving score: high support giving group and low support giving group. Second, we conducted linear regression analyses. Here, the support receiving was the independent variable and depression the dependent variable. The analyses showed that in the high support giving group, support receiving correlated negatively and marginally with depression, $F\,(1, 88) = 3.33, p < .10$. This result suggests that high school students who perceived their mother as caring and affectionate reported the lowest degree of depression when they gave and received more support with their friend.

Next, for the students in the high parental care group, we carried out a regression analysis with the squared value of support reciprocity as the independent variable and depression as the dependent variable. The regression was marginally significant, $F\,(1, 167) = 3.21, p < .10$. This result indicates that high school students who perceived their mother as caring and affectionate expressed the lowest degree of depression when support receiving and support giving were equal.

These findings almost supported hypothesis 3: for high school students who perceived their parents as caring and affectionate, support reciprocity in a friendship will correlate strongly with lower depression but not for those who perceived their parents as distant and dismissive.

DISCUSSION

Consistent with hypothesis 1, in a friendship, support reciprocity correlated more strongly with lower depression than in a parent-child relationship. Because solidarity-oriented groups such as friendships have the tendency to use the principle of equality, caring-oriented groups such as parent-child relationships to use the principle of need as the basic value underlying the system of distributive justice (Deutsch, 1975), support reciprocity with friends rather than with parents would be strongly related to lower depression. Our results agree with Antonucci and Jackson's (1990) suggestion that in more longitudinal relationships such as parent-child relationships, support giving and receiving can be considered as long-term support deposits or debts. Thus, in parent-child relationships, long term reciprocity rather than current reciprocity may have a strong connection with lower depression.

Hypothesis 2 proposed that support reciprocity in a friendship would relate strongly to lower depression among high school students but not among elementary school and middle school students. The results of this study were in support of this hypothesis. As students grow older, they have more intimate friendships with just a few friends (Ochiai and Satoh, 1996) and regard reciprocal friendships as more important (Kusumi and Kano, 1986). Therefore, support reciprocity in a single intimate relationship would have stronger influence on depression among older students than younger students. Our results also showed that for all students more support giving correlated significantly with lower depression. The results of support giving are consistent with Hachiya (1990) who found that the more support giving was associated with lower loneliness. Feelings of indebtedness or obligation to restore reciprocity by repaying support may follow support receiving (Barrera, 1986). It seems that support giving decreases depression or increases self-esteem through mitigating such feelings.

According to hypothesis 3, for high school students who perceived their parents as caring and affectionate, support reciprocity in a friendship correlated strongly with lower depression but not for those who perceived their parents as distant and dismissive. Because secure attachment working models promote support exchange in intimate relationships (Simpson et al., 1992), support reciprocity seems to be more characteristic of secure persons' friendships than insecure persons'. Accordingly, support reciprocity would be associated more strongly with lower depression among secure students than insecure students. The results of our study also provided additional evidence that only among students with secure attachments to their parents did more support giving relate to lower depression. The quality of parents' attachment with their children has a significant influence on the children's expectations and mobilization of available support from others (Larose and Boivin, 1997; Ura, 1997). Thus, securely attached persons are likely to receive more support from others. For secure persons, therefore, more support giving may lead to recovery of reciprocity, which, in turn, lessens depression.

A limitation of this study is that the cross-sectional design of the study prevents us from determining the causal direction of the association between support reciprocity and depression. It may be that depression status has an effect on support reciprocity. Future studies should use respondents' current feelings of loneliness and/or satisfaction with their social relationships, instead of depression, as indicators of mental health. States of loneliness and satisfaction are probably affected by current interpersonal contexts and it seems reasonable to assume that support reciprocity influences these individual states. Future work also should examine whether the effect of support reciprocity on depression changes as the duration of relationships increases. The effect of equity or equality of social exchange on emotional states and commitment in friendships has been shown to vary with the length of relationships or intimacy stage (Moroi, 1989; Nakamura, 1990).

AUTHOR NOTE

Hirokazu Taniguchi, Graduate School of Biosphere Sciences, Hiroshima University; Mitsuhiro Ura, Faculty of Integrated Arts and Science, Hiroshima University.

Hirokazu Taniguchi is now at Faculty of Education, Okayama University.

Parts of the previous version of this study were presented at the 44th Annual Conference of the Japanese Group Dynamics Association and at the 38th Annual Conference of the Japanese Association of Educational Psychology. The original version of this article was published in *Japanese Psychological Research*, 2002, *44*, 247-253.

REFERENCES

Acitelli, L. K., and Antonucci, T. C. (1994). Gender differences in the link between marital support and satisfaction in older couples. *Journal of Personality and Social Psychology*, *67*, 688-698.

Antonucci, T. C., Fuhrer, R., and Jackson, J. S. (1990). Social support and reciprocity: A cross-ethnic and cross-national perspective. *Journal of Social and Personal Relationships*, *7*, 519-530.

Antonucci, T. C., and Jackson, J. S. (1990). The role of reciprocity in social support. In B. R. Sarason, I. G. Sarason, and G. R. Pierce (Eds.), *Social support: An interaction view* (pp. 173-198). New York: John Wiley and Sons.

Barrera, M., Jr. (1986). Distinctions between social support concepts, measures, and models. *American Journal of Community Psychology*, *14*, 413-445.

Beck, A. T. (1972). *Depression: Causes and treatment.* Philadelphia: University of Pennsylvania Press.

Bowlby, J. (1969). *Attachment and loss. Vol. 1. Attachment.* New York: Basic Books.

Buunk, B. P., Doosje, B. J., Jans, L. G. J. M, and Hopstaken, L. E. M. (1993). Perceived reciprocity, social support, and stress at work: The role of exchange and communal orientation. *Journal of Personality and Social Psychology*, *65*, 801-811.

Deutsch, M. (1975). Equity, equality, and need: What determines which value will be used as the basis of distributive justice? *Journal of Social Issues*, *31*, 137-149.

Hachiya, Y. (1990). Sosyaru sapoto to tekio [Social support and adjustment]. *Proceedings of the Japanese Society of Social Psychology the 31st Annual Conference*, 54-55.

Ingersoll-Dayton, B., and Antonucci, T. C. (1988). Reciprocal and nonreciprocal social support: Contrasting sides of intimate relationships. *Journal of Gerontology*, *43*, S65-73.

Jones, D. C., and Vaughan, K. (1990). Close friendships among senior adults. *Psychology and Aging*, *5*, 451-457.

Jung, J. (1990). The role of reciprocity in social support. *Basic and Applied Social Psychology, 11*, 243-253.

Kusumi, S., and Kano, S. (1986). Seinenki ni okeru yujingainen hattatu no inshibunseki teki kenkyu [Developmental change in adolescent conceptions of friendship]. *Research Bulletin of Educational Psychology, the Faculty of Education, Kyushu University, 31*, 97-104.

Larose, S., and Boivin, M. (1997). Structural relations among attachment working models of parents, general and specific support expectations, and personal adjustment in late adolescence. *Journal of Social and Personal Relationships, 14*, 579-601.

Levitt, M. J., Guacci, M., and Weber, R. A. (1992). Intergenerational support, relationship quality, and well-being: A bicultural analysis. *Journal of Family Issues, 13*, 465-481.

Main, M., Kaplan, N., and Cassidy, J. (1985). Security in infancy, childhood, and adulthood: A move to the level of representation. *Monographs of the Society for Research in child Development, 50*, 66-104.

Moroi, K. (1989). Taijinkankei heno kouheiriron no tekiyou (2): Dousei sinyu tono kankei ni okeru kouheisei to jyoudou teki jyoutai [An application of equity theory to interpersonal relations (2): Equity and emotional states in close relationships with same-sex friends]. *Japanese Journal of Experimental Social Psychology, 28*, 131-141.

Nagata, Y. (1987). Syudan to kojin [Group and individual]. In K. Sasaki, and Y. Nagata (Eds.), Syudan kodo no shinrigaku (pp. 138-168). Tokyo: Yuhikaku.

Nakamura, M. (1990). Daigakusei no yujinkankei no hattenkatei ni kansuru kenkyu: Kankei kanyosei wo yosoku suru syakaiteki kokan moderu no hikaku kento [A study on the developmental process of friendship in college students: A comparative examination of social exchange models predicting relationship commitment]. *Japanese Journal of Social Psychology, 5*, 29-41.

Ochiai, Y., and Satoh, Y. (1996). Seinenki ni okeru tomodati tono tukiaikata no hattatuteki henka [The developmental change of friendship in adolescence]. *Japanese Journal of Educational Psychology, 44*, 55-65.

Okayasu, T., Shimada, H., and Sakano, Y. (1993). Tyugakusei ni okeru sosyaru sapoto no gakko sutoresu keigen koka [Alleviation effects of social support on school stress in junior high school students]. *Japanese Journal of Educational Psychology, 41*, 302-312.

Parker, G., Tupling, H., and Brown, L. B. (1979). A parental bonding instrument. *British Journal of Medical Psychology, 52*, 1-10.

Rook, K. S. (1987). Reciprocity of social exchange and social satisfaction among older women. *Journal of Personality and Social Psychology, 52*, 145-154.

Sakurai, S. (1989). Jido no zetubokan to geninkizoku tono kankei [A study of relation between hopelessness and causal attribution in school-aged children]. *Japanese Journal of Psychology, 60*, 304-311.

Sarason, B. R., Pierce, G. R., Bannerman, A., and Sarason, I. G. (1993). Investigating the antecedents of perceived social support: Parents' views of and behavior toward their children. *Journal of Personality and Social Psychology, 65*, 1071-1085.

Shaver, P., and Buhrmester, D. (1983). Loneliness, sex-role orientation and group life: A social needs perspective. In P. B. Paulus (Ed.), *Basic group process* (pp. 259-288). New York: Springer-Verlag.

Simpson, J. A., Rholes, W. S., and Nelligan, J. S. (1992). Support seeking and support giving within couples in an anxiety-provoking situation: The role of attachment styles. *Journal of Personality and Social Psychology, 62*, 434-446.

van Tilburg, T. (1992). Support networks before and after retirement. *Journal of Social and Personal Relationships, 9*, 433-445.

Ura, M. (1997). Shigoto to katei no intafeisu no kento: Taijin kankei no dogusei to jyotyosei no baransu ni tyakumoku site [An examination of work-family interface: Focusing on the balance of instrumentality and emotionality of interpersonal relationships]. *The report of the research supported by a Grant-in-Aid for Scientific research, Ministry of Education, Science and Culture, No. 07610130.*

In: Trends in Depression Research
Editor: Maurice J. Henri, pp. 125-143

ISBN 1-60021-394-4

Chapter 7

POSTPARTUM DEPRESSION: LATIN-AMERICAN PERSPECTIVES

Johann Vega-Dienstmaier
Professor of Psychiatry, Universidad Peruana Cayetano Heredia, Lima, Peru
Maria I. Zapata-Vega
Assistant Professor of Psychiatry, Mount Sinai School of Medicine, New York, USA

ABSTRACT

In the past two decades there has been increasing recognition that mood disorders, particularly depression, are a significant cause of pregnancy-related morbidity. Latin-American researchers have been actively contributing to the field of perinatal psychiatry.

This article presents a review of the scientific literature on postpartum depression, available in MEDLINE and LILACS/BIREME databases, developed in Latin-American countries including studies conducted mostly in Brazil, Peru, and Chile. Furthermore, due to the known vast migration of Latin-American individuals into developed countries, selected studies on postpartum depression in women of Latino heritage in the United States of America were also reviewed.

Significant efforts involving the adaptation and validation of widely used instruments for the assessment of postpartum depression in Spanish and Portuguese language, such as the Edinburgh Postnatal Depression Scale, have been reported.

Estimates of the prevalence of depression in puerperal women varied from 5.92% and 48% in different clinical settings. The time at which the maternal assessments were conducted ranged from as early as one day to after up to one year postpartum.

Demographic characteristics, availability of social and financial resources, affective support from partners and family, history of depression and/or other psychiatric symptomatology, other pregnancy-related pathologies, premature births, and neonatal illness, among others, have been consistently identified as associated risk factors for the development of postpartum depression in different studies throughout Latin America. Similar findings, in addition to migration and acculturation factors, may play a roll in the development of depression in Latino women in the USA.

The impact of perinatal depression in the wellbeing of mothers and their children, and perinatal and pediatric care and beneficial interventions for risk groups such as premature children were addressed in other contributions.

The need for appropriate assessment, diagnosis, and treatment of postpartum depression, and the development of preventive strategies and specific services are discussed.

INTRODUCTION

Since the times of Hippocrates (4th Century BC), it was known that there was some association between childbirth and mental disorders (Miller, 1999). In most recent times, there has been growing evidence that mood disorders, particularly depression, are a significant cause of pregnancy-related morbidity.

Disorders in the postpartum state may involve the recurrence of preexisting mental conditions or the onset of a new disorder; the severity may range from the most benign syndromes such as the "postpartum blues" or "baby blues" to other potentially lethal conditions like postpartum psychosis (Wyszynski and Lusskin, 2005).

Research on postpartum disorders have been conducted mostly in industrialized countries and presented in the scientific literature in English language. Nevertheless, researchers in other geographical areas have made significant contributions to the field.

This article is intended to review the studies on postpartum depression (PPD) developed in Latin America and published in the international medical literature. In addition, due to the growing number of women of Hispanic/Latino origin in developed countries like the USA (US Census, 2000), studies conducted on this particular population were also reviewed.

METHODOLOGY

The authors conducted a literature search in the LILACS/BIREME and Medline databases searching for all original articles published until March 2006. Inclusion criteria were as followed: only original papers with an abstract, conducted in any Latin-American country or involving Latino women in the USA, and addressing "postpartum", "postnatal", "perinatal", or "maternal" depression, as well as, early mother-child interactions.

The first search was conducted in LILACS using the keywords: "depression" and "postpartum" or "puerperium". A second search was conducted in Medline using the following keywords: "postpartum depression" and "Latinos/Hispanics", "Latin-America", "Spanish", "Portuguese", names of the eighteen Spanish-speaking Latin-American countries and "Brazil".

SEARCH RESULTS

The search through the LILACS/BIREME database yielded 22 original articles in Spanish or Portuguese languages. The second search in Medline resulted in a total of 23 papers, meeting the above criteria and documenting studies on PPD conducted in Latin-American countries (n= 11, five of these articles were already included in the LILACS search results) or on Latino women in the USA (n= 12). Full articles were retrieved through the Latin American and Caribbean Center on Health Sciences Information.

Articles were classified into four areas: validation of instruments for the assessment of PPD, epidemiology of the disorder, risk factors, and impact on mother-child interaction.

Instruments for the Assessment of PPD

The DSM-IV-TR adds the specifier "postpartum onset" to diagnosis of Major Depressive Disorder, whenever the depressive episode occurs within 4 weeks after childbirth, it is not considered as a separate class of affective disorder. However, most studies do not use standardized criteria and more frequently diagnose the presence of depression based on positive scores using depression assessment instruments. In Latin America significant efforts have been made to adapt and validate widely used instruments for, specifically, the assessment of postpartum depression in Spanish and Portuguese languages.

Most studies involved the validation of the Spanish version of the Edinburgh Postnatal Depression Scale (EPDS), originally developed in England (Cox et al., 1987), specifically reported in Peru (Vega-Dienstmaier et al, 2002) and Chile (Jadresic et al., 1995; Alvarado et al., 1992b); and its Portuguese version, was studied in Brazil (Santos et al, 1999). A summary of the main psychometric findings for each study are showed in Table 1, and in addition, we calculated the number-needed-to-diagnose (NND) based on the sensitivity and specificity reported by the investigators for the best cut-off points (Bandolier, 1996).

Brazil

The Portuguese version of the EPDS was studied in the city of Brasilia (Santos et al., 1999), where a sample of 236 women, and a sub-sample of 63 subjects for additional statistical analysis, were assessed during the 6 to 24 weeks after childbirth. The cut-off score found to have the lowest NND (1.52) was 10.5, with a sensitivity of 84% and specificity of 82%.

Chile

Two studies validating the EPDS were conducted in Chile by different research teams (Alvarado et al, 1992b; Jadresic et al, 1995). Both studies in this country suggests 9.5 as the best cut-off score for detection of depression, having a NND of 1.51 (sensitivity = 85.71% and specificity = 80.41) in the first one and of 1.25 (sensitivity = 100% and specificity = 80) in the second one.

Table 1. Validation studies of assessment instruments for PPD: psychometrics properties and best cut-off scores

Country (City) Author/Year	Scale	Language	Sample size	Time frame (after childbirth)	Cronbach's alpha	Diagnostic reference	Cut-off point	Sensibility	Specificity	NND
Brazil (Brasilia) Santos et al, 1999	EPDS	Portuguese	N= 236 (and sub-sample of N= 69)	6 - 24 weeks	0.8	Major/minor depression- RDC	10.5	84	82	1.52
Chile (Santiago and and Codegua) Alvarado et al, 1992b	EPDS	panish	28 depressed and 97 non-depressed	8 weeks	0.844	Depressive Episode - DSM-III-R	9.5 12.5 13.5	85.71 71.43 67.86	80.41 94.85 95.88	1.51 1.51 1.57
Chile (Santiago and Codegua) Alvarado et al, 1993b	BDI	Spanish	28 depressed and 97 non-depressed	8 weeks	0.848	Depressive Episode - DSM-III-R	13.5	85.71	96.91	1.21
Chile (Santiago) Jadresic et al, 1995	EPDS	Spanish	N=108 (11 depressed)	2-3 months	0.77	Major/minor depression - RDC / PAS	9.5	100	80	1.25
Peru (Lima) Vega-Dienstmaier et al, 2002	EPDS	Spanish	19 depressed and 302 non-depressed	1st year	0.7043	Major Depression- SCID / DSM-IV	7.5 13.5	100.00 84.21	25.50 79.47	3.92 1.57
USA Beck and Gable, 2003	PDSS	Spanish	N=377	12 weeks	0.95	-	-	-	-	-
USA Beck and Gable, 2005	PDSS	Spanish	N=150	2-12 weeks	0.95	Major/minor depression - SCID / DSM-IV	60	84	84	1.47
	PDSS 7-Item				0.79		13	84	80	1.56

EPDS = Edinburgh Postnatal Depression Scale
PDSS = Postpartum Depression Screening Scale
BDI = Beck Depression Inventory
PAS = Psychiatric Assessment Schedule
RDC = Research Diagnostic Criteria
SCID = Structured Clinical Interview for DSM-IV
NND = Number-needed-to-diagnose, NND = 1 / [Sensitivity - (1 - Specificity)]

Another scale, the Beck Depression Inventory (BDI), was also validated in Chile for its use in the screening of pregnancy and postpartum depression (Alvarado et al, 1993b). A cut-off point of 13.5 for this scale had the lowest NND of all instruments reviewed here for the diagnosis of PPD (NND=1.21,sensitivity=85.71% and specificity= 96.91%).

This finding does not support the idea that for the assessment of PPD is necessary to use specific instruments for puerperium like EPDS.

Peru

The study of the EPDS in Peru, included women evaluated within the first year after childbirth and found, for a total score of 13.5, a sensitivity of 84.21% and a specificity of 79.47%. It was also reported that the items assessing nervousness/worries, ability to cope, crying spells and panic feelings, were those that contributed the most to the predictive ability of the instrument. This finding may suggest that anxiety is a predominant aspect in the evaluation of postpartum depression (Vega-Dienstmaier et al, 2002). A higher cut-off point in this study may be related to the fact that only women diagnosed with major depression were included as cases, whereas other validation studies included also subjects with minor depression.

Spanish-Speaking Women in the USA

In the USA, the Postpartum Depression Screening Scale (PDSS), the original 35-item version and a 7-item Short Form, were translated into Spanish (Beck et al., 2003) and its psychometric properties were found to be "slightly lower, but still in the acceptable range" when compared to the measurements of the original English version (Beck and Gable, 2003 and 2005).

Epidemiology of Postpartum Depression in Latin America

International studies on postpartum depression estimate its prevalence between 10 and 15% (Beck, 2001; O'Hara and Swain, 1996); however, studies around the world have shown a great heterogeneity of results. Symptoms, complaints, and syndromes may vary across cultures; therefore, cross-cultural considerations have to be taken when attempting to determine the epidemiology of this disorder (Halbreich and Karkun, 2006).

An additional challenge for clinicians and researchers seems the discrimination between the diagnosis of "postpartum depression" versus more benign and transient conditions such as "postpartum blues" or "postpartum dysphoria" presented in the very firsts days after childbirth.

Studies reporting prevalence of depressive symptoms in Latin America and in Hispanic women in the USA are shown in Table 2. Estimates on the prevalence of depressive symptoms in Latin-American countries, without making a distinction between "blues" and postpartum depression, ranged between 5.92% and 48%. Almost all reports described the use of the EPDS or other instruments for the diagnosis of depression, and the authors cited, in the majority of cases, previous adaptation and validation of the instrument in their targeted population. The assessment of depressive symptoms was, in most cases, conducted only once and sometimes in the early puerperium; therefore, symptoms may represent postpartum dysphoria or "blues". Study subjects were recruited not only in specialized obstetric settings, but also in primary care clinics and during pediatric visits.

Table 2. Prevalence of postpartum depressive symptoms in Latin-American women and Hispanic women in the USA

Country (City) Author, Year	Sample size	Evaluation setting	Time frame (after childbirth)	Diagnostic Instrument or Criteria	Prevalence of depressive symptoms
Brazil (São Paulo) Coutinho et al, 2002	N = 73	Health Center, Pediatric visit	3 - 6 months	EPDS ≥ 13	32.9%
Brazil (Rio de Janeiro) Da-Silva et al , 1998	N = 33	Home visits	Monthly, for 6 months	EPDS ≥ 13	42.8%
Brazil (São Paulo) Faisal-Cury et al, 2004	N = 113	Obstetrics clinic	10th day	BDI ≥ 15	15.9%
				Pitt's Blues Scale > 20 Stein's Blues Scale >8	30.1% 32.7%
Brazil (Ribeirão Preto) Luis and Oliveira, 1998	N = 135	Psychiatric Emergency and Obstetrics clinic	Not specified	ICD-9 Criteria for (648.4) "Mental Disorders in Pregnancy, Childbirth and Puerperium" (Chart review)	8.1%, of all 648.4-ICD-9 *
Brazil (Pelotas) Moraes et al, 2006	N = 410	Home visits	30 - 45 days	HAM-D ≥ 18	19.1%
Brazil (Brasilia) Moreno et al, 2004	N = 123	Pediatric clinic	8 -12 weeks	EPDS ≥ 12	22.2%
Brazil (Pelotas) Pinheiro et al, 2006	N = 386 couples	Home visits	6 - 12 weeks	BDI ≥10 BDI > 18	23.6% (Mothers) 11.9% (Fathers) 7.8% (mothers) 4.1% (fathers)
Brazil (Porto Alegre) Rohde et al, 1997	N = 86 (postpartum) vs. N = 75 (hospital workers, women 'out of puerperium')	Maternity ward and home visits	Daily, for 8 days	Blues Questionnaire	Symptomatic peak at 5th day postpartum. No specific prevalence was reported.
Chile Alvarado et al, 1992a and 2000	N = 125	Three Primary Care Centers	2nd and 8th weeks	Psychiatric interview (based on DSM-III-R criteria)	20.5-22.4%

Table 2. Prevalence of postpartum depressive symptoms in Latin-American women and Hispanic women in the USA (Continued)

Country (City) Author, Year	Sample size	Evaluation setting	Time frame (after childbirth)	Diagnostic Instrument or Criteria	Prevalence of depressive symptoms
Chile (Antofagasta) Evans et al, 2003	N = 106	Obstetrics clinic	5 - 6 months	ICD-10 criteria (5 or more, for at least 2 weeks)	32.07%
Chile (Santiago) Hasbun et al, 1999	N = 103	Two hospitals	3rd day (n= 103) and 12th week (n=43, completed 2nd evaluation)	HAM-D >10	6.8% (3rd day) 27.9% (12th week)
				EPDS ≥ 10	27.2% (3rd day) 48% (12th week)
Chile (Santiago) Jadresic et al, 1992a	N = 108	University diagnostic center, Home visits, and Pediatric visits	2 - 3 months	Major / minor depression - RDC	10.2%
Chile (Santiago) Jadresic and Araya, 1995	N = 542	Five Health Centers, Pediatric visits and Home visits	2 - 3 months	EPDS ≥ 10	36.7%
Costa Rica (Hatillo and Desamparados) Wolf et al, 2002	N = 151 (Hatillo)	Home visits, Pediatric visits	5 years	"Postpartum dysphoria" (interview)	38.0%
	N = 80 (Desamparados)		12 - 23 months **		35.0%
Peru (Cuzco) Betalleluz and Quiroz, 1997	N = 360	Obstetrics clinic	1st, 4th, and 8th days	"postpartum sadness syndrome" based on items of BDI and ZSRAS	34.44%
Peru (Lima) Vega-Dienstmaier et al, 1999	N=321	Family Planning and Pediatric Services	Within 1st year postpartum	Major depression SCID / DSM-IV	5.92%
USA (San Mateo County) Chaudron et al, 2005	N = 218	Telephone surveys, participants of outreach program	6 - 18 months	EPDS ≥ 10	23%
USA (Tucson) Freeman et al, 2005	N = 96 (53.2% of Hispanic ethnicity)	Pediatric visits	30 - 103 days	EPDS ≥ 12	14.6% of he total sample (no specific data for Hispanic women was reported)

* 648.4-ICD-9: Mental disorders in pregnancy, childbirth and puerperium

** Unclear information.

HAM-D = Hamilton Scale for Depression

BDI = Beck Depression Inventory

EPDS = Edinburgh Postnatal Depression Scale

SCID = Structured Clinical Interview for DSM-IV

ZSRAS= Zung Self-Rating Anxiety Scale

Brazil

Eight studies conducted in Brazil and reporting data on postpartum depressive symptomatology were found. One of these studies, specifically, used "postpartum blues" scales but no reference to previous validation of the scales in the population was cited; the prevalence of depression, as measured by the "blues" scales, varied within 30.1% - 32.7% by the 10th day (Faisal-Cury et al., 2004). Additionally, Rohde et al., used the Blues Questionnaire (Kennerley and Gath, 1989) to assessed postpartum women (n=86) on a daily basis during the first 8 days and compared them with a sample of 'out of postpartum' female hospital workers (n=75); the symptom peak was found at the 5th day, however no specific prevalence was reported (Rohde et al., 1997).

The EPDS was used in three studies, using cut-off points above 12 or 13 (Moreno et al., 2004; Coutinho et al., 2002; Da Silva et al., 1998). One study assessed the subjects on six monthly home visits and found a rate of 42.8% (Da Silva et al., 1998), however this study enrolled only a small sample (N=33) of puerperal women. Two larger studies using the EPDS found prevalence of 22.2 % and 32.9%, recruiting, in both cases, women bringing their children for pediatric visits. They, respectively, assessed 123 women between 8 and12 weeks after childbirth (Moreno et al., 2004), and 73 women between 3 and 6 months postpartum (Coutinho et al., 2002).

Two other studies were conducted in the city of Pelotas. One study used the HAM-D on 410 women interviewed 1-1.5 months after childbirth; it found occurrence of depression in 19.1% of cases (Moraes et al, 2006). The other study, evaluated the presence of depressive symptoms not only in the mother but also in the child's father (N = 386 couples). In this case, the BDI was used during home visits at 6 to 12 weeks after childbirth, and found a prevalence of 23.6% of maternal depression and 11.9% of paternal depression with a cut-off score of 10 or higher. The presence of paternal depression was higher among men whose wives had moderate or severe depression (Pinheiro et al., 2006).

An additional report documented the review of 135 cases that met ICD-9 criteria for "Mental Disorders in Pregnancy, Childbirth, and Puerperium" evaluated in the psychiatric emergency and obstetrics clinic in the city of Ribeirão Preto. Results were not specified for each perinatal phase, but it found that 8.1% of the cases with the above broad diagnosis presented with depressive symptoms, the majority related to suicide attempts. Since it seemed that these evaluations necessitated some level of emergency care, it could be anticipated that other serious disorders (e.g. psychosis) accounted for a considerable percentage of cases (Luis and Oliveira, 1998).

Chile

Five studies in Chile containing epidemiological data were identified. Clinical psychiatric interviews were conducted in two studies to appraise standardized diagnostic criteria. Evans et al (2003) reported a 32.07% of depression in 106 women interviewed 5 to 6 months after childbirth based on ICD-10 criteria. Other authors reported a prevalence of depression of 20.5-22.4% in 125 women interviewed between their 2nd and 8th week postpartum using DSM-III-R criteria (Alvarado et al., 1992a; and 2000).

Hasbun et al (1999) used two scales, HAM-D and EPDS, in 103 women assessed at the 3rd day postpartum and followed 43 of them to complete a second evaluation by the 12th week. At the 3rd day, the prevalence of depression ranged between 6.8% and 27.2%, and it increased by the 12th week to a range between 27.9% and 48%. The latest was the highest prevalence of PPD found in the studies reviewed for this report.

Two studies conducted by Jadresic and collaborators in 1995 and earlier in 1992, recruited women at 2-3 months postpartum. One study used the EPDS (n=542) and found a prevalence of 36.7% (Jadresic and Araya, 1995). Whereas, the earlier study, reported a prevalence of 10.2% using the CSD-20 by Florenzano et al. (1984) followed by a semi-structured psychiatric interview, the PAS, on a smaller sample (n=108) (Jadresic et al, 1992a).

Costa Rica

Wolf et al (2002) studied two samples of mothers of infants included in a research on iron deficiency anemia and infant behavior. At 12-23 months in one sample or 5 years in the other, Costa Rican mothers were interviewed about recollection of episodes of depressed mood following childbirth; however this later interview did not distinguish between "baby blues" and more serious postpartum mood disorders. Dysphoric mood following delivery of a child was documented in 35%-38% of the mothers included in the two Costa Rican samples.

Peru

Postpartum "blues" were studied in 360 puerperal women in the city of Cuzco. Women were assessed for "postpartum sadness syndrome" using items from the BDI and the Zung Self-Rating Anxiety Scale; the diagnosis was based on five established criteria: depressed mood, crying spells, sleep disturbance, anxiety, and mood changes/irritability/decreased attention span/forgetfulness. Women were recruited in the maternity wards of three local hospitals and interviewed in their first, fourth, and eighth days after childbirth. It was found that 34.44% of the women developed the syndrome with a symptomatic peak in the third day (Betalleluz and Quiroz, 1997).

Vega-Dienstmaier et al (1999) studied a total of 425 women divided into 3 samples: nulliparous (n=41), up to one year postpartum (n=321), and over one year after childbirth (n=63). The assessment included the SCID for current and past major depressive episodes, and other psychiatric disorders. The study found that 5.92% of women presented major depression in their first puerperal year, and in women, whose children were born over a year before the assessment, the prevalence of major depression was 14.29%, this difference was statistically significant.

Hispanic Women in the USA

Two recent studies on Hispanic women in the USA were found, both using the EPDS. One study involved 218 women in San Mateo County, California, who were participants of a countywide initiative to improve comprehensive outreach services to pregnant women and those with children aged 4 and under. Women with children ages 6-18 months, most of them immigrants, were included. Data was collected through telephone surveys using the EPDS. A 23% of women scored positively to the EPDS (Chaudron et al., 2005). The other study, conducted in Tucson, Arizona, does not present specific data on Latinas, but was considered in this review because the sample of 96 women was composed of over 50% of Hispanics; 14.6% of the total sample scored positively to the EPDS (Freeman et al., 2005).

Risk Factors Associated to PPD

Risks factors found in association to DPP in Latin American studies are shown in Table 3. The variables described here include: life events (stressors), socioeconomic status, demographic characteristics (e.g. age, ethnicity), educational level, social and family support, relationship with partner, expectations about the pregnancy, number of previous pregnancies, and mental and general medical problems.

Table 3: Risk Factors for the Development of Postpartum Depression

Country Author, Year	Criteria or scale used for the diagnosis of depression	Variables associated to Postpartum Depression	Significance of the association
Brazil Coutinho et al, 2002	EPDS	Dysphoria during current or after previous pregnancies	P=0.033
		Mother had a diagnosis of depression in her lifetime	P=0.005
		Poor social support from mother's family	$P<0.05$
Brazil Da-Silva et al, 1998	EPDS (Score $\geq$ 13)	Ethnicity (Black)	$P<0.05$
		Fewer previous pregnancies	$P<0.05$
Brazil Eizirik, 1984	6 cards of the TAT by Welch et al. (1961)	Premature child	$P<0.05$
		Newborn with some life risk	$P<0.05$
Brazil Faisal-Curry et al, 2002	BDI (Score >15)	Lower educational level	P=0.004
		Having 3 or more children	P=0.004
		Not been a primiparous	P=0.008
		Having previous pregnancies	P=0.015
		6 or more years of marital life	P=0.036
		Ethnicity (White)	P=0.02
Brazil Moraes et al, 2006	HAM-D (Score $\geq$ 18)	Low family income	P=0.005
		Low social class	P=0.025
		Poor maternal education	P=0.003
		Young maternal age	P=0.005
		Marital status: Single, separated or widow	P=0.012
		Poor prenatal care (low number of visits)	P=0.016
		Lack of support from child's father	P=0.030
		Thought of terminating pregnancy	P=0.005
		Tried to terminate pregnancy	P=0.031
		Preference for a child of male gender	$P<0.001$

Table 3: Risk Factors for the Development of Postpartum Depression (Continued)

Country Author, Year	Criteria or scale used for the diagnosis of depression	Variables associated to Postpartum Depression	Significance of the association
Brazil Pinheiro et al, 2006	BDI	Paternal depression	P<0.001
Chile Alvarado et al, 1992a	DSM-III-R	Age extremes (< 19 or > 34 year-old)	P=0.021
		Depression during 3rd trimester	P<0.001
		Negative attitude towards pregnancy	P=0.011
		Unsatisfactory relation with partner before childbirth	P=0.018
		Unsatisfactory relation with partner after childbirth	P<0.001
Chile Alvarado et al, 1993a	DSM-III-R	Urinary tract infection during pregnancy	P=0.039
		Stopping breast-feeding	P=0.015
Chile Alvarado et al, 1994	DSM-III-R	Having an abortion immediately before the pregnancy	P=0.048
		Life events	P<0.001
Chile Evans et al, 2003	ICD-10	Some illness during pregnancy	Statist. Signif.*
		Child required hospitalization as a newborn or while breast-fed	Statist. Signif.*
		History of previous depression	Statist. Signif.*
Chile Hasbun et al, 1999	EPDS HAM-D	Unexpected pregnancy	P=0.0041
		Having 3 or more children	P=0.034
		Absence of the child's father	P=0.003
		Vaginal delivery	P=0.009
		Conflicts with the child's father	P=0.0068
		Being a single mother	P=0.023
Chile Jadresic et al, 1992b	RDC	Life events in general	P<0.001
		Child with low-weight or small-size at birth	P<0.001
		Previously seen by a specialist due to emotional problems	P<0.01
		Being separated from family or close friend	P<0.01
		Severe economic problems	P<0.01
		Marital conflict	P<0.025
		Difficulties with breast-feeding	P<0.025
		Anxiety or depressive symptoms during pregnancy	P<0.025
		Development of varicose veins	P<0.025
		Having serious conflicts with her own mother	P<0.05
		Close person became seriously ill	P<0.05
		Having several urinary tract infections	P<0.05

Table 3: Risk Factors for the Development of Postpartum Depression (Continued)

Country Author, Year	Criteria or scale used for the diagnosis of depression	Variables associated to Postpartum Depression	Significance of the association
Chile Jadresic and Araya, 1995	EPDS	Familiar income (low)	P<0.01
		Single/widow (vs. Married / living together)	P=0.01
Costa Rica Wolf et al, 2001	"Postpartum dysphoria"	Higher educational level	P=0.04
		Less crowded household	P=0.02
Peru Betalleluz and Quiroz, 1997	"Postpartum dysphoric syndrome"	Insufficient prenatal care	P=0.009
		Non-complex occupation	P<0.05
		Worries about financial expenses	P<0.05
		Partner's absence	P<0.05
		Limited presence of the partner at home	P<0.05
		Poor support from the partner	P<0.05
		Sleep deprivation	P<0.05
		Excessive work	P<0.05
		Need to meet multiple demands simultaneously	P<0.05
		Mother's upbringing was under adverse circumstances.	P<0.05
Peru Vega-Dienstmaier et al, 1999	SCID for DSM-IV	Obsessive-compulsive disorder	P=0.0004
		Past major depressive episode	P=0.002
		Premenstrual dysphoric disorder	P=0.007
		Maternity blues	P=0.016
		Age < 25 year-old	P=0.018
		Young maternal age	B=-0.13, SE=0.08
		Lower educational level	B=-0.23, SE=0.15
		Larger number of pregnancies	B=-0.32, SE=0.28
USA, Hispanic women Beck et al, 2005	PDSS SCID	Marital status (single)	Statist. Signif.*
		Number of days postpartum (more)	Statist. Signif.*
		Puerto Rican ethnicity	Statist. Signif.*
		Delivery by cesarean-section	Statist. Signif.*
Country Author, Year	Criteria or scale used for the diagnosis of depression	Variables associated to Postpartum Depression	Significance of the association
USA, > 50% Hispanic sample Freeman et al, 2005	EPDS	Smoking	P=0.0025
		Family history of mental health problems	P=0.0093

Table 3: Risk Factors for the Development of Postpartum Depression (Continued)

Country Author, Year	Criteria or scale used for the diagnosis of depression	Variables associated to Postpartum Depression	Significance of the association
USA, Mexican-American women Heilemann et al, 2004	CES-D	Mastery (inverse correlation)	<0.001
		Satisfaction with life (inverse correlation)	<0.001
		Resilience subscale 1: personal competence (inverse correlation)	<0.008
		Resilience subscale 2: Acceptance of self and life (inverse correlation)	<0.001
		Importance of spiritual beliefs (inverse correlation)	0.02
USA, Hispanic women Howell et al, 2005	2-items from the Primary Care Evaluation of Mental Disorders Procedure	Age < 25 year-old	P<0.01
		Educational level ≤ high school	P<0.05
		Infant colic	P<0.01
		Poor social support	P<0.01
		Less access to their health care providers	P<0.05
		Less self-efficacy in managing the infant and household affairs	P<0.01
		Physical symptoms	P<0.01
		Physical function limitations	P<0.01
USA, Mexican-American women Martinez-Schallmoser et al, 2003	CES-D	Prenatal depression	P=0.0001
		Postpartum family health (inverse correlation)	P=0.0001
		Postpartum support need	P=0.03
		Prenatal support need	P<0.05
		Prenatal support satisfaction (inverse correlation)	P<0.05
		Prenatal conflict network size	P<0.05
		Postnatal support satisfaction (inverse correlation)	P<0.05
		Postnatal conflict network size	P<0.05

HAM-D = Hamilton Scale for Depression
BDI = Beck Depression Inventory
EPDS = Edinburgh Postnatal Depression Scale
TAT = Thematic Apperception Test
RDC = Research Diagnostic Criteria
ICD-10 = International Classification of Diseases- 10th revision
SCID = Structured Clinical Interview for DSM-IV
PDSS = Postpartum Depression Screening Scale
CES-D = Center for Epidemiologic Studies - Depression
* Reported by authors as "statistically significant"
B = regression coefficient
SE = standard error

One of the most significant factors is the number of life events or stressors the mother needs to cope with. Life events had a strong association to DPP ($p<0.001$) in two studies conducted in Chile (Alvarado et al, 1994; Jadresic et al, 1992b). Among those stressors, the most relevant are the ones related to some risk to the pregnancy or the newborn, for example, low-weight at birth (Jadresic et al., 1992b) and premature birth or some risk to the newborn's life (Eizirik, 1984). Other significant stressors include having an abortion immediately before the current pregnancy (Alvarado et al, 1994), having a close person with a serious illness or the onset of severe economic difficulties (Jadresic et al. 1992b).

A lower socio-economic status was associated to the development of DPP in Brazil (Moraes et al, 2006) and Chile (Jadresic and Araya, 1995), and worries about pregnancy-related expenses were related to postpartum dysphoria in Peru (Betalleluz and Quiroz, 1997). Similar findings in the work by Betalleluz and Quiroz (1997) in Peru and the one by Moraes et al (2006) in Brazilian population documented a low number of prenatal visits as an associated factor for the development of depression.

Several studies reported that low educational level is a risk factor for the development of PPD (Moraes et al, 2006; Faisal-Curry et al, 2002; Vega-Dienstmaier et al, 1999; Howell et al, 2005). However, a study in Costa Rica found an association between "postpartum dysphoria" and higher level of education (Wolf et al, 2001). This finding may be explained by the fact that women were asked to remember the presence of postnatal dysphoria up to 5 years after their child's birth; therefore, a better education may have influenced the recollection of better-detailed information.

Inadequate social support has been identified also as a factor in some studies (Howell et al, 2005; Coutinho et al, 2002; Martinez-Schallmoser et al, 2003). Being away from her family or close friends or having serious conflicts with her own mother seems to be also linked to PDD (Jadresic et al, 1992b). Other identified factors are those concerning the mother's relationship with her partner, among these: unsatisfactory relation with the partner before or after childbirth (Alvarado et al, 1992a), marital conflicts (Jadresic et al, 1992b), relational difficulties with the child's father (Moraes et al, 2006), limited presence or absence of the partner (Hasbun et al, 1999; Betalleluz and Quiroz, 1997), and being single, separated or widow (Moraes et al, 2006; Hasbun et al, 1999; Jadresic and Araya, 1995).

Other factors found associated to PPD involved the mother's attitude and expectations attached to her pregnancy. For example: having contemplated to terminate the pregnancy or having in fact attempted to do it (Moraes et al, 2006), having a negative attitude towards the pregnancy (Alvarado et al, 1992a), and if the pregnancy was unplanned (Hasbun et al, 1999). Moraes et al (2006) found a peculiar relationship between the preference for a child of male gender and the development of depression.

A larger number of children or previous pregnancies were found associated to PPD in several studies (Faisal-Curry et al, 2002; Hasbun et al, 1999; Vega-Dienstmaier et al, 1999). On the contrary, Da-Silva et al (1998) found an opposite relation between the number of children and the risk for PPD.

About mental illness, the history of depression at anytime prior to the puerperium was consistently found associated to PPD in several studies (Vega-Dienstmaier et al, 1999; Coutinho et al, 2002; Evans et al, 2003), particularly if the depressive episode occurred during the pregnancy (Jadresic et al, 1992b; Alvarado et al, 1992a; Martinez-Schallmoser et al, 2003). Other mental health conditions found to be risk factors are: obsessive-compulsive disorder, premenstrual dysphoric disorder and "maternity blues" (Vega-Dienstmaier et al,

1999); also, having previously consulted a mental health specialist for emotional problems (Jadresic et al, 1992b), and the history of dysphoria after a previous pregnancy o during the present one (Coutinho et al, 2002). Other interesting and very important finding by Pinheiro et al (2006) involved the association of maternal depression and the occurrence of paternal depression after childbirth.

Factors related to maternal and the newborn's general health were also linked to PPD: any pathology during the pregnancy (Evans et al, 2003), presence of significant physical symptoms (Howell et al, 2005), physical function limitations (Howell et al, 2005), urinary tract infections (Alvarado et al, 1993a; Jadresic et al, 1992b), development of varicose veins (Jadresic et al, 1992b), child required to be hospitalized as a newborn or while still being breast-fed (Evans et al, 2003), problems related to breast-feeding (Alvarado et al, 1993a; Jadresic et al, 1992b) and a child suffering of colic (Howell et al, 2005).

Young maternal age seems a consistent finding connected to PPD (Moraes et al, 2006; Vega-Dienstmaier et al, 1999; Howell et al, 2005; Alvarado et al, 1992a). One study found that maternal age over 34 year-old was also an additional risk factor (Alvarado et al, 1992a).

Ethnicity represents a controversial factor, Da-Silva et al (1998) found black race as a risk factor; however, Faisal-Curry (2002) reported that white mothers are at higher risk for the development of PPD than black females.

Latino Women in the USA

Howell et al (2005) found several risk factors including a maternal age less than 25 year-old, low educational level, a child suffering form colics, having a poor social support, physical symptoms and functional limitations, feeling decreased self-efficiency in managing the infant and household affairs and a limited access to health services.

Martinez-Schallmoser et al (2003), found several factors similar to those previously described and specifically sought correlations between several variables related to acculturation, social support, quality of life, and depression. Key finding involved social/cultural factors related to antenatal depression, and that during the postpartum period a greater conflict with the mother's social network ($r = -0.38$, $p < 0.05$) was related to dissatisfaction with postpartum support, particularly from their husbands or partners.

Significant predictors for postpartum depression in Hispanic mothers according to Beck et al (2005) were Puerto Rican ethnicity, cesarean delivery and single marital status.

Freeman et al (2005) studying a sample of women predominantly Hispanic (53.2%) identified smoking and family mental health problems as risk factors for high EPDS.

Heilemann et al (2004) studied women of Mexican descent and found that postpartum depression inversely correlated with mastery, satisfaction with life, personal competence acceptance of self and life, and importance of spiritual beliefs. In this study also was found in childbearing women (pregnant and postpartum) a relation between "exposed to USA in childhood" and higher depressive symptoms. Women who spent their childhood in Mexico had lower depression levels.

Mother and their Children: The Impact of Postpartum Depression

We found a study regarding the relationship between PPD and child care (Medeiros and Furtado, 2004) conducted in Brazil. This study compared the care provided by mothers with (n=10) and without depression (n=12). Results showed that PPD was linked to events suggestive of maternal negligence and with the lack of breast-feeding. Hence, mothers with higher numbers of events suggestive of negligence (e.g. episodes of fever, skin irritation, colics, accidents, forgetting to give prescribed medications) presented with EPDS scores significantly higher than those of mothers with lower incidents of such events (EPDS score 18.2 vs. 9.7, $p<0.05$). Mothers providing exclusively breast-feeding to their children had significantly lower mean EPDS scores than those that were no longer exclusively breast-feeding.

As discussed in a previous section, premature birth seems to be an associated risk factor; consequently a study in Argentina presented a report on intervention with mothers of premature children (Ruiz et al., 2005) targeted to the needs of the child and their parents and their parenting abilities and factors that may interfere with child care and safety. Mothers of premature children were included in a program developed by Lester and collaborators (1996). The level of stress and depression in these women were significantly lower than a control group who did not receive the intervention. Mean scores of the BDI used to assess depression was 9.0 in the group of mothers participants of the program versus 19.6 in the control group.

Conclusion

Studies in Latin America report a prevalence of postpartum depressive symptomatology that varies between 5.92% and 48%, evaluations were usually conducted with previously validated assessment instruments in Spanish or Portuguese language.

A number of risk factors are consistent with the international literature, and involved a diversity of variables including: stressors, demographic and socioeconomic status, educational level, social and family support, relationship with partner, expectations about the pregnancy, number of previous pregnancies, newborn health, and maternal mental and general medical problems.

Depression, both maternal and paternal, may interfere with their parenting abilities and the care and safety of the child, therefore appropriate interventions to diagnose, treat, and educate families is needed. Effective evaluation should not be limited to obstetric settings but should also involve multidisciplinary teams such pediatricians, nurses, psychiatrists, psychologists and primary care professionals in general.

References

Alvarado M, R., Rojas C, M., Morandé, J., Neves G, E., Olea, E., Perucca, E., and Vera, A. (1992a). Cuadros depresivos en el postparto y variables asociadas en una cohorte de 125 mujeres embarazadas. *Rev. psiquiatr. (Santiago de Chile), 9*(3/4), 1168-1175.

Alvarado M., R., Vera C., A., Rojas C., M., Olea, E., Morandes, J., and Neves, E. (1992b). La escala de Edinburgo para la detección de cuadros depresivos en el postparto. *Rev Psiquiatr (Santiago de Chile), 9*(3/4), 1177-1181.

Alvarado M., R., Perucca P., E., Rojas, M., Monardes, J., Olea, E., Neves G., E., and Vera C., A. (1993a). Aspectos gineco-obstétricos en mujeres que desarrollan una depresión en el postparto. *Rev Chil Obstet. ginecol, 58*(3), 239-244.

Alvarado Muñoz, R., Vera C., A., Monardes, J., Rojas, M., Olea, E., and Neves, E. (1993b). El inventario de depresión de Beck en los cuadros depresivos del embarazo y del postparto. *Rev Psiquiatr (Santiago de Chile), 10*(2), 4-13.

Alvarado Muñoz, R., Vera C., A., Rojas, M., Olea, E., Monardes, J., Neves, E., and Perucca, E. (1994). Eventos vitales, soporte social y depresión en el postparto. *Rev Psiquiatr. (Santiago de Chile), 11*(3), 121-126.

Alvarado, R., Rojas, M., Monardes, J., Perucca Páez, E., Neves G., E., Olea, E., and Vera C., A. (2000). Cuadros depresivos en el postparto en una cohorte de embarazadas: construcción de un modelo causal. *Rev Chil Neuro-psiquiatr, 38*(2), 84-93.

Bandolier (1996): How Good is That Test II. Bandolier Evidence-based health care 27, 64-66.

Beck, C. T. (2001). Predictors of postpartum depression: an update. *Nurs Res, 50*(5), 275-285.

Beck CT, Bernal H and Froman RD (2003). Methods to document semantic equivalence of a translated scale. Res Nurs Health 26(1), 64-73.

Beck, C. T., and Gable, R. K. (2003). Postpartum depression screening scale: Spanish version. *Nurs Res, 52*(5), 296-306.

Beck, C. T., Froman, R. D., and Bernal, H. (2005). Acculturation level and postpartum depression in Hispanic mothers. *MCN Am J Matern Child Nurs, 30*(5), 299-304.

Beck, C. T., and Gable, R. K. (2005). Screening performance of the postpartum depression screening scale--Spanish version. *J Transcult Nurs, 16*(4), 331-338.

Betalleluz Pallardel, J. R., and Quiroz Valdivia, R. (1997). Síndrome de tristeza postparto hospitalario en la ciudad del Cusco. *SITUA, 5 (9):8-13.*

Chaudron, L. H., Kitzman, H. J., Peifer, K. L., Morrow, S., Perez, L. M., and Newman, M. C. (2005). Self-recognition of and provider response to maternal depressive symptoms in low-income Hispanic women. *J Womens Health (Larchmt), 14*(4), 331-338.

Coutinho, D. S., Baptista, M. N., and Morais, P. R. (2002). Depressäo pós-parto: prevalência e correlaçäo com o suporte social. *Infanto Rev. Neuropsiquiatr Infanc Adolesc, 10*(2), 63-71.

Cox JL, Holden JM, Sagovsky R (1987). Development of the 10-item, Edinburgh Postnatal Depression Scale. Br J Psychiatry 150, 782-786.

Da-Silva, V. A. d., Moraes-Santos, A. R., Carvalho, M. S., Martins, M. L. P., and Teixeira, N. A. (1998). Prenatal and postnatal depression among low income Brazilian women. *Braz J Med Biol Res, 31*(6), 799-804.

Eizirik, L. S. (1984). Depressäo puerperal: efeitos de prematuridade e risco de vida do recém-nascido no estado emocional da puérpera. *Ciênc Cult. (Säo Paulo), 36*(6), 1002-1007.

Evans M., G., Vicuña M., M., and Marín, R. (2003). Depresión postparto realidad en el sistema público de atención de salud. *Rev Chil Obstet Ginecol, 68*(6), 491-494.

Faisal-Cury, A., Tedesco, J. J., Kahhale, S., Menezes, P. R., and Zugaib, M. (2004). Postpartum depression: in relation to life events and patterns of coping. *Arch Women Ment Health, 7*(2), 123-131.

Florenzano, R., Feuerhake, O., Hinrichsen, M., and Figueroa, C. (1984). La calibración de una escala cuantitativa para medir el nivel de depresión en poblaciones. *Rev Chil Neuro-Psiquiat, 22*, 17-23.

Freeman MP, Wright R, Watchman M, Wahl RA, Sisk DJ, Fraleigh L, Weibrecht JM (2005). Postpartum depression assessments at well-baby visits: screening feasibility, prevalence, and risk factors. J Womens Health (Larchmt) 14(10), 929-935.

Halbreich, J., and Karkun, S. (2006). Cross-cultural and social diversity of prevalence of postpartum depression and depressive symptoms. *J Affect Disord, in press*.

Hasbún Hernández, J., Risco Neira, L., Jadresic Marinovic, E., Galleguillo U., T., González A., M., and Garay S., J. (1999). Depresión postparto: prevalencia y factores de riesgo. *Rev Chil Obstet Ginecol, 64*(6), 466-470.

Heilemann, M., Frutos, L., Lee, K., and Kury, F. S. (2004). Protective strength factors, resources, and risks in relation to depressive symptoms among childbearing women of Mexican descent. *Health Care Women Int, 25*(1), 88-106.

Howell, E. A., Mora, P. A., Horowitz, C. R., and Leventhal, H. (2005). Racial and ethnic differences in factors associated with early postpartum depressive symptoms. *Obstet Gynecol, 105*(6), 1442-1450.

Jadresic Vargas, E., Jara V., C., Miranda, M., Arrau, B., and Araya, R. (1992a). Trastornos emocionales en el embarazo y el puerperio: estudio prospectivo de 108 mujeres. *Rev Chil Neuro-psiquiatr, 30*(2), 99-106.

Jadresic M., E., Jara V., C., and Araya B., R. (1992b). Depresión en el embarazo y el puerperio: estudio de factores de riesgo. *Acta Psiquiátr Psicol Am Lat, 39*(1), 63-74.

Jadresic, E., Araya, R., and Jara, C. (1995). Validation of the Edinburgh Postnatal Depression Scale (EPDS) in Chilean postpartum women. *J Psychosom Obstet Gynaecol, 16*(4), 187-191.

Jadresic Marinovic, E., and Araya B., R. (1995). Prevalencia de depresión postparto y factores asociados en Santiago, Chile . *Rev Méd Chile, 123*(6), 694-699.

Kennerley, H., and Gath, D. (1989). Maternity blues. Detection and measurement by questionnaire. *Br J Psychiatry, 155*, 356-362.

Lester, B., Bigsby, R., High, P., Wu, S. (1996) Principles of intervention for preterm infant in the NICU. Paper presented at the 10 Canadian Ross Conference in Pediatrics. Optimizing the neonatal intensive care environment.

Luis, M. A. V., and Oliveira, E. R. d. (1998). Transtornos mentais na gravidez, parto e puerpério, na região de Ribeirão Preto-SP-Brasil. *Rev. Esc. Enfermagem USP, 32*(4), 314-324.

Martinez-Schallmoser, L., Telleen, S., and MacMullen, N. J. (2003). The effect of social support and acculturation on postpartum depression in Mexican American women. *J Transcult Nurs, 14*(4), 329-338.

Medeiros, P. P. V., and Furtado, E. F. (2004). Perfil dos cuidados maternos em mäes deprimidas e näo-deprimidas no período puerperal. *J Bras Psiquiatr, 53*(4), 227-234.

Miller, L. J. (1999). Introduction. In L. J. Miller (Ed.), *Postpartum mood disorders*. Washington, DC: American Psychiatric Press, Inc.

Moraes, I. G. d. S., Pinheiro, R. T., Silva, R. A. d., Horta, B. L., Sousa, P. L. R., and Faria, A. D. (2006). Prevalência da depressão pós-parto e fatores associados. *Rev Saúde Pública, 40*(1), 65-70.

Moreno Zaconeta, A., Domingues Casulari Da Motta, L. l., and França, P. S. (2004). Depresión postparto: prevalencia de test de rastreo positivo en puérperas del Hospital Universitario de Brasilia, Brasil. *Rev Chil Obstet Ginecol, 69*(3), 209-213.

O'Hara, M. W., and Swain, A. M. (1996). Rate and risk of postpartum depression. A meta-analysis. *Int Rev Psychiatry, 8*, 37-54.

Pinheiro RT, Magallanes PV, Horta BL, Pinheiro KA, Silva RA, Pinto RH (2006). Is paternal postpartum depression associated with maternal postpartm depression? Population-based study in Brasil. Acta Psychiatr Scand 113(3), 230-232.

Rohde, L. A., Busnello, E., Wolf, A., Zomer, A., Shansis, F., Martins, S., and Tramontina, S. (1997). Maternity blues in Brazilian women. *Acta Psychiatr Scand, 95*(3), 231-235.

Ruíz, A. L., Ceriani Cernadas, J. M., Cravedi, V., and Rodríguez, D. (2005). Estrés y depresión en madres de prematuros: un programa de intervención. *Arch Argent Pediatr, 103*(1), 36-45.

Santos, M. F. d., Martins, F. C., and Pasqual, L. (1999). Escala de auto-avaliação de depressão pós-parto: estudo no Brasil. *Rev Psiquiatr Clín. (São Paulo), 26*(2), 90-95.

US Census Bureau. (2001). *The Hispanic population. Census 2000 Brief.* Washington DC: US Department of Commerce.

Vega-Dienstmaier, J. M., Mazzotti, G., Stucchi-Portocarrero, S., and Campos, M. (1999). Prevalencia y factores de riesgo para depresión en mujeres postparto. *Actas Esp Psiquiatr, 27*(5), 299-303.

Vega-Dienstmaier, J. M., Mazzotti Suarez, G., and Campos Sanchez, M. (2002). [Validation of a Spanish version of the Edinburgh Postnatal Depression Scale]. *Actas Esp Psiquiatr, 30*(2), 106-111.

Welch B, Schafer R, Dember CH (1961). TAT stories of hypomanic and depressed patients J Proj Tech 25, 221-232

Wolf, A. W., De Andraca, I., and Lozoff, B. (2002). Maternal depression in three Latin American samples. *Soc Psychiatry Psychiatr Epidemiol, 37*(4), 169-176.

Wyszynski, A., and Lusskin, S. (2005). The obstetrics patient. In A. Wyszynski and B. Wyszynski (Eds.), *Manual of psychiatric care for the medically ill.* Arlington: American Psychiatric Publishing, Inc.

In: Trends in Depression Research
Editor: Maurice J. Henri, pp. 145-160

ISBN 1-60021-394-4

Chapter 8

STIMULANT AND DEPRESSANT BEHAVIORAL ACTIONS OF ALCOHOL IN NON-SELECTED WISTAR RATS

Fabiola Hernández-Vázquez and Milagros Méndez*

Departamento de Neuroquímica, Subdirección de Investigaciones Clínicas,
Instituto Nacional de Psiquiatría Ramón de la Fuente,
Calzada México Xochimilco, México D.F., Mexico

ABSTRACT

Low doses of alcohol have been reported to induce psychomotor activation in rodents, whereas high doses produce sedation. However, locomotor responses to alcohol may be influenced by different factors, including the dose and route of administration, the duration of drug exposure, the distinct sensitivity of rodent strains, the light-dark cycle and stressful situations. The aim of this work was to investigate locomotor responses in Wistar rats in normal and reverse light-dark cycles, as well as the effect of different doses of alcohol. Behavioral responses were assessed in an activity meter and scores of slow and fast horizontal movements, as well as slow and fast stereotyped movements were recorded. Rats were habituated for 30 min, then received an intraperitoneal (i.p.) saline injection and saline or alcohol was administered (0.25, 1 or 2.5 g/kg i.p.) after 30 min. A control group of animals was registered but not injected. Animals in the reverse light-dark cycle exhibited a higher motor response than those in the normal cycle. Thus, behavioral responses to alcohol were studied in reverse cycle animals. Forty four and 49 % significant decreases in total horizontal movements were observed in response to alcohol at doses of 0.25 and 2.5 g/kg, respectively, versus the control group. In contrast, a 69 % increase was found with 1 g/kg versus the saline group. This dose also increased total stereotyped movements by 41 and 92 % versus the control and saline groups, respectively, whereas a dose of 2.5 g/kg induced a 38 % decrease versus the control group. Total activity (total horizontal

* Corresponding author : Dr. Milagros Méndez. Tel. : (52) 56 55 28 11, ext. 212; Fax : (52) 55 13 37 22; Email adress : ubach@imp.edu.mx

movements plus total stereotyped movements) was significantly increased (40 %) and decreased (43 %) by alcohol doses of 1 and 2.5 g/kg, respectively, versus the control group. The stimulant effect of alcohol was even higher (a 78 % increase) when compared to the saline group. Opposite behavioral alcohol effects were observed, 1 g/kg stimulating motor activity and 2.5 g/kg exhibiting a sedative effect. Our results suggest that stimulant alcohol effects may be mainly due to fast horizontal and fast stereotyped movements. In contrast, the sedative alcohol effects may involve similar contributions of slow and fast horizontal, as well as fast stereotyped movements. Alcohol behavioral effects may be closely related to activation of brain dopaminergic circuits.

INTRODUCTION

Alcohol consumption affects several biological functions and induces important behavioral changes, which are associated with alterations in several neuronal systems. Activation of brain dopaminergic pathways is involved in actions elicited by drugs of abuse, including alcohol. The dopaminergic mesocorticolimbic system plays an important role in the development of the positive reinforcing and rewarding actions of alcohol, which may lead to addictive behavior [34, 63]. Otherwise, alcohol also affects dopaminergic neurotransmission in the nigrostriatal pathway [21, 55], which may be implicated in determining brain sensitivity to alcohol [66]. Alcohol also interacts with other neurotransmitter and neuromodulator systems, including glutamate [29], serotonin [7], γ-aminobutyric acid (GABA) [57] and opioid peptides [26]. These interactions may contribute to the positive reinforcing actions of the drug.

Alcohol affects several neurobiological processes, such as temperature regulation, sleep and motor coordination [46]. Alcohol decreases body temperature and severe intoxication in a cold environment has been suggested to produce life-threatening declines in temperature (hypothermia). In addition, alcohol interferes with normal sleep patterns. Low doses of alcohol produce sleepiness and suppression of rapid eye-movement (REM) sleep. Chronic alcohol consumption may result in the loss of muscular coordination, which may be associated with peripheral neuropathy, a disorder commonly seen in alcoholics [46]. These data indicate that alcohol consumption may have serious repercussions in the functioning of the entire nervous system.

Alcohol exhibits biphasic behavioral effects in animals and humans. Low doses of alcohol have been reported to induce locomotor stimulation in most mouse [6] and some rat [28] strains, as well as psychomotor activation and euphoria in humans [41]. In contrast, high doses of alcohol decrease locomotor activity in mice and rats, and induce sedation in both animals and humans [17, 18]. Important conclusions on the biphasic effects of alcohol on locomotor activity have been provided by studies using animal models. However, conflicting data have been reported. Waller et al. (1986) [62] have shown that alcohol doses of 0.12 to 0.25 g/kg increase locomotor activity in alcohol preferring (P) inbred line of rats, while alcohol non-preferring (NP) animals failed to show increases in locomotor activity at any alcohol dose tested. Other studies have reported that alcohol doses of 0.12 to 0.5 g/kg do not affect locomotor activity in P, NP or Fawn-Hooded (FH) rats, whereas a dose of 1g/kg diminish motor activity in FH rats, as well as in Flinders Sensitive Line (FSL) and Flinders Resistant Line (FRL) rats [11]. In addition, Imperato and Di Chiara (1986) [31] reported increases and decreases in locomotor activity with doses of alcohol of 0.5 and 1 g/kg, respectively, in Sprague Dawley rats. Similar results were obtained by Schaeffer et al. (1988) [58], who reported a reduction in motor activity with a dose of alcohol of 1g/kg in the same strain of rats. Koros et al. (1998, 1999) [37, 38] did not observe a positive correlation between alcohol intake and locomotor activity in Wistar rats. These data indicate that alcohol's actions on locomotor activity may be importantly influenced by several factors, including the alcohol dose and the rodent strain used. The route of administration and the duration of alcohol exposure [47] may also contribute to the behavioral responses elicited by the drug.

Stress situations and light-dark cycle conditions may also affect the behavioral responses to alcohol. Studies in animals have suggested a close relationship between alcohol and stress. For instance, alcohol-seeking behavior is restored in abstinent rats by a stressor (an electrical shock in their feet) [40]. In humans, a positive correlation between stress and alcohol consumption has been observed, since alcohol intake relieves anxiety and helps people with stressful situations [50]. Other studies have shown that some stressors (i.e., a novel environment or a tail pinch) and alcohol administration increase locomotor activity in animals [2, 19, 52]. On the other hand, alcohol sensitivity is altered according to the light-dark phase during which the drug is consumed [24, 25]. Reinberg (1992) [51] has shown that the same dose of alcohol in human drinkers produces different effects depending on the hour of the day alcohol is ingested. In animals, this behavior is also observed. Animals consume more alcohol in the dark compared with the light phase of the day [25] and the absorption and elimination of alcohol is faster when the drug is consumed at midnight [24]. In addition, stress and circadian rhythms are closely linked, since higher responses to stressors (food restriction) are observed in the morning [56]. Thus, stressful and light-dark cycle conditions are critical in determining alcohol sensitivity and responsiveness, which may reflect differential behavioral responses. These factors may specifically affect different features of locomotor activity. Therefore, the aim of this work was to study the patterns of locomotor activity in non-selected Wistar rats in normal and reverse light-dark cycles. We investigated the effects of different doses of alcohol on motor activity as well, since alcohol dose-response studies have provided conflicting data.

Materials and Methods

Animals

Male Wistar rats (200 - 300g) were housed five per cage and maintained in a 12h normal cycle (lights on at 7:00 h) (group A) or reverse cycle (lights on at 19:00 h) (group B). Rats of group B were changed to the reverse cycle one week before activity recording and were tested with red light. All animals had free access to standard laboratory chow and water (except during the test) and were habituated to the test room for 1 h. Experiments were conducted between 10:00 and 14:00 h.

Locomotor Activity Test

Locomotor activity was measured in an activity meter (Panlab, s.I., Letica Scientific Instruments) provided with a 45 x 45 cm arena and 16 infra-red beams, which are intended to measure forward locomotion by beam interruption. Locomotor activity was defined as the distance (number of beam interruptions) traveled by the rat during the 30 min test session at 2 min intervals. The activity meter was set to measure fast (F-MOV) and slow (S-MOV) horizontal movements and fast (F-STE) and slow (S-STE) stereotyped movements.

Normal and Reverse Cycle Experiments

Motor activity was measured in rats in normal or reverse light-dark cycles in 30 min sessions and records were compared.

Alcohol Administration and Activity Experiments

Animals in the reverse light-dark cycle were tested with different doses of alcohol, since their motor activity was higher than in the normal cycle rats. Animals were placed in the activity meter for a period of 30 min in order to habituate them to the testing environment (habituation phase). Then, all animals received an intraperitoneal (i.p.) saline injection with the purpose of diminish stress and activity was measured during 30 min (saline phase). Finally, animals received an i.p. injection of saline or alcohol (0.25, 1 or 2.5 g ethanol per kg) and activity was monitored for a period of 1 h (drug phase). Two control groups were included in the study, one receiving saline solution during the drug phase (saline group), the other not injected but recorded during the whole experiment (2 h) (control group).

Statistical Analyses

Statistical differences between animal groups in the normal and reverse cycles were determined by one way ANOVA. In alcohol administration experiments data were also analyzed by ANOVA, considering differences between alcohol doses tested and control groups. Significant differences between groups were investigated by the post hoc Tuckey-HSD test.

Results

Motor Activity in Normal and Reverse Cycle Rats

Highest activity scores in all animals were observed during the first 10 min. Exploratory behavior and stereotyped movements were higher in animals in reverse than those in normal cycle. These differences were higher in fast horizontal (F-MOV) (Figure 1A) and fast stereotyped movements (F-STE) (Figure 1C) than in slow horizontal (S-MOV) and slow stereotyped movements (S-STE) (Figures 1B and 1D). Significant differences in F-MOV between normal and reverse cycle animals were only observed during the first 10 min (Figure 1A), whereas differences in S-SMOV, S-STE and F-STE were observed almost in the whole 30 min recording activity period (Figures 1B, 1C and 1D). Cumulated activity scores (beam interruptions) in 10 or 30 min periods in reverse compared with normal cycle animals showed significant increases of 51 and 72 % in F-MOV, 22 and 39 % in S-MOV, 46 and 53 % in F-STE and 8 and 24 % in S-STE (Figures 1A, 1B, 1C and 1D, inserts).

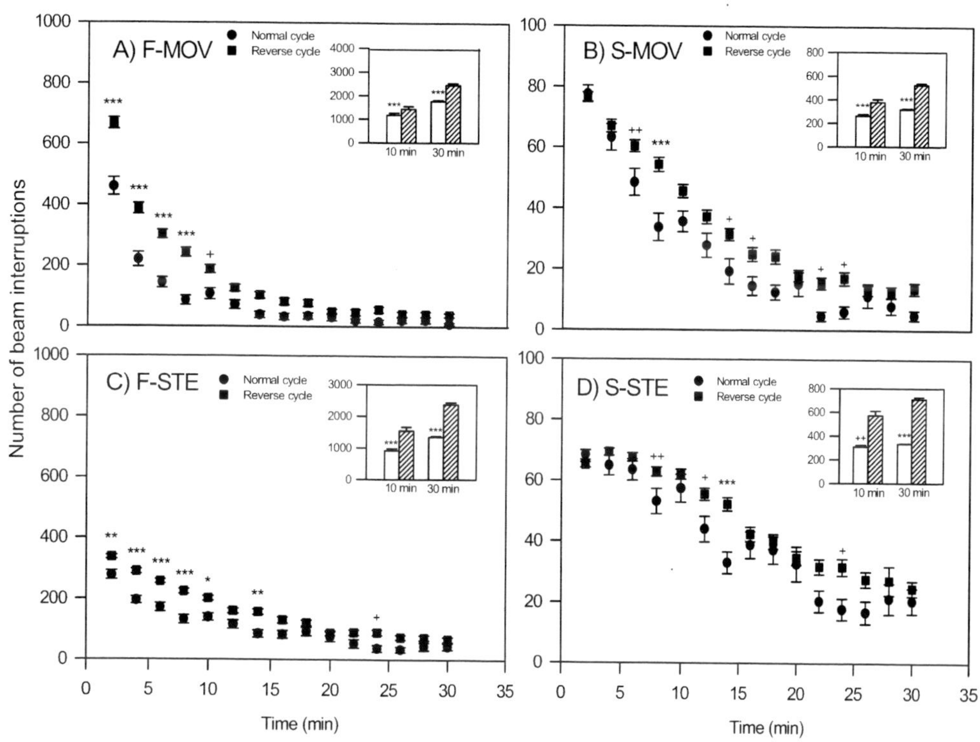

Figure 1. Time course of motor activity in normal and reverse cycle rats. F-MOV (A), S-MOV (B), F-STE (C) and S-STE (D) were measured in 2 min intervals during 30 min. Data represent the mean ± S.E.M. of 25 (normal cycle) or 30 (reverse cycle) animals. Activity is also shown as cumulated scores in the first 10 min of the test and total activity in 30 min (inserts). Inserts : white bars = normal cycle; hatched bars = reverse cycle. ***$p < 0.0001$; **$p < 0.001$; *$p < 0.005$; $^{++}p < 0.01$; $^{+}p < 0.05$.

Total horizontal activity (fast plus slow horizontal movements), total stereotyped movements (fast plus slow stereotyped movements) and total activity (total horizontal activity plus total stereotyped movements) were higher in rats in reverse cycle than in animals in normal cycle (Figures 2A, 2B and 2C). Cumulated scores in 10 or 30 min periods in reverse compared with normal cycle animals showed significant increases of 40 and 65 % in total horizontal activity, 36 and 45 % in total stereotyped movements and 41 and 52 % in total activity (Figures 2A, 2B and 2C, inserts).

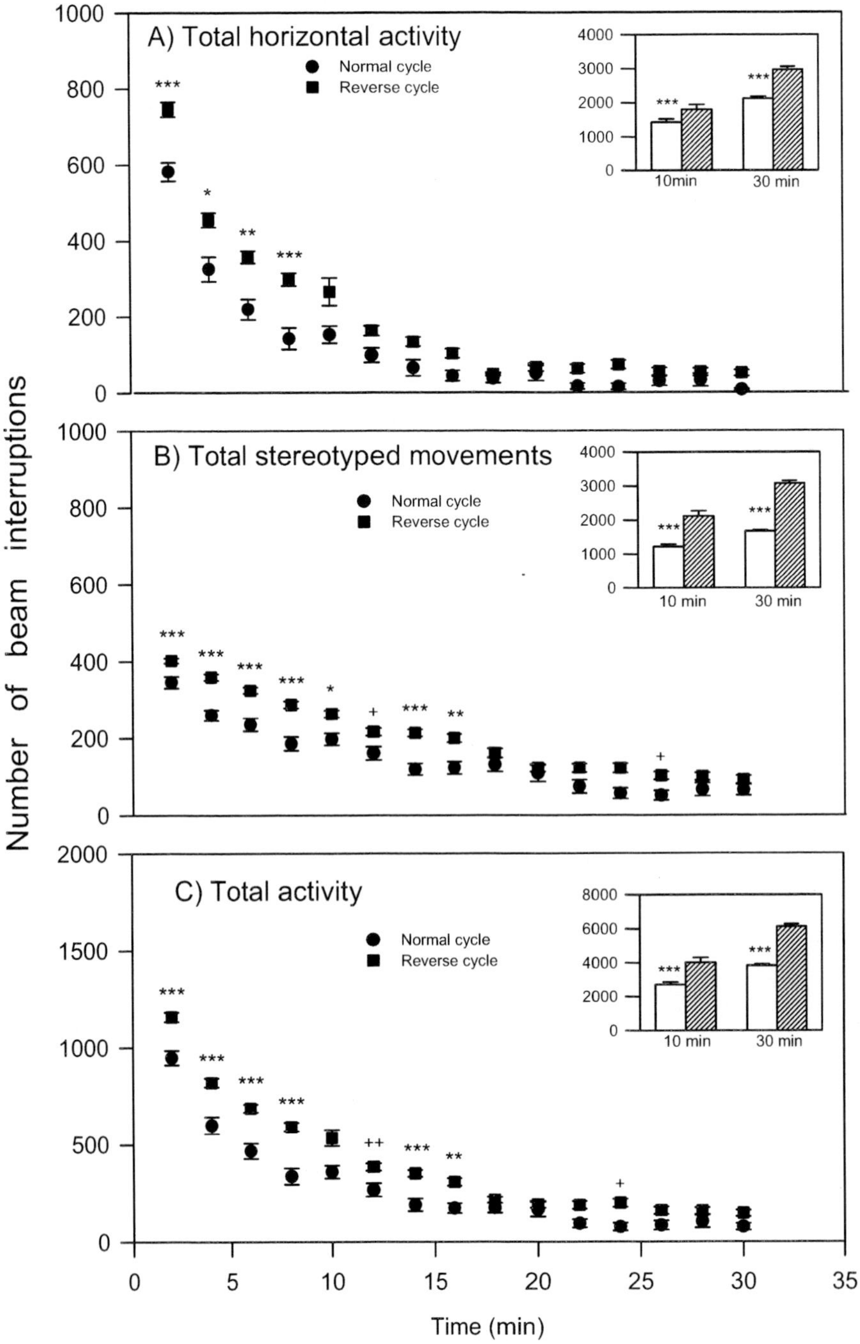

Figure 2. Time course of total motor activity in normal and reverse cycle rats. Total horizontal activity (A), total stereotyped movements (B) and total activity (C) were measured in 2 min intervals during 30 min. Data represent the mean ± S.E.M. of 25 (normal cycle) or 30 (reverse cycle) animals. Activity is also shown as cumulated scores in the first 10 min of the test and total activity in 30 min (inserts). Inserts : white bars = normal cycle; hatched bars = reverse cycle. ***$p < 0.0001$; **$p < 0.001$; *$p < 0.005$; $^{++}$ $p < 0.01$; $^{+}$ $p < 0.05$.

Effect of Different Doses of Alcohol on Motor Activity

Habituation Phase

Since reverse cycle animals exhibited higher motor activity than those in normal cycle, we investigated the effect of different doses of alcohol in reverse cycle rats. No significant differences were observed in all activity parameters studied (F-MOV, S-MOV, F-STE and S-STE) during the habituation period (data not shown).

Saline Phase

Saline injection after a 30 min habituation period did not produce differences in F-MOV between animal groups (Figure 3). Saline injection decreased F-MOV when compared with the control (non-injected) group, although this difference was not significant (Figure 3). No significant differences were observed when examining S-MOV, F-STE and S-STE (data not shown).

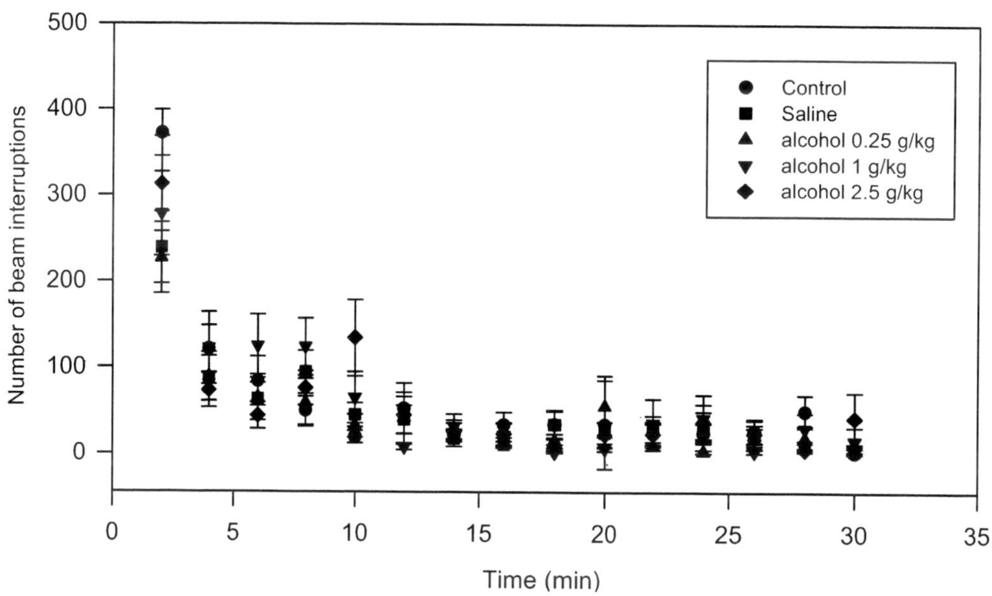

Figure 3. Effect of a saline injection on horizontal fast movements in reverse cycle rats. Animals were divided in 4 groups, which were subsequently re-injected with saline or alcohol at doses of 0.25, 1 or 2.5 g/kg. An additional non-injected group (control) was examined. Data represent the mean ± S.E.M. of 9 (control), 10 (saline), 9 (0.25 g/kg), 10 (1 g/kg) and 11 (2.5 g/kg) animals.

Drug Phase

Since the effects of different doses of alcohol were only significant during the first four intervals (8 min), results are presented as cumulated scores in 8 min. An alcohol dose of 1g/kg significantly increased F-MOV by 90 % when compared with saline-injected animals, but not with the control group. In contrast, alcohol doses of 0.25 and 2.5 g/kg were not significantly different from the saline group, but decreased F-MOV by 58 and 63 % respectively, when compared with the control group (Figure 4A). Significant differences were detected between alcohol groups : 186 and 226 % increases in F-MOV were observed when comparing 0.25 versus 1 g/kg and 2.5 g/kg versus 1 g/kg, respectively (Figure 4A). Alcohol at doses of 0.25, 1 or 2.5 g/kg did not significantly affect S-MOV, F-STE or S-STE, although the dose of 2.5 g/kg decreased S-MOV and F-STE by 46 %. An alcohol dose of 1 g/kg increased S-SMOV by 107 % compared with the dose of 2.5 g/kg (Figures 4B, 4C and 4D). Fast stereotyped movements were 86 % higher in response to an alcohol dose of 1 g/kg than the dose of 2.5 g/kg (Figure 4C). Since no significant differences were observed between the different groups of animals during the saline phase of the experiment (Figure 3), the observed effects during the drug phase are due to alcohol administration and not to a stress response (i.p. saline injection).

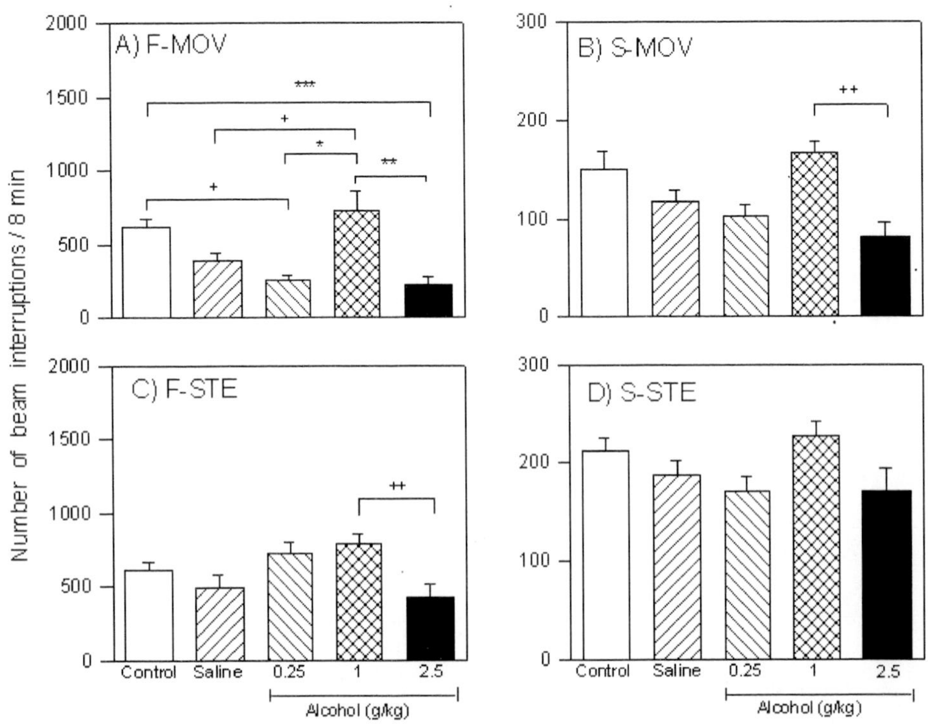

Figure 4. Effect of different doses of alcohol on horizontal activity and stereotyped movements in reverse cycle rats. Cumulated scores in 8 min are shown for F-MOV (A), S-MOV (B), F-STE (C) and S-STE (D). Data represent the mean ± S.E.M. of 9 (control), 10 (saline), 9 (0.25 g/kg), 10 (1 g/kg) and 11 (2.5 g/kg) animals. *** $p < 0.001$; ** $p < 0.005$; * $p < 0.01$; $^{+}$ $p < 0.05$.

Alcohol administered at doses of 0.25 and 2.5 g/kg significantly decreased total horizontal activity by 44 and 49 % in comparison with the control group (Figure 5A). In contrast, a dose of 1g/kg significantly increased total horizontal activity when compared with all groups tested : 69 % (saline), 117 % (0.25 g/kg) and 141 % (2.5 g/kg), except with the control group (Figure 5A). Alcohol at the same dose (1 g/kg) significantly increased total stereotyped movements when compared with all groups tested : 41 % (control), 92 % (saline), 51 % (0.25 g/kg) and 129 % (2.5 g/kg). A dose of 2.5 g/kg significantly decreased total stereotyped movements by 38 % versus the control group (Fig 5B). Alcohol at a dose of 1g/kg also increased total activity when compared with all groups tested : 40 % (control), 78 % (saline), 97 % (0.25 g/kg) and 150 % (2.5 g/kg), whereas a dose of 2.5g/kg decreased total activity by 43% when compared with the control group. Total activity was not significantly affected by an alcohol dose of 0.25g/kg (Figure 5C). No significant differences were observed between the saline and control groups (Figures 4 and 5).

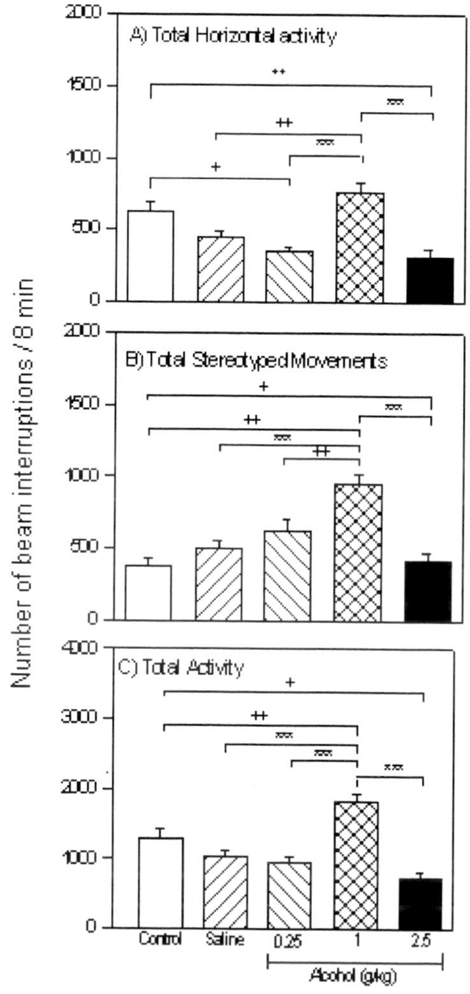

Figure 5. Effect of different doses of alcohol on total motor activity in reverse cycle rats. Cumulated scores in 8 min are shown for total horizontal activity (A), total stereotyped movements (B) and total activity (C). Data represent the mean ± S.E.M. of 9 (control), 10 (saline), 9 (0.25 g/kg), 10 (1 g/kg) and 11 (2.5 g/kg) animals. *** $p < 0.0001$; ** $p < 0.01$, * $p < 0.05$.

Discussion

Alcohol doses with stimulant properties are difficult to establish in humans, since the same dose may have stimulant or depressant effects in different subjects [15, 16]. This difference is also seen in animals, given that there are several factors that affect the behavioral responses to alcohol. In this study, we have shown that alcohol, at a dose of 1g/kg, increased total horizontal activity and total stereotyped movements in non-selected Wistar rats. A slight but not significant increase in locomotor activity in Wistar rats has also been reported in response to the same dose of alcohol [45]. In contrast, this alcohol dose has been reported to decrease locomotor activity and to induce sedation in Sprague-Dawley rats [31, 58], as well as in FH, FSL and FRL strains of rats, with no effect in P and NP rats [11]. A depressant effect of an alcohol dose of 1 g/kg was also reported by Gingras and Cools (1996) [28] in selected Nijmegen Wistar rats. Stimulant alcohol effects have been obtained with lower doses (0.1 - 0.5 g/kg i.p.) [11, 28, 30, 31], although no effect has also been reported [42, 58]. Therefore, discrepancies regarding the variable responses to various doses of alcohol might be due to the different strains of rats used in the reported studies.

Behavioral responses may also be affected by other factors, including the light-dark cycle and the presence of stressful stimuli [52, 53]. Stimulant actions of alcohol on locomotor activity have been reported in rats in both normal and reverse light-dark cycles, although most studies have been carried out in normal cycle. For instance, alcohol at doses of 0.25 and 0.5 g/kg increased locomotor activity in FRL and Nijmegen Wistar rats, respectively [11, 28], whereas no effect was observed with alcohol doses of 0.1 – 0.5 g/kg in Sprague-Dawley, P, NP, FH and FSL rats [11, 42, 58]. On the other hand, alcohol-induced increases in horizontal activity with doses of 0.1 and 0.25 g/kg have been reported in Sprague-Dawley rats in reverse light-dark cycle [30, 43]. We have shown that a higher dose of alcohol (1 g/kg) also stimulates locomotor activity in non-selected Wistar rats in a reverse light-dark cycle. Thus, lower doses of alcohol are required to induce locomotor activity in Sprague-Dawley than in non-selected Wistar rats, suggesting the existence of differences in sensitivity to alcohol effects between different strains of rodents, as described by other authors [9, 10, 65, 66]. Moreover, alcohol low doses do not stimulate locomotor activity in Sprague-Dawley rats maintained in a normal cycle, while these doses elicit activating responses in reverse cycle animals. These findings indicate that behavioral responses to low doses of alcohol in the same rat strain are altered depending on the light-dark cycle.

In the present study we investigated the effects of alcohol in non-selected Wistar rats in reverse cycle, since motor activity was higher than that in normal cycle animals. However, a higher motor activity does not necessarily predict a higher alcohol stimulant effect. To our knowledge, the effects of different doses of alcohol have not been compared in both normal and reverse light-dark cycles in the same rat strain. Therefore, it would be interesting to determine if the alcohol stimulant actions observed in the present study are similar in both light-dark cycles.

Numerous studies have consistently shown that alcohol high doses (more than 2 g/kg) produce depressant effects in rodents [28, 31, 58, 62]. Accordingly, we have shown that an alcohol dose of 2.5 g/kg significantly decreased horizontal and stereotyped movements. These findings suggest that motor responses to high doses of alcohol may not be related to the rodent strain or the light-dark cycle and may be associated to the sedative effects of the drug.

Animal exposure to a certain stressful stimuli, such as a novel environment, triggers specific neural changes which determine behavioral responses to drugs of abuse. The environmental context in which drugs are administered modulates their ability to induce forms of drug experience-dependent plasticity [3, 12]. Behavioral responses to drugs, as well as gene expression patterns in specific brain regions are differentially modulated by the exposure to a novel environment [4, 13, 22, 23, 32, 54, 60, 61]. In addition, animals exhibit different responses to drugs depending on how they respond to a novel environment. Animals showing high motor activity in a novel environment (High Responders, HR) are more susceptible to self-administrate drugs than animals exhibiting low activity (Low Responders,

LR) [8, 48]. These responses have been observed with amphetamine [48], dexamphetamine [20] and morphine [1]. Studies with alcohol have provided inconsistent results. Several reports have shown that spontaneous locomotor activity during a single exposure to a novel environment failed to predict alcohol intake [5, 38, 44]. In contrast, Gingras and Cools (1995) [27] found an inverse correlation between exposure to novelty and alcohol intake in Nijmegen Wistar rats, HR animals showing a significantly less alcohol intake than LR animals. Interestingly, the i.p. administration of alcohol doses of 0.25 and 0.5 g/kg stimulated locomotor activity in HR but not in LR animals [28, 30], suggesting that a novel stimulus predicts alcohol sensitivity in these animals. In contrast, high alcohol doses (i.e., 2 g/kg) produced sedative effects in both types of animals [28], indicating that depressant effects of alcohol are not altered by a novel stimulus. Therefore, alcohol stimulant and depressant actions on motor activity may involve different neural mechanisms. The behavioral response to an alcohol dose of 1 g/kg observed in the present study is worth mentioning, since this dose significantly increased horizontal and stereotyped movements, despite the fact that animals were not selected as High (HR) and Low (LR) responders. Research is currently carried out in our laboratory in order to study the dose-dependent actions of alcohol on locomotor activity in animals selected by their response to a novel stimulus.

Dopaminergic neurotransmission in the nucleus accumbens and the caudate-putamen plays a critical role in the mechanisms underlying the locomotor and stereotyped responses elicited by psychostimulant drugs, respectively [14, 33, 49, 59]. On the other hand, alcohol modulates the activity of dopaminergic reinforcement and reward circuits (i.e., the mesocortical and meso-accumbens systems) [34, 35, 36, 63], as well as the nigrostriatal pathway [66]. Regulation of dopaminergic transmission in these pathways plays a major role in controlling motor activity in response to alcohol exposure [39, 42, 62, 64]. Studies regarding the behavioral actions of alcohol have been mainly focused on horizontal activity [11, 28]. A few reports have assessed the effects of the drug on vertical activity [43], whereas the stereotyped movements induced by alcohol have been poorly investigated. We have shown that total horizontal activity and total stereotyped movements were significantly affected by alcohol administration at doses of 1g/kg and 2.5 g/kg : an alcohol dose of 1 g/kg increased, while a dose of 2.5 g/kg diminished both parameters. The locomotor and stereotyped responses induced by these alcohol doses might be related to dopaminergic activation in the nucleus accumbens and the caudate-putamen, respectively, as suggested by other authors for psychostimulants [14, 33, 49, 59]. Further research is needed in order to elucidate the mechanisms of action of alcohol in these brain circuits.

Conclusion

Behavioral responses to alcohol exposure are affected by several factors, including the dose and route of administration, the rodent strain, the light-dark cycle and the presence of stressful stimuli, such as a novel environment. In this study we have shown that non-selected Wistar rats in a reverse light-dark cycle exhibited a higher motor activity than animals in normal cycle. Alcohol administration in reverse cycle animals produced stimulant and depressant effects depending on the dose. An alcohol dose of 1 g/kg increased total horizontal activity and total stereotyped movements, while a dose of 2.5 g/kg showed opposite effects.

Our results suggest that stimulant alcohol effects may be mainly attributed to fast horizontal and fast stereotyped movements. In contrast, the sedative alcohol effects may involve similar contributions of fast and slow horizontal, as well as fast stereotyped movements. Alcohol behavioral responses might be closely related to activation of brain dopaminergic circuits in the nucleus accumbens and the caudate-putamen.

ACKNOWLEDGMENTS

We thank Dr. L. Mayagoitia for helpful discussions and J.M. Luna and S. Rodriguez for technical assistance. This work was supported by Consejo Nacional de Ciencia y Tecnología (CONACyT) (34359-N and 42095-M).

REFERENCES

[1] Ambrosio, E., Goldberg S. R. and Elmer, G. I. (1995). Behavior genetic investigation of the relationship between spontaneous locomotor activity and the acquisition of morphine self-administration behavior. *Behav Pharmacol 6,* 229-237.

[2] Antelman, S. M., Eichler, A. J., Black, C. A. and Kocan, D. (1980). Interchangeability of stress and amphetamine in sensitization. *Science 207,* 329-331.

[3] Badiani, A., Browman, K. E. and Robinson, T. E. (1995). Influence of novel versus home environments on sensitization to the psychomotor stimulant effects of cocaine and amphetamine. *Brain Res 674,* 291-298.

[4] Badiani, A., Oates, M. M., Day, H. E. W., Watson, S. J., Akil, H. and Robinson, T. E. (1999). Environmental modulation of amphetamine-induced c-fos expression in D_1 versus D_2 striatal neurons. *Behav Brain Res 103*, 203-209.

[5] Bisaga, A. and Kostowski, W. (1993). Individual behavioral differences and ethanol consumption in Wistar rats. *Physiol Behav 54,* 1225-1131.

[6] Carlsson, A., Engel, J. and Svensson, T. H. (1972). Inhibition of ethanol induced excitation in mice and rats by alpha-methyl-p-tyrosine. *Psychopharmacologia 26*, 307-312.

[7] Chen, H. T., Casanova, M. F., Kleinman, J. E., Zito, M., Goldman, D. and Linnoila, M. (1991). ^{3}H-Paroxetine binding in brains of alcoholics. *Psychiatry Res 38,* 293-299.

[8] Cools, A. R. and Gingras, M.A. (1997). Nijmegen high and low responders to novelty: A new tool in the search after the neurobiology of drug abuse liability. *Pharmacol Biochem Behav 60*, 151-159.

[9] Crabbe, J. C., Kosobud, A., Young, E. R., Tam, B. R. and McSwigan, J. D. (1985). Bidirectional selection for susceptibility to ethanol withdrawal seizures in *mus musculus*. *Behav Gene*t *15,* 521-536.

[10] Crabbe, J. C., Feller, D. J., Terdal, E. S. and Merril C. D. (1990). Genetic compounds of ethanol response. *Alcohol 7,* 245-248.

[11] Criswell, H. E., Overstreet, D. H., Rezvani, A. H., Johnson, K. B., Simson, P. E., Knapp, D. J., Moy, S. S. and Breese, G. R. (1994). Effects of ethanol, MK-801, and

chlordiazapoxide on locomotor stimulation from ethanol preference. *Alcohol Clin Exp Res 18*, 917-923.

[12] Crombag, H.S., Badiani, A. and Robinson, T. E. (1996). Signalled versus unsignalled intravenous amphetamine: large differences in the acute psychomotor response and sensitization. *Brain Res 722*, 227-231.

[13] Day, H. E. W., Badiani, A., Uslaner, J. M., Oates, M. M., Vittoz, N. M., Robinson T. E., Watson, S. J. Jr. and Akil, H. (2001). Environmental novelty differentially affects c-fos mRNA expression induced by amphetamine or cocaine in subregions of the bed nucleus of the stria terminalis and amygdala. *J Neurisc 21*, 732-740.

[14] Delfs, J. M., Schreiber, L. and Kelley, A. E. (1990). Microinjection of cocaine into the nucleus accumbens elicits locomotor activation in the rat. *J Neurosci 10*, 303-310.

[15] de Wit, H., Uhlenhuth, E. H. and Johanson, C. E. (1987). Individual differences in behavioral and subjective responses to alcohol. *Alcohol Clin Exp Res 11*, 52-59.

[16] de Wit, H., Pierri, J., Johanson, C. E. (1989). Assessing individual differences in ethanol preference using a cumulative dosing procedure. *Psychopharmacology 98*, 113-119.

[17] Duncan, P. M. and Baez, A. M. (1981). The effect of ethanol on wheel running in rats. *Pharmacol Biochem Behav 15*, 819-821.

[18] Earleywine, M. (1994). Anticipated biphasic effects of ethanol's psychomotor stimulant effect. *Alcohol Clin Exp Res 18*, 956-963.

[19] Erickson, C. K. and Kochhar, B. S. (1985). An animal model for low dose ethanol-induced locomotor stimulation: behavioral characteristics. *Alcohol Clin Exp Res 9*, 310-314.

[20] Exner, E. and Clark, D. (1993). Behavior in the novel environment predicts responsiveness to d-amphetamine in the rat: A multivariate approach. *Behav Pharmacol 4*, 47-56.

[21] Fadda, F., Argiolas, A., Melis, M. R., Serra, G. and Gessa, G. L. (1980). Differential effects of acute and chronic ethanol on dopamine metabolism in frontal cortex, caudate nucleus and substancia nigra. *Life Sci 27*, 979-986.

[22] Ferguson, S. M., Norton, C. S., Watson, S. J., Akil, H. and Robinson T. E. (2003). Amphetamine-evoked c-fos mRNA expression in the caudate-putamen: the effects of DA and NMDA receptor antagonists vary as a function of neuronal phenotype and environmental context. *J Neurochem 86*, 33-44.

[23] Ferguson, S. M. and Robinson, T. E. (2004). Amphetamine-evoked gene expression in striatopallidal neurons: regulation by corticostriatal afferents and the ERK/MAPK. *J Neurochem 91*, 337-348.

[24] Gauvin, D. V, Baird, T. J., Vanecek, S. A., Briscoe, R. J., Ballet, M. and Holloway, F. A. (1997). Effects of time-day and photoperiod phase shifts on voluntary ethanol consumption in rats. *Alcohol Clin Exp Res 21*, 817-825.

[25] Geller, I. (1971). Ethanol preference in the rat as a function of photoperiod. *Science 173*, 456-459.

[26] Gianoulakis, C. (1998). Alcohol-seeking behavior. *Alcohol Health Res World 27*, 202-210.

[27] Gingras, M. A. and Cools, A. R. (1995). Differential ethanol intake in high and low responders to novelty. *Behav Pharmacol 6*, 718-723.

[28] Gingras, M. A. and Cools, A. R. (1996). Analysis of the biphasic locomotor response to ethanol in high and low responders to novelty: a study in Nijmegen wistar rats. *Psychopharmacology 125,* 258-264.

[29] Grant, K. A. and Colombo, G. (1993). Discriminative stimulus effects of ethanol. Effect of training dose on the substitution of N-methyl-D-aspartate antagonists. *J Pharmacol Exp Ther 264,* 1241-1247.

[30] Hoshaw, B. A. and Lewis, M. J. (2001). Behavioral sensitization to ethanol in rats: Evidence from the Sprague-Dawley strain. *Pharmacol Biochem Behav 68,* 685-90.

[31] Imperato, A. and di Chiara, G. (1986). Preferential stimulation of dopamine release in the nucleus accumbens of freely moving rats. *J Pharmacol Exp Ther 239*, 219-228.

[32] Jaber, M., Cador, M., Dumartin, B., Normand, E., Stinus, L. and Bloch, B. (1995). Acute and chronic amphetamine treatments differently regulate neuropeptide messenger RNA levels and Fos immunoreactivity in rat striatal neurons. *Neuroscience 65*, 1041-1050.

[33] Kelly, P. H., Seviour, P. W. and Iversen, S. D. (1975). Amphetamine and apomorphine response in the rat following 6-OHDA lesions of the nucleus accumbens septi and corpus striatum. *Brain Res 94,* 507-522.

[34] Koob, G.F. (1992). Neural mechanisms of drug reinforcement. *Ann NY Acad Sci 654,* 171-191.

[35] Koob, G. F. (2003). Neuroadaptive mechanisms of addiction: studies on the extended amygdala. *Eur Neuropsychopharmacol 1*3, 442-52.

[36] Koob, G. F., Ahmed, S. H., Boutrel, B., Chen, S. A., Kenny, P. J., Markou, A., O'Dell, L. E., Parsons, L. H. And Sanna, P. P. (2004). Neurobiological mechanisms in the transition from drug use to drug dependence. *Neurosci Biobehav Rev 27,* 739-49.

[37] Koros, E., Piasecki, J., Kostowski, W. and Bienkowski, P. (1998). Saccharin drinking rather than open field behavior predicts initial ethanol acceptance in Wistar rats. *Alcohol Alcohol 33,* 131-40.

[38] Koros, E., Plasecki, J., Kostowski, W. and Bienkowski, P. (1999). Development of alcohol deprivation effect in rats: lack of correlation with saccharin drinking and locomotor activity. *Alcohol Alcohol 34*, 542-50.

[39] Krimmer, E. C. and Schechter, M. D. (1992). HAD and LAD rats respond differently to stimulating effect but not discriminative effects of ethanol. *Alcohol 9*, 71-74.

[40] Lê, A. D., Quan, B., Juzytch, W., Fletcher, P. J., Joharchi, N. and Shaham, Y. (1998). Reinstatement of alcohol-seeking by priming injections of alcohol and exposure to stress in rats. *Psychopharmacology 135*, 169-174.

[41] Martin, C. S., Earleywine, M., Musty, R. E., Perrine, M. W. and Swift, R. M. (1993). Development and validation of the biphasic alcohol effects scale. *Alcohol Clin Exp Res 17*, 140-146.

[42] Milton, G. V., Patrick, K. and Erickson C. K. (1995). Low dose effects of ethanol on locomotor activity induced by activation of the Mesolimbic System. *Alcohol Clin Exp Res* 19, 3, 768-776.

[43] Moore, T. O., June, H. L. and Lewis, M. J. (1993). Ethanol induced stimulation and depression on measures of locomotor activity: effects of basal activity levels in rats. *Alcohol 10,* 537-40.

[44] Nadal, R. A., Pallares, M. A. and Ferre, N. S. (1996). Oral intake of sweetened or sweetened alcoholic beverages and open field behavior. *Pharmacol Biochem Behav 54*, 739-743.

[45] Nestby, P., Vanderschuren, L. J., de Vries, T. J., Hogenboom, F., Wardeh, G., Mulder, A. H. and Schoffelmeer, A. N. (1997). Ethanol, like psychostimulants and morphine, causes long-lasting hyperreactivity of dopamine and acetylcholine neurons of rats nucleus accumbens: possible role in behavioral sensitization. *Psychopharmacology 133*, 69-76.

[46] Oscar-Berman, M., Shagrin, B., Evert, D. L. and Epstein, C. (1997). Impairments of Brain and Behavior. *Alcohol Health Res World 21*, 65-75.

[47] Phillips, T. J. and Shen, E. H. (1996). Neurochemical basis of locomotion and ethanol stimulant effects. *Int Rev Neurobiol 39*, 243-82

[48] Piazza, P. V., Deminière, J. M., Maccari, S., Mormède, P., Le Moal, M. and Simon, H. (1990). Individual reactivity to novelty predicts probability of amphetamine self-administration. *Behav Pharmacol 1*, 339-345.

[49] Pijnenburg, A. J. J., Honing, W. M. M. and Van Rossum J. M. (1975). Inhibition of the d-amphetamine-induced locomotor activity by injection of haloperidol into the nucleus accumbens of the rat. *Psychopharmacologia 41*, 87-95.

[50] Pohorecky, L. A. (1991). Stress and alcohol interactions: An update of human research. *Alcoholism Clin Exp Res 15*, 438-58.

[51] Reinberg, A. (1992). Circadian changes in psychologic effects of ethanol. *Neuropsychopharmacology 7*, 149-56.

[52] Rosario, L. A. and Abercrombie, E. D. (1999). Individual differences in behavioral reactivity: correlation with stress-induced norepinephrine eflux in the hippocampus of Sprague-Dawley rats. *Brain Res Bull 48*, 595-602.

[53] Rosenwasseer A.M. (2001) Alcohol, antidepresants, and Circadian Rhythms. *Alcohol Research and Health* 25, 126-135.

[54] Ruskin, D. N., and Marshall, J. F. (1994). Amphetamine- and cocaine-induced fos in the rat striatum depends on D2 dopamine receptor activation. *Synapse 18*, 233-240.

[55] Russell, V. A., Lamm, M .C. L. and Taljaard, J. J. F. (1988). Effect of ethanol on (^{3}H) dopamine release in rat nucleus accumbens and striatal slices. *Neurochemical Res 13*, 487-92.

[56] Rybkin, I. I., Zhou, Y., Volaufova, J., Smagin, G. N., Ryan, D. H. and Harris, R. B. (1997). Effect of restraint stress on food intake and body weight is determined by time of day. *Am J Physiol 273*, 1612-1622.

[57] Samson, H. H., Haraguchi, M., Tolliver, G. A. and Sadeghi, K. G. (1989). Antagonism of ethanol-reinforced behavior by the benzodiazepine inverse agonist Ro 15-4513 and FG 7142: relation to sucrose reinforcement. *Pharmacol Biochem Behav 33*, 601-608.

[58] Schaeffer, G. J., Richardson, W. R., Bonsall, R. W. and Michael, R. P. (1988). Brain self-stimulation, locomotor activity and tissue concentrations of ethanol in male rats. *Drug Alcohol Depend 21*, 67-75.

[59] Sharp, T., Zetterström T., Ljungberg T., Ungerstedt U. (1987). A direct comparison of amphetamine-induced behaviors and regional brain dopamine release in the rat using intracerebral microdialysis. *Brain Res* 401, 322-330.

[60] Uslaner, J., Badin, A., Norton, C. S., Day, H. E. W., Watson, S. J., Akil, H. and Robinson, T. E. (2001). Amphetamine and cocaine induce different patterns of *c-fos*

mRNA expression in the striatum and subthalamic nucleus depending on environmental context. Eur J *Neurosci 13*, 1977-1983.

[61] Uslaner, J. M., Norton, C. S., Watson, S. J., Akil, H., and Robinson, E. (2003). Amphetamine-induced *c-fos* mRNA expression in the caudate-putamen and subthalamic nucleus: interactions between dose, environment and neuronal phenotype. *J Neurochem 85*, 105-114.

[62] Waller, M. B., Murphy, J. M., McBride, W. J., Lumeng, L. and Li, T. K. (1986). Effect of low-dose ethanol on spontaneous motor activity in alcohol-preferring and non-preferring lines of rats. *Pharmacol Biochem Behav 24,* 617-623.

[63] Wise R. A. and Bozarth, M. A. (1982). Action of drugs of abuse on brain reward systems: an update with specific attention to opiates. *Pharmacol Biochem Behav 17,* 239-243.

[64] Wise R. A. and Bozarth, M. A. (1987). A psychomotor stimulant theory of addiction. *Psychol Rev 94,* 469-492.

[65] Yanai, J., Bergman, A., Keltz, M. and Pick, C. G. Mechanism of sensitivity and tolerance to ethanol and barbiturates. In: Yanai, J., Rosenfeld, J.M., Eldar, P. and Bauml, R. Alcohol dependence, the family and the community. London: Freund; 1988; pp. 143-158.

[66] Yanai, J., Shaanani, R. and Pick, C. G. (1995). Altered brain sensitivity to ethanol in mice after MPTP treatment. *Alcohol 12,* 127-30.

INDEX

A

absorption, 147
abuse, 146, 154, 160
academic performance, viii, 61
acceptance, 16, 18, 54, 139, 158
access, 36, 54, 56, 137, 139, 147
accommodation, 15
accounting, 40
acculturation, ix, 125, 139, 142
accumulation, 20
acetylcholine, 159
achievement, 21, 22, 23
acid, 146
activation, x, 107, 145, 146, 155, 156, 157, 158, 159
activity level, 24, 158
adaptation, ix, 14, 125, 130
adaptive functioning, 74
addiction, 158, 160
adjunctive therapy, 92
adjustment, 64, 102, 122, 123
adjuvant, 92
adolescence, 16, 81, 114, 123
adolescents, viii, 54, 60, 61, 62, 63, 64, 65, 74, 75, 76, 77, 78, 79, 80, 81, 82, 83, 84, 85, 86, 114
adult population, 47
adulthood, viii, 61, 79, 81, 84, 123
adults, 28, 29, 62, 64, 74, 84, 104, 122
adverse event, 79, 109
advertisements, 80
advertising, 75
affect, 3, 4, 11, 12, 13, 17, 18, 23, 75, 76, 114, 146, 147, 152, 153
affective disorder, 82, 127
affective experience, 17
age, vii, 23, 24, 51, 53, 54, 55, 56, 58, 59, 60, 64, 75, 76, 77, 84, 88, 114, 134, 136, 139
agent, 74, 76, 91, 93, 94
aggressive behaviour, 8
agonist, 93, 94, 159
akathisia, 59
alcohol, x, 145, 146, 147, 148, 151, 152, 153, 154, 155, 157, 158, 159, 160
alcohol consumption, 146, 147
alcoholics, 146, 156
allergy, 97
alternative, viii, 35, 36, 44, 87, 94, 103
alternatives, 91
Alzheimer's disease, 110
ambivalence, 13, 14
American Psychiatric Association, 28, 35, 43, 45, 81, 82, 85, 88, 90, 104
American Psychological Association, 29, 30, 48
amines, 111
amphetamine, 155, 156, 157, 158, 159
amygdala, 157, 158
anemia, 133
anger, 3, 5, 16, 18, 19, 23
animals, x, 93, 145, 146, 147, 148, 149, 150, 151, 152, 153, 154, 155
ANOVA, 148
antidepressant, vii, viii, 31, 32, 34, 35, 36, 37, 39, 40, 42, 43, 44, 48, 49, 53, 54, 55, 56, 57, 58, 59, 79, 85, 86, 87, 88, 89, 90, 91, 92, 93, 95, 96, 100, 101, 102, 104, 105, 106, 107, 108, 109, 110, 111
antidepressant medication, 32, 34, 35, 36, 37, 39, 40, 42, 43, 44, 48, 54, 55, 57, 58, 59, 79, 90, 91, 93
antidepressant medications, 91
antidepressants, viii, 43, 46, 87, 89, 90, 91, 93, 94, 95, 96, 102, 103, 105, 106, 107, 110, 111
antihypertensive drugs, 99
antipsychotic, 107, 112
antipsychotics, 93, 94
antisocial personality, 97

antisocial personality disorder, 97
anxiety, 3, 6, 8, 9, 10, 13, 14, 15, 17, 19, 21, 23, 27, 30, 39, 44, 46, 50, 62, 67, 71, 73, 76, 77, 82, 83, 92, 106, 124, 129, 133, 147
anxiety disorder, 39, 46, 50, 67, 71
anxiety disorders, 39, 46
appetite, 76
aptitude, 30
Argentina, 140
AS, 106, 107
aspartate, 158
assertiveness, 15
assessment, vii, ix, 1, 2, 8, 24, 29, 60, 67, 70, 74, 78, 81, 82, 83, 84, 85, 89, 125, 126, 127, 128, 129, 130, 133, 140
assignment, 42, 78
association, 105, 121, 126, 134, 135, 136, 137, 138, 139
assumptions, 6, 17, 18, 19
atrophy, 93
attachment, 2, 3, 10, 11, 12, 23, 27, 28, 29, 30, 121, 123, 124
attachment theory, 2
attention, 6, 14, 23, 37, 96, 133, 160
attitudes, 41, 42, 46, 60, 106, 114, 116
authenticity, 18
authority, 9, 14, 15, 19
autonomy, 18, 44
availability, ix, 31, 34, 40, 42, 125
avoidance, 12, 23
awareness, 2, 4, 5, 13, 14, 16, 17, 29, 33, 55
axons, 93

B

barbiturates, 160
barriers, 56
beams, 148
Beck Depression Inventory, 38, 73, 128, 129, 131, 137
behavior, 2, 4, 12, 13, 15, 16, 23, 30, 41, 44, 56, 114, 116, 123, 133, 146, 147, 148, 156, 157, 158, 159
behavior therapy, 44
behavioral change, 146
behaviors, 3, 4, 6, 13, 22, 159
benign, 126, 129
benzodiazepine, 92, 159
beverages, 159
bias, 42, 59
bilateral, 90
binding, 102, 111, 156
biology, 112
bipolar disorder, 23, 91, 97, 107
birth, 53, 135, 138, 140
births, ix, 125
blame, 7, 16, 18, 22, 23
blood, 99, 100, 102, 103
blood pressure, 99, 100, 103
BMI, 24
body, vii, 24, 31, 40, 41, 43, 146, 159
body mass index, 24
body weight, 159
bonding, 123
borderline personality disorder, 21
boredom, 23
boys, 115
brain, x, 93, 101, 105, 106, 107, 108, 111, 146, 154, 155, 156, 159, 160
brain dopaminergic circuits, x, 146, 156
Brazil, ix, 125, 126, 127, 128, 130, 132, 134, 135, 138, 140
bulimia, 28, 29

C

California, 133
Canada, viii, 1, 53, 54, 55, 60
Canadian, 24, 35, 36, 43, 49
cardiac, 95
Caribbean, 127
case study, 49, 104
catalyst, 11
causal attribution, 123
cell, 101, 108, 112
cells, 93
Census, 126, 143
central nervous system (CNS), 104, 105
cerebellum, 108
cerebral cortex, 109
channels, 96
chi, 97
child bearing, 97
child rearing, 114, 116
childhood, 16, 65, 83, 123, 139
children, viii, x, 8, 54, 60, 61, 62, 63, 65, 74, 75, 76, 77, 78, 81, 82, 83, 84, 85, 86, 114, 116, 121, 123, 126, 132, 133, 134, 135, 138, 140
Chile, ix, 125, 127, 128, 129, 130, 131, 132, 135, 136, 138, 141, 142
chronic, 90, 91, 92, 102, 103, 106, 108, 109, 111, 112, 157, 158
chronically, 90, 106
circadian rhythm, 147
circadian rhythms, 147
citalopram, 77, 92, 97, 101, 103, 105, 112
classes, 89, 91

classification, 89
clients, 4, 5, 8, 9, 12, 23, 24
clinical depression, 106
clinical trials, 34, 40, 46, 59, 88
close relationships, 123
closure, 21
clustering, 55
CNS, 104, 105
cocaine, 156, 157, 159
cognition, 17, 18
cognitions, 5
cognitive therapy, 30, 32, 35, 38, 46, 49
cohesion, 11, 14, 30
cohort, viii, 42, 53, 55
colic, 137, 139
collaboration, 62
college students, 113, 123
combination therapy, 92, 95, 100
commitment, 14, 122, 123
communication, 4, 6, 10, 11, 17, 77
community, vii, 45, 48, 50, 84, 160
comorbidity, 39, 47, 59, 65, 67, 71, 80, 81
compensatory, 22
competence, 137, 139
competency, 36
complement, 8
complementarity, 2, 6, 7
complex, 9, 18, 44
complexity, 36
compliance, 62
complications, 57
components, 4, 5, 9, 11, 12, 13, 17, 19, 21, 27, 29, 33
compounds, 91, 102, 156
concentration, 93, 101, 102
concept, 6, 10, 44
conceptualization, 10, 11, 22
conduct, 79
conduct disorder, 79
conduction, 74
conflict, 12, 15, 16, 17, 19, 23, 135, 137, 139
conflicts, 20
confrontation, 17
confusion, 101
conscious awareness, 5, 16, 17
consensus, 34, 89, 106
consent, 99
constipation, 74
construct validity, 117
consumption, 146, 147, 156, 157
context, 2, 4, 8, 9, 16, 17, 28, 41, 44, 154, 157, 160
control, viii, x, 7, 10, 19, 20, 22, 27, 36, 41, 42, 61, 63, 92, 96, 140, 145, 148, 151, 152, 153
control condition, 22
control group, x, 63, 96, 140, 145, 148, 151, 152
controlled studies, 63, 65, 74, 92, 94
controlled study, 94, 95, 100, 105, 106
controlled trial, 92, 93, 102, 104, 108, 110
controlled trials, 31, 63, 64, 65, 84, 92, 93, 102
coping, 2, 9, 16, 23, 41, 142
coping strategies, 41
coping strategy, 2
core, 5, 10, 12, 16, 17, 22, 38
correlation, 102, 137, 147, 155, 158, 159
cortex, 94, 105, 106, 107, 108, 109, 112, 157
cortisol, 93
Costa Rica, 131, 133, 136, 138
costs, 43
counseling, vii, 31, 32, 34, 40, 42, 44, 46
couples, 114, 122, 124, 130, 132
coverage, 34
criterion, 37, 38
criticism, 13, 15, 16, 19, 20, 22
CRP, 4, 5, 6, 9, 10, 11, 12, 14, 15, 16, 19
crying, 129, 133
CT, vii, 31, 35, 37
cues, 11
cumulative, 157
cycles, x, 145, 147, 148, 154
cytochrome, 95, 102

D

data collection, 59
data set, 35
database, viii, 34, 37, 39, 43, 62, 83, 126
death, 20, 55
debts, 121
decision, 37, 40, 42, 49
decision making, 42
decisions, 19, 42, 50, 56, 89
defense, 11, 17
defense mechanism, 11
defense mechanisms, 11
defensiveness, 12
deficiency, 133
definition, 2, 29, 77, 80, 91, 110
delivery, 43, 54, 133, 135, 139
demographic characteristics, 134
dendritic cell (DC), 108, 111
Department of Health and Human Services, 106
dependent variable, 25, 119, 120
deposits, 121
depression, vii, viii, ix, 1, 8, 10, 21, 22, 23, 24, 25, 27, 28, 29, 31, 32, 33, 34, 35, 36, 37, 39, 40, 41, 42, 43, 44, 45, 46, 47, 48, 49, 50, 51, 53, 54, 55, 57, 58, 59, 60, 61, 62, 63, 64, 65, 73, 74, 75, 76,

77, 78, 79, 81, 82, 83, 84, 85, 86, 88, 89, 90, 91, 93, 94, 96, 100, 101, 103, 104, 105, 106, 107, 108, 109, 110, 111, 112, 113, 114, 115, 116, 117, 118, 119, 120, 121, 125, 126, 127, 128, 129, 130, 131, 132, 133, 134, 135, 136, 137, 138, 139, 140, 141, 142, 143, 158
depressive, vii, 1, 21, 22, 23, 27, 28, 29, 34, 35, 36, 37, 38, 39, 40, 43, 45, 46, 47, 49, 50, 51
depressive symptomatology, 21, 43, 132, 140
depressive symptoms, vii, 1, 21, 22, 23, 27, 28, 46, 47, 51, 63, 65, 75, 91, 93, 96, 97, 129, 130, 131, 132, 135, 139, 141, 142
deprivation, 136, 158
desensitization, 93
desire, 23
destruction, 93
detection, 79, 106, 127
developed countries, ix, 125, 126
developmental change, 123
developmental process, 123
diabetes, 91
diagnosis, 88, 91, 97, 100
Diagnostic and Statistical Manual of Mental Disorders, 22
diagnostic criteria, 24, 37, 62, 64, 65, 75, 76, 132
dialogue, 16
diaphoresis, 103
differences, vii, 18, 20, 24, 30, 31, 34, 35, 36, 42, 148, 151, 153, 154, 156, 157, 159
dimensions, 6, 7, 29, 30, 44
diminishing returns, 56
disability, 88
disappointment, 19, 40
discipline, 36
disclosure, 11, 13, 14, 17
discomfort, 11, 13
discrimination, 129
disequilibrium, 10
disorder, vii, viii, 1, 22, 23, 28, 29, 30, 31, 32, 35, 36, 37, 39, 40, 43, 44, 46, 48, 50, 53, 60, 61, 62, 67, 71, 81, 83, 88, 91, 93, 97, 107, 108, 126, 127, 129, 136, 138, 146
dissatisfaction, 40, 139
distress, 9, 22, 113
distribution, 57, 60
distributive justice, 114, 121, 122
diversity, 140, 142
divorce, 20
dizziness, 76
doctors, 88
domain, 21, 27
dominance, 8, 11, 14, 15
dopamine, 94, 95, 105, 107, 112, 157, 158, 159
dorsal, 92, 110
dosage, 78, 90, 96, 100
dosing, 80, 157
double-blind trial, 74, 77
drinking, 158
drive, 2
drive theory, 2
drug, x, 32, 34, 36, 46, 145, 146, 147, 148, 152, 154, 155, 156, 158
drug abuse, 156
drug dependence, 158
drug interaction, 56
drug treatment, 36
drug use, 55, 158
drugs, 46, 83, 99, 101, 104, 105, 110, 146, 154, 155, 160
DSM, 22, 24, 55, 58, 60, 62, 65, 66, 68, 70, 73, 74, 75, 76, 77, 78, 81, 84, 85, 97, 99, 111, 127, 128, 130, 131, 132, 135, 136, 137
DSM-II, 60, 65, 66, 70, 73, 74, 76, 84, 85, 128, 130, 132, 135
DSM-III, 60, 65, 66, 70, 73, 74, 76, 84, 85, 128, 130, 132, 135
DSM-IV, 22, 24, 55, 58, 62, 66, 70, 73, 75, 77, 78, 81, 97, 99, 111, 127, 128, 131, 136, 137
duration, x, 33, 38, 50, 59, 64, 66, 70, 76, 80, 84, 89, 91, 97, 100, 108, 122, 145, 147
dysphoria, 22, 129, 130, 131, 136, 138, 139
dysthymia, 63

E

eating, 22, 23, 24, 28, 29, 30
eating disorders, 23, 29
echoing, 16
economic problem, 135
economic status, 138
education, 24, 41
effective, 4, 13, 22, 28, 35, 37, 40, 43, 44, 45, 50
efficacy, 89, 92, 96, 100, 102, 104, 109
elderly, 39, 46, 48, 50
elementary school, ix, 113, 114, 115, 116, 117, 119, 121
emergence, 13, 19
emission, 106
emotion, 17
emotional disorder, 48, 85
emotional disorders, 48
emotional state, 122, 123
emotionality, 124
emotions, 3, 18, 29
employees, 114
energy, 12, 22, 24, 27

England, 28, 47, 127
environment, 9, 142, 146, 147, 148, 154, 155, 157, 160
enzyme, 95, 102
enzymes, 102
epidemiology, 85, 106, 127, 129
equality, 114, 121, 122
equity, 122, 123
estimating, 11
ethanol, 148, 156, 157, 158, 159, 160
ethics, 24
ethnicity, 131, 134, 136, 139
etiology, 31, 32, 44
euphoria, 146
evaluation, 49
evidence, viii, 22, 33, 36, 37, 47, 53, 58, 62, 65, 79, 80, 89, 92, 93, 94, 97, 102, 104, 105, 114, 121, 126
excitation, 156
exclusion, 21, 23, 80
expectation, 16
expectations, 4, 11, 19, 22, 121, 123, 134, 138, 140
experiment, 148, 152
exposure, x, 23, 38, 55, 145, 147, 154, 155, 158
expression, 13, 17, 18, 106, 108, 112, 154, 156, 157, 160
extracellular, 101, 105, 106, 108, 112

F

factor analysis, 117
factor i, 91
factors, x, 30, 39, 42, 44, 46, 145, 147, 153, 154, 155
failure, 15, 19, 24, 27, 40, 90
family, viii, ix, 8, 11, 18, 24, 61, 62, 63, 75, 76, 80, 82, 113, 124, 125, 134, 135, 137, 138, 139, 140, 160
family functioning, 75
family history, 76
family income, 24, 134
family members, 18, 62, 113
family relationships, viii, 61
family support, 134, 140
family therapy, 63
fear, 12, 13, 14
fears, 3, 12, 21, 42
feedback, 13, 18
feelings, 6, 8, 13, 14, 18, 19, 121, 129
feet, 147
female, 2, 40
females, 67, 71, 139
fever, 140
fibroblast, 108
fibroblast growth factor, 108
financial resources, ix, 125
Finland, 61, 84
flexibility, 15
fluoxetine, 70, 73, 74, 75, 76, 78, 79, 81, 82, 85, 93, 95, 97, 102, 103, 104, 106, 108, 109, 111, 112
fluvoxamine, 95
focus groups, 41
focusing, 12, 19, 21, 33, 96, 100
follow-up, 90, 108, 111
food, 147, 159
food intake, 159
Ford, 32, 41, 46, 90, 106
forebrain, 105
forgetting, 140
framing, 50
frequency, 19
friends, ix, 113, 114, 115, 121, 123, 138
friendship, 115, 116, 117, 118, 119, 120, 121, 123
frontal, 157
frontal cortex, 94, 106, 107, 157
functioning, 24, 27, 39, 146

G

ganglion, 93
gender, 40, 76, 134, 138
gene, 108, 109, 154, 157
gene expression, 154, 157
gene promoter, 109
general practitioner, 36, 50
generalization, 18
generalized anxiety disorder, 39, 50
generation, 78
genotype, 80
gift, 20
girls, 115
glial cells, 96
glutamate, 146
Glutamate, 146
glycogen, 93
goal setting, 30
goals, 9, 14, 21, 33, 62
Gray, 45, 48
grief, 18, 33
group identity, 11
group interactions, 10, 20
group therapy, vii, 1, 2, 8, 9, 14, 24, 28
group work, 10
groups, vii, ix, x, 14, 15, 17, 20, 24, 28, 30, 37, 41, 53, 54, 55, 63, 68, 69, 72, 73, 74, 77, 78, 88, 94, 97, 98, 114, 119, 120, 121, 126, 145, 148, 151, 152

growth, vii, 17, 108
growth factor, 108
guidance, 43
guidelines, 2, 34, 54, 55
guilt, 22

H

habituation, 148, 151
harm, 42
Hawaii, 85
HE, 109
headache, 76
headache,, 76
health, 33, 37, 38, 41, 43, 44, 47, 49, 50, 54, 55, 56, 57, 59, 83, 100, 106, 114, 137, 139, 140, 141
health care, 41, 137, 141
health care professionals, 41
health services, 47, 139
heart block, 74
heart rate, 74
height, 24
hepatic, 95, 102
heterogeneity, 80, 129
heuristic, 2, 10
high blood pressure, 99, 103
high school, ix, 24, 113, 114, 115, 116, 117, 118, 119, 120, 121, 137
hippocampus, 92, 94, 108, 112, 159
Hispanic population, 143
Hispanics, 126, 134
homeostasis, 13
homogeneity, 14, 101
hopelessness, 21, 24, 27, 39, 123
Hops, 82, 84
hormone, 91, 93, 108, 112
hospitalization, 80, 135
hospitals, 131, 133
hostility, 3, 8, 12, 13, 16
human development, 2, 29
hyperreflexia, 103
hypertension, 103
hypothermia, 146
hypothesis, 119, 120, 121
hypothyroidism, 91, 93, 97, 105

I

ICD, 111, 130, 131, 132, 135, 137
ideas, 14
identification, 14, 18
identity, 11, 14, 21, 22
imagery, 63
images, 15, 16, 17
immigrants, 134
immunoreactivity, 158
implementation, 33
in vitro, 101, 105, 109
in vivo, 101, 105, 107
incidence, 59, 100
inclusion, 33, 55
income, 24, 136, 141
incus, 35
independence, 117
independent variable, 119, 120
indication, 55
indicators, 59, 121
indices, 34, 102
individual differences, 157
inducible protein (IP), 107
industrialized countries, 126
industry, 32
infancy, 123
infants, 133
infection, 135
influence, 5, 9, 15, 35, 39, 41, 44
Influence, 156
informed consent, 24, 44
inhibition, viii, 87, 93, 96, 102, 109
inhibitor, 90, 102, 103, 104, 111
injections, 158
injury, 18
inner tension, 13, 14
insecurity, 6
insight, 10, 41
insomnia, 76, 92
instinct, 2
institutions, 54
instruments, ix, 33, 64, 76, 84, 125, 127, 128, 129, 130, 140
insurance, 34
integration, 1, 19
integrity, 11, 13, 18
intensity, 38
intent, vii, 1, 4, 12, 13, 26, 40
interaction, 4, 8, 15, 16, 28, 30, 93, 95, 97, 101, 102, 103, 110, 117, 119, 120, 122, 127
interaction effect, 119, 120
interactions, 6, 7, 8, 10, 12, 18, 20, 27, 80, 126, 146, 159, 160
interdependence, 17, 18
interest, 16, 24, 27, 34, 62
interface, 10, 124
interleukin (IL), 112
internal working models, 114

internalization, 2, 16
International Classification of Diseases, 137
interpersonal conflict, 12, 18
interpersonal interactions, 27
interpersonal processes, 2
interpersonal relations, viii, 21, 33, 61, 123, 124
interpersonal relationships, viii, 21, 33, 61, 124
interpretation, 11, 12, 19
interval, 55
intervention, 10, 12, 13, 17, 34, 35, 38, 40, 42, 43, 44, 47, 63, 64, 86, 102, 140, 142
interventions, 4, 14, 16, 17, 19, 21, 28, 31, 32, 35, 36, 39, 40, 41
interview, 24, 41, 54, 55, 58, 66, 70, 77, 82, 83, 85, 86, 111, 130, 131, 133
intimacy, 12, 18, 122
intoxication, 146
intravenous, 92, 157
intravenous (IV), 90, 96, 97, 99, 111
intravenously, 65
iron, 133
irritability, 76, 133
isolation, 14

J

Japan, 113
judges, 24
judgment, 10, 19, 37, 38
junior high school, 123
justification, 56

K

knowledge, 9, 20, 32, 96, 100, 154

L

lack of control, 42
language, ix, 12, 125, 126, 140
Latin America, ix, 125, 126, 127, 129, 134, 140, 143
Latino women, ix, 125, 126, 127
Latinos, 126
lead, 4, 9, 20, 40, 41, 121, 146
learning, 18, 33, 63
lesions, 158
liability, 156
life experiences, 41
lifetime, 39, 46, 71, 88, 134
light, x, 32, 145, 147, 148, 154, 155
likelihood, 41, 89
limitation, 102, 103, 121
literacy, 47
lithium, 91, 92, 93, 94, 96, 101, 102, 103, 105, 106, 109, 112
Locke, 29
locus, 107, 110
logic, 15
loneliness, 19, 22, 114, 121
longitudinal study, 54
love, 23

M

major depression, vii, viii, 31, 32, 34, 35, 36, 37, 39, 43, 44, 46, 47, 48, 49, 50, 53, 54, 55, 57, 58, 59, 60, 61, 62, 74, 77, 78, 79, 81, 82, 83, 84, 85, 90, 91, 93, 100, 104, 106, 107, 108, 109, 110, 111, 129, 133
major depressive disorder, viii, 45, 47, 49, 50, 54, 74, 81, 84, 87, 89, 91, 97, 99, 104, 106, 108, 109, 110
maladaptive, 6, 9, 12, 13, 15, 16
male, 159
management, 34, 37, 45, 50, 60, 66, 70, 81, 112
mania, 74
manic, 76, 99
manic symptoms, 76
marital conflict, 138
marital life, 134
marital status, 139
marketing, 56
mastery, 15, 139
mean, 24, 25, 35, 38, 95, 97, 98, 100, 149, 150, 151, 152, 153
measurement, 64, 66, 76, 88, 142
measures, viii, 25, 28, 55, 58, 62, 65, 66, 70, 74, 75, 76, 77, 78, 80, 122, 158
median, 24
medication, 32, 34, 35, 36, 37, 39, 40, 42, 43, 44, 46, 48, 55, 59, 62, 64, 65, 76, 78, 80, 89, 90, 92, 93
membranes, 101
men, 53, 88, 132
mental disorder, 28, 50, 59, 73, 81, 86, 97, 126
Mental Disorders, 48
mental health, 33, 38, 43, 45, 50, 55, 56, 57, 59, 113, 114, 121, 136, 138, 139
mental health professionals, 45, 50
mental illness, 138
messenger RNA, 158
messenger RNA (mRNA), 112, 157, 158, 160
meta-analysis, 46, 50, 93, 96, 104, 111
metabolism, 102, 157
metabolites, 102, 109, 111
methodology, 32, 42, 66, 70, 74

Mexico, 139, 145
mg, ix, 88, 90, 95, 96, 97, 98, 100, 101, 103
mice, 105, 107, 146, 156, 160
microcosms, 28
migration, ix, 125
military, 54
Ministry of Education, 124
minority, 36, 40
moclobemide, 78, 81
mode, 18, 24
modeling, 16
models, 2, 4, 29, 32, 40, 44, 102, 114, 121, 122, 123, 146
monitoring, 44, 63, 100
monoamine oxidase inhibitors, 89, 95
mood, ix, 23, 31, 32, 35, 36, 37, 40, 43, 44, 62, 75, 93, 97, 108, 125, 126, 133, 143
mood change, 133
mood disorder, ix, 31, 32, 35, 36, 37, 40, 43, 44, 93, 125, 126, 133, 143
mood disorders, 43
mood states, 23
morbidity, viii, ix, 46, 61, 125, 126
morning, 147
morphine, 155, 156, 159
mortality, viii, 59, 61
mothers, x, 126, 130, 133, 139, 140, 141
motivation, 4
motor activity, x, 146, 147, 148, 149, 150, 151, 153, 154, 155, 160
movement, 10, 15, 146
mRNA, 112, 157, 160
multiple regression, 117, 118, 120
multiple regression analyses, 117, 118, 120
multiple sclerosis (MS), 111
mutual, 9, 41, 42
mutuality, 18
myoclonus, 103

N

national community, 60
natural, 20, 28
nausea, 76, 95, 99
needs, 3, 4, 5, 6, 12, 13, 23, 27, 33, 41, 55, 57, 59, 60, 123, 138, 140
negative mood, 23
neglect, 58
negotiation, 41, 42
nervous system, 93, 146
nervousness, 129
network, 37, 137
neurobiology, 156
neurogenesis, 93, 94, 105
neuron, 93, 94
neuronal systems, 146
neurons, 92, 93, 96, 105, 156, 157, 158, 159
neuropathy, 146
neuropeptide, 158
neuroticism, 39
neurotransmission, 93, 105, 146, 155
neurotransmitter, 79, 146
neurotrophic, 93, 95, 96, 106
neurotrophic factors, 95
New South Wales, 51
New Zealand, 51
non-pharmacological treatments, 54, 56
norepinephrine, 93, 94, 104, 105, 109, 112, 159
norepinephrine (NE), 93, 94, 104, 105, 109, 112, 159
novelty, 155, 156, 157, 158, 159
NP, 146, 154
nucleus, 110, 155, 156, 157, 158, 159, 160
nurses, 33, 36, 44, 48, 140
nurturance, 21

O

obesity, 22, 29
obligation, 121
obsessive-compulsive disorder, 138
olanzapine, 93, 104, 106, 108, 112
old age, 55
older adults, 114
opiates, 160
organization, 28, 37
orientation, 32, 122, 123
outliers, 24
outpatients, 35, 63, 64, 67, 71, 74, 76, 77, 78, 80, 85, 89, 90, 109
ownership, 18
oxidation, 109

P

pain, 16, 17, 20, 21
panic disorder, 39, 91
parental care, 120
parenting, 140
parents, ix, 2, 20, 113, 114, 115, 116, 120, 121, 123, 140
paroxetine, 70, 73, 74, 75, 76, 77, 83, 84, 95, 97, 101, 104, 105, 108, 109, 110, 111
passive, 8, 14, 23, 41, 42
passive-aggressive, 8
pathology, 39, 139

pathophysiology, 88
pathways, 146, 155
patterns of behavior, 16
peers, 11
peptides, 110, 146
perception, 42, 46
perceptions, 5
performance, 21
perinatal, ix, 125, 126, 132
peripheral neuropathy, 146
permit, 43
personality, 2, 10, 11, 21, 22, 28, 29, 39, 42, 48
personality disorder, 21, 28, 39, 48
personality disorders, 28
personality factors, 39
perspective, 7, 30, 42, 83, 122, 123
Peru, ix, 125, 127, 128, 129, 131, 133, 136, 138
pharmacological treatment, 55, 57
pharmacotherapy, 32, 35, 36, 37, 43, 44, 46, 47, 48, 49, 50, 62, 78, 81, 84, 85, 91, 100, 106, 109
phase shifts, 157
phenotype, 157, 160
pilot study, 83, 116
placebo, viii, 34, 35, 48, 62, 64, 65, 73, 74, 75, 76, 77, 78, 79, 81, 82, 83, 84, 85, 89, 90, 93, 94, 103, 104, 105, 108, 110
planning, 41
plasma, 66, 80, 83, 95, 102
plasma levels, 80, 95, 102
plasticity, 95, 154
PM, 82, 84
polymorphism, 102, 109
polymorphisms, 102, 107
poor, viii, 8, 40, 61, 102, 139
population, viii, 22, 30, 42, 47, 53, 54, 55, 56, 58, 59, 60, 75, 89, 126, 130, 132, 138
positive correlation, 147
positive reinforcement, 33
postpartum depression, ix, 125, 126, 127, 129, 139, 141, 142, 143
posture, 12
power, 6, 8, 9, 79
predictability, 15
prediction, 114
predictors, 47, 50, 75, 108, 109, 117, 120, 139
preference, 32, 40, 41, 42, 43, 44, 46, 138, 157
prefrontal cortex, 105, 108, 112
pregnancy, ix, 125, 126, 129, 131, 134, 135, 138, 139, 140
preparation, 8, 9, 10, 13, 24, 32
pressure, 100
prevention, 85, 86, 94
priming, 158
principle, 2, 7, 36, 55, 114, 121
probability, 44, 59, 159
probe, 110
problem solving, 17, 18, 32, 33, 35, 38, 42, 48
problem-solving, 34, 35, 38, 39, 48
production, 110
professionalism, 9
prognosis, 89
program, 41, 66, 131, 140
progression, 89
prolactin, 92, 93
proliferation, 108
promoter, 109
protein, 108
proteins, 93
protocol, 78, 96
psychiatric disorders, viii, 61, 62, 91, 133
psychiatric patients, 31, 36, 83, 85
psychiatrist, 88, 95, 97
psychoanalysis, 2, 30, 63, 85
psychologist, 24
psychology, 14, 29, 50
psychometric properties, 129
psychopathology, 4, 29, 39
psychopharmacological treatments, 80
psychopharmacology, 64, 84
psychosis, 126, 132
psychosocial functioning, 63, 64, 76, 85
psychostimulants, 155, 159
psychotherapy, vii, 4, 9, 22, 28, 29, 30, 31, 32, 33, 34, 35, 36, 37, 38, 39, 40, 43, 44, 46, 47, 48, 49, 50, 51, 57, 62, 63, 64, 66, 70, 78, 81, 82, 83, 84
psychotropic medications, 48
public health, 54, 56, 58, 59
Puerto Rico, 106
pulse, 64, 65
pumps, 101, 102

Q

quality improvement, 41, 47
quality of life, 139
questioning, 42
quetiapine, 104

R

RA, 105, 108
race, 139
racial, 40
radio, 75

range, 18, 33, 37, 38, 58, 67, 71, 75, 92, 97, 100, 115, 116, 117, 126, 129, 133
rating scale, 47, 64, 73, 80, 82, 83, 85, 107
ratings, 72, 74, 88, 114
reasoning, 114
recall, 20
receptor, 94, 102, 105, 107, 111, 112, 157, 159
receptors, 92, 93, 94, 95, 96, 101, 102, 105, 109
reciprocity, ix, 7, 113, 114, 115, 117, 118, 119, 120, 121, 122, 123
recognition, ix, 125, 141
recollection, 133, 138
recovery, viii, 34, 35, 36, 37, 39, 46, 55, 61, 63, 79, 80, 82, 106, 121
recruiting, 44, 132
recurrence, 36, 75, 79, 81, 84, 106, 126
reduction, 34, 37, 38, 65, 75, 76, 89, 94, 98, 147
reflection, 14
regression, 117, 118, 119, 120, 137
regression analysis, 119, 120
regulation, 101, 108, 112, 146, 157
reinforcement, 155, 158, 159
rejection, 3, 13
relapses, 79
relational, 3, 6, 12, 15, 16, 21
relationship, ix, 2, 3, 6, 8, 17, 19, 21, 22, 23, 35, 38, 40, 47, 54, 107, 113, 115, 117, 118, 119, 120, 121, 123, 134, 138, 140, 147, 156
relationship quality, 123
relationships, ix, 2, 3, 6, 9, 10, 16, 18, 19, 20, 21, 27, 29, 33, 41, 47, 113, 114, 121, 122
relaxation, 63
rem, 146
REM, 146
remission, ix, 37, 39, 40, 58, 63, 65, 75, 76, 78, 88, 89, 90, 94, 95, 96, 100, 101, 103, 110
replacement, 93
resentment, 19
resistance, 89, 90, 91, 100
resolution, 19, 20
resources, 4, 32, 36, 142
response, viii, x, 5, 7, 8, 14, 15, 16, 17, 19, 20, 33, 36, 50, 87, 88, 90, 91, 92, 93, 94, 95, 96, 97, 100, 101, 102, 103, 104, 106, 107, 108, 109, 110, 111, 112, 145, 147, 152, 154, 155, 156, 157, 158
responsiveness, 92, 147, 157
restructuring, 30
retaliation, 17
retirement, 124
reward, 155, 160
rice, 92
risk, ix, 12, 13, 42, 43, 53, 76, 79, 85, 88, 95, 108, 125, 126, 127, 134, 138, 139, 140, 142, 143
risk factors, ix, 85, 125, 127, 138, 139, 140, 142
risperidone, 94, 104
RNA, 158
robustness, 37
rodents, x, 145, 154
RS, 108, 110
Russell, 47, 159

S

saccharin, 158
sadness, 18, 20, 24, 27, 131, 133
safety, 11, 12, 13, 14, 59, 97, 103, 140
sample, 24, 25, 27, 54, 60, 63, 65, 74, 75, 77, 78, 79, 83, 114, 127, 128, 131, 132, 133, 134, 136, 139
sample mean, 24
sampling, 54, 55
satisfaction, 41, 49, 121, 122, 123, 137, 139
saturation, 59
schizophrenia, 93, 97
school, ix, 24, 62, 113, 114, 115, 116, 117, 119, 120, 121, 123
scores, ix, x, 24, 25, 26, 27, 38, 65, 75, 76, 77, 78, 80, 88, 93, 94, 97, 98, 116, 117, 127, 128, 140, 145, 148, 149, 150, 151, 152, 153
Scores, x, 145, 148, 149, 150, 151, 152, 153
search, viii, 11, 28, 62, 126, 156
searching, 126
security, 6, 9, 19
sedative, x, 146, 154, 155, 156
seizure, 97
seizures, 156
selection, 36, 156
selective attention, 6
selective serotonin reuptake inhibitor, 104, 109, 110, 111
self, 2, 3, 4, 5, 6, 8, 9, 10, 11, 12, 13, 14, 15, 16, 17, 19, 20, 21, 22, 23, 27, 28, 29, 30, 42, 50, 58, 63, 64, 65, 80, 82, 114, 121, 137, 139, 154, 156, 159
self esteem, 8, 23, 27
self-awareness, 29
self-concept, 3, 4, 5, 6, 9, 10, 11, 16
self-definition, 22, 29
self-efficacy, 137
self-esteem, 3, 10, 21, 121
self-evaluation, 8
self-observation, 11
self-reflection, 14
self-reports, 63
sense of failure, 15
sensitivity, x, 102, 127, 129, 145, 146, 147, 154, 155, 160
sensitization, 156, 157, 158, 159

separation, 20
series, 94
serotonin, viii, 74, 87, 90, 92, 93, 94, 96, 99, 101, 102, 103, 104, 105, 106, 107, 109, 110, 111, 112, 146
serotonin syndrome, 103
sertraline, ix, 77, 82, 88, 90, 96, 97, 98, 99, 102, 103, 108, 109, 111, 112
services, x, 47, 126, 133
severity, 22, 31, 34, 35, 36, 37, 38, 39, 40, 44, 49, 50, 59, 68, 69, 73, 75, 76, 80, 97, 126
sex, 75, 123
sexual, 2, 3
sexuality, 18
shame, 13, 14
shape, 16
sharing, 13, 20
shock, 107, 147
side effects, viii, 41, 59, 87, 89, 90, 92, 95, 97, 100, 103
side-effects, 100
sign, 9
significance level, 79
sites, 59, 80, 102
situation, 8
skill, 9, 33
skills, viii, 33, 61
skin, 140
sleep disturbance, 74, 133
smoking, 139
social anxiety, 21
social class, 134
social exchange, 122, 123
social network, 139
social norms, 12
social psychology, 14
social relations, 121
social relationships, 121
social skills, viii, 33, 61, 63
social skills training, 63
social support, 41, 113, 122, 123, 134, 137, 138, 139, 142
social workers, 44
socioeconomic status, 134, 140
sodium, 96
solidarity, 121
solution, 148
specificity, 127, 129
speculation, 96, 102
speed, 94
spirituality, 41
Sprague-Dawley rats, 154, 159
stabilizers, 108
stages, 9, 10, 12, 13, 89, 90, 96
standard deviation, 24, 25, 98
Standard Deviation, 25, 26
standard error, 137
standards, 34, 37
statistics, 88
stigma, 41, 55, 56
stimulant, x, 146, 153, 154, 155, 156, 157, 159, 160
stimuli, 154, 155
stimulus, 155, 158
strain, 147, 154, 155, 158
strains, x, 145, 146, 154
strategies, viii, x, 10, 11, 33, 41, 56, 58, 60, 87, 89, 91, 92, 94, 100, 108, 111, 126
strength, 142
stress, vii, 11, 29, 122, 123, 140, 147, 148, 152, 156, 158, 159
stressor, 147
stressors, 23, 134, 138, 140, 147
striatum, 158, 159, 160
students, ix, 113, 114, 115, 116, 117, 118, 119, 120, 121, 123
substance abuse, 79, 91
substance use, 23, 62, 97
substitution, 158
sucrose, 159
suicidal ideation, 46, 47, 65, 77
suicide, 54, 59, 84, 85, 132
suicide attempts, 54, 59, 132
summaries, 20
superiority, ix, 88
supervision, 24, 45
suppression, 146
surveillance, 59
survival, 15, 36
survival rate, 36
susceptibility, 156
Sweden, 106
switching, viii, 87, 92, 95, 99
symptom, vii, 1, 2, 17, 21, 22, 31, 39, 74, 76, 80, 82, 89, 93, 132
symptoms, vii, ix, 1, 2, 6, 8, 19, 21, 22, 23, 27, 28, 39, 46, 47, 51, 62, 64, 65, 68, 69, 75, 76, 81, 88, 89, 91, 92, 94, 95, 96, 99, 109, 113, 129, 137, 139
syndrome, ix, 21, 88, 99, 103, 104, 131, 133, 136
synergistic, 94, 108
synergistic effect, 94, 108
synthesis, 5, 92
systems, 41, 95, 146, 155, 160

T

t3, 93, 107

targets, 16, 17, 21, 107
tb, 106
teachers, 62, 115
technical assistance, 156
telephone, 23, 134
temperature, 146
tension, 8, 11, 13, 14, 15, 16
theory, vii, 1, 2, 4, 6, 10, 15, 24, 28, 29, 30, 33, 59, 123, 160
therapeutic benefits, 37
therapeutic change, 27
therapeutic interventions, 2
therapeutic process, 18, 28
therapeutic relationship, 62
therapists, 10, 11, 12, 13, 14, 15, 18, 20, 21, 24, 34
therapy, vii, 1, 2, 3, 5, 8, 9, 14, 16, 20, 21, 24, 28, 29, 30, 32, 33, 34, 35, 36, 38, 39, 44, 46, 49, 50, 63, 78, 81, 82, 83, 90, 91, 92, 93, 94, 95, 96, 100, 104, 106, 108, 110
Therapy, 22, 30, 45, 48
threat, 9, 11, 13, 15, 18
threats, 23
thyroid, 91, 93, 104, 108, 112
time, viii, ix, 8, 14, 15, 17, 18, 19, 20, 24, 30, 34, 36, 38, 43, 45, 47, 54, 55, 64, 68, 69, 72, 73, 76, 78, 79, 80, 84, 87, 88, 89, 92, 93, 100, 102, 125, 157, 159
tissue, 159
toxicity, 79, 95
training, 9, 24, 33, 36, 44, 63, 85, 158
traits, 10
trajectory, 22
transactions, 2
transference, 17
transition, 33, 158
transitions, 33
transmission, viii, 87, 92, 93, 94, 96, 101, 102, 155
transport, 107
treatment, viii, ix, 87, 88, 89, 90, 91, 92, 93, 95, 96, 97, 98, 99, 100, 101, 102, 103, 104, 105, 106, 107, 108, 109, 110, 111, 112, 160
treatments, 33, 37, 40, 41, 46, 48, 49, 50, 158
tremor, 103
trend, 12, 35, 43, 59
trial, vii, 1, 22, 28, 30, 33, 40, 46, 48, 50, 51, 63, 64, 65, 66, 70, 75, 76, 77, 78, 80, 82, 83, 84, 85, 86, 89, 90, 91, 93, 100, 101, 103, 104, 106, 107, 108, 110
tricyclic antidepressant, 65, 66, 67, 68, 69, 89, 92, 95, 96, 104, 105, 107
tricyclic antidepressants, 65, 66, 67, 68, 69, 89, 92, 95, 104, 107
triggers, 154
triiodothyronine, 107, 111
trust, 9, 18
tryptophan, 92, 94, 105
Turkey, 87, 88
turnover, 92
tyrosine, 156

U

UK, 54, 76
uncertainty, 9, 17, 50
unconscious, 2, 3, 6, 15, 20
uniform, 37
United Kingdom, 54
United States, ix, 53, 54, 59, 125
universality, 14
urban areas, 36
urinary retention, 74
urinary tract, 135, 139
urinary tract infection, 135, 139
US Department of Commerce, 143

V

validation, ix, 29, 111, 125, 127, 129, 130, 132, 158
validity, 49, 86
values, 25, 26, 68, 69, 72, 73, 98
variability, 14
variable, 25, 26, 34, 43, 56, 57, 75, 154
variables, 24, 25, 36, 39, 74, 75, 101, 117, 134, 139, 140, 141
variance, 55
variation, 80
varicose veins, 135, 139
varimax rotation, 117
vein, 44
venlafaxine, viii, ix, 70, 73, 74, 78, 81, 87, 88, 96, 100, 101, 102, 103, 104, 105, 107, 108, 109, 110, 111
vision, 74
voice, 13, 14, 21, 116
voicing, 13
vomiting, 22
vulnerability, 15, 21, 22, 56
vulnerability to depression, 22

W

war, 133
water, 147
Watson, 156, 157, 159, 160
weight gain, 76, 95

weight loss, 23
well-being, 123
withdrawal, 91, 156
wives, 132
women, ix, 24, 29, 53, 88, 97, 114, 123, 125, 126, 127, 129, 130, 131, 132, 133, 136, 137, 138, 139, 140, 141, 142, 143
words, 10, 17, 18
workers, 44, 130, 132

Y

yield, 15
young adults, 29, 59, 60, 81, 83, 86

Z

ziprasidone, 104

Filename: Henri-Trends in Depression Research-FR.doc
Directory: C:\00 books and journals\Frank Fixes- PF to FR\Henri- Trends in Depression Research
Template: C:\Documents and Settings\Owner\Application Data\Microsoft\Templates\Normal.dot
Title: Chapter 1
Subject:
Author: Frank Columbus
Keywords:
Comments:
Creation Date: 3/13/2007 3:47 PM
Change Number: 3
Last Saved On: 3/13/2007 3:50 PM
Last Saved By: Owner
Total Editing Time: 4 Minutes
Last Printed On: 3/13/2007 3:50 PM
As of Last Complete Printing
Number of Pages: 183
Number of Words: 93,004 (approx.)
Number of Characters: 530,128 (approx.)